PRAISE FOR *BORN LUCKY*

"*Born Lucky* is a story of father-son heroism that will keep the reader riveted. Together, Leland 'Lucky' Vittert and his dad overcome tremendous obstacles with perseverance and love. If every American read this book, we would have a much better country."
—BILL O'REILLY, SEVENTEEN-TIME *NEW YORK TIMES* BESTSELLING AUTHOR

"*Born Lucky* is a beautiful, emotional, true story that will help readers understand the challenge Leland Vittert and his family faced and overcame dealing with his autism. If you like honest, true stories, today is your lucky day: read *Born Lucky*."
—JAMES PATTERSON, AUTHOR OF SIXTY-ONE *NEW YORK TIMES* BESTSELLERS

"*Born Lucky* is a parenting book written from the perspective of a child—an autistic child who struggled with coordination and social cues and making friends and fitting in, until his father dropped everything to become his coach, mentor, companion, and lifeline. Vittert's gorgeous, heart-wrenching book details how his father helped him work within the parameters of his autism diagnosis to become the wildly successful news anchor he is. His father taught Leland to recognize the rhythm of human interaction, one that didn't come naturally, stressing that character matters above all else and self-esteem is earned, not given. *Born Lucky* will inspire anyone who reads it, but especially families with children on the spectrum, as well as the children themselves. A beautiful book with the potential to redefine the autism spectrum."
—BATYA UNGAR-SARGON, JOURNALIST AND AUTHOR

"Leland's story gripped me in a way few things ever have. This book isn't just inspiring—it's soul-shaking. It's a masterclass in resilience, vulnerability, and unapologetic courage. Page after page, I found myself moved to tears, then fired up to push harder, be better, live louder. Leland doesn't just tell his story—he hands you the permission to rewrite your own."
—JILLIAN MICHAELS, FITNESS TRAINER, MEDIA PERSONALITY, AND AUTHOR

"A feel-good read about an autistic kid with a big heart who wanted success and earned it as a national TV host. FYI—I didn't know he had autism, but I always knew my pal was weird!"
—JUAN WILLIAMS, AUTHOR OF *EYES ON THE PRIZE* AND FOX NEWS SENIOR POLITICAL ANALYST

Born Lucky

A DEDICATED FATHER,
A GRATEFUL SON, AND MY
JOURNEY WITH AUTISM

LELAND VITTERT

WITH DON YAEGER

HARPER HORIZON

Born Lucky

Copyright © 2025 by Leland Vittert

All rights reserved. No portion of this book may be reproduced, stored in a retrieval system, or transmitted in any form or by any means—electronic, mechanical, photocopy, recording, scanning, or other—except for brief quotations in critical reviews or articles, without the prior written permission of the publisher.

Published by Harper Horizon, an imprint of HarperCollins Focus LLC, 501 Nelson Place, Nashville, TN 37214, USA.

Unless otherwise noted, Scripture is from the Holy Bible, New International Version®, NIV®. Copyright © 1973, 1978, 1984, 2011 by Biblica, Inc.™ Used by permission of Zondervan.

Scripture quotations marked KJV are taken from the King James Version. Public domain.

Some names and identifying characteristics have been changed. Some dialogue has been reconstructed.

Any internet addresses, phone numbers, or company or product information printed in this book are offered as a resource and are not intended in any way to be or to imply an endorsement by Harper Horizon, nor does Harper Horizon vouch for the existence, content, or services of these sites, phone numbers, companies, or products beyond the life of this book.

ISBN 978-1-4002-5475-0 (ePub)
ISBN 978-1-4002-5468-2 (HC)

Without limiting the exclusive rights of any author, contributor or the publisher of this publication, any unauthorized use of this publication to train generative artificial intelligence (AI) technologies is expressly prohibited. HarperCollins also exercise their rights under Article 4(3) of the Digital Single Market Directive 2019/790 and expressly reserve this publication from the text and data mining exception.

HarperCollins Publishers, Macken House, 39/40 Mayor Street Upper,
Dublin 1, D01 C9W8, Ireland (https://www.harpercollins.com)

Library of Congress Control Number: 2025909811

Art direction: Belinda Bass
Cover design: Richard Ljoenes
Interior design: Mallory Collins

Printed in the United States of America

25 26 27 28 29 LBC 5 4 3 2 1

To Dad with love—
For all the parents and children now struggling the way I did.
—Leland

To Will—
There isn't a day since you were born that I don't consider myself the luckiest dad alive. I love you.
—Don

CONTENTS

FOREWORD BY GEORGE F. WILL   IX

CHAPTER 1: DISCOVERING I'M WEIRD   1

CHAPTER 2: BORN LUCKY   15

CHAPTER 3: THE MEASURE OF A MAN   25

CHAPTER 4: MY FATHER'S PROMISE   39

CHAPTER 5: THE SOCIAL BLUEPRINT   51

CHAPTER 6: DO IT RIGHT THE FIRST TIME, EVERY TIME   63

CHAPTER 7: WALKING THROUGH HELL   75

CHAPTER 8: MY BEST AND ONLY FRIEND   85

CHAPTER 9: WHAT WILL YOU BE GREAT AT?   99

CHAPTER 10: PRACTICE YOUR CRAFT   115

CHAPTER 11: IF YOU QUIT, THEY WIN   127

CHAPTER 12: CHOOSING MY PATH   141

CHAPTER 13: FINALLY HAVING FRIENDS   151

CHAPTER 14: I'LL TELL MY KIDS ABOUT IT   161

CONTENTS

CHAPTER 15: MOM, NO MATTER WHAT
YOU SEE ON TV, I'M OKAY   177

CHAPTER 16: WAR CHANGES YOU   187

CHAPTER 17: JUST BE YOU   199

CHAPTER 18: SPEAKING THE TRUTH   211

CHAPTER 19: LEARNING TO BE ME   223

CHAPTER 20: THE ROAD AHEAD   233

AFTERWORD FROM DAD   241

ACKNOWLEDGMENTS   245

NOTES   247

ABOUT THE AUTHOR   251

FOREWORD BY GEORGE F. WILL

From early on, Leland Vittert's nickname has been "Lucky." This might seem odd, considering the impediments strewn in front of him by life.

But as has been well said, luck is the residue of design. Leland's luck has included having a father who, when told that there was not much he could do for his son, said, *We'll just see about that.* And he designed a path for his son through medical and social thickets to today's success and happiness.

The lottery of life begins at life's beginning. As early as possible: at conception. We know that a lot depends—although we do not know *how much* of each life's trajectory depends—on genetic inheritance. And that is just a portion of the importance of shrewdly picking one's parents.

In our first years, we are with our parents at bath and bedtime, and most of the hours in between. Later, if we are fortunate to avoid the all-too-widespread fraying of family structure, we join our parents at the dinner table, where we learn the truth of the axiom that the family is the smallest school. One of life's great determinants is this 9/91 fact: Children from birth to age 18 spend 9 percent of their time in school, and 91 percent elsewhere, mostly with family members.[1]

From this book you will learn that Leland Vittert chose his parents well. And you will learn something astonishing: He, who did not speak a single word until he was three, has thrived in the communications business. This is an uncommon destination for people who, as children, are located somewhere on the autism spectrum.

Readers of this book also will come to understand the wonderful, amazing amalgam of ferocity and tenderness that can appear in parents who are confronted with the sobering and sometimes life-shattering news that their child has a serious disability. Leland had several.

"I was," he writes, "born severely cross-eyed—almost cartoon-character-like—and had surgery at six months to correct it." The surgery was less than completely successful, but that was the least of Leland's problems. He was, he writes, "socially lost yet intellectually advanced." The drama of his youth was his parents' quest to find out what was wrong—and then to prevent identifying the cause of his problems from making them worse.

Parents confronted with a diagnosis such as autism are often confused and fearful, for good reason. This was especially so in the 1980s and early 1990s, when the absence of scientific understanding about autism bred, with the help of the internet, the proliferation of misunderstandings and false certitudes. And of cruel, wounding speculations about whether parental behavior—something done or not done—was a cause of autism.

Permit me here a brief personal digression. In 1972, my first child, Jon, was born with Down syndrome. We knew his disability within twenty-four hours because he had some physical abnormalities that are facets of the syndrome, and because genetic testing quickly confirmed the condition. There was much we could not immediately know about: other possible physical problems, and the degree of Jon's mental disability, which can vary widely in people with Down syndrome. But at least we knew from Jon's first hours what we were dealing with.

So we were spared the torments that Leland's parents experienced with their agonizingly drawn-out realization that something was wrong with him. It would be a long, winding road to identifying Leland's problem.

FOREWORD

Once it was identified, his parents made a decision that was unusual, bold, risky—and right. They did not want him diagnosed, *even correctly*, with autism. They understood that categories have consequences.

In health matters, to diagnose is to label. And to label is to attach a stigma that can complicate many things, including access to treatments and to socialization processes and institutions such as school. Leland made it through school and into the upper reaches of broadcast journalism, which took him to war zones. Meanwhile, in the United States, health policy was becoming a kind of war zone.

The internet is an endless melee of often truculent people belaboring one another with opinions, information, misinformation, and disinformation. For some strange reason, when something is said on the internet, it thereby acquires momentum for respect by many people who should keep their skepticism unsheathed. Credulousness, and misplaced confidence, does not much matter if the subject is the best ingredients for macaroni and cheese. (Hint: Start, and pretty much end, with macaroni and cheese.) Or in arguments for and against baseball's designated hitter. When, however, the subject is even more important than baseball—when it concerns a serious health condition—the internet can become a serious subtraction from understanding.

In the 1950s, when television was in its infancy, a wit who was unenthralled with the new device said that television enabled you to have in your living room people you probably would not want to have in your living room. Today, the internet enables millions to read and see things they would be better off not reading or seeing. And the internet fills people with an often spurious confidence in their understanding of a subject.

It was because of the internet that during a 2012 debate between candidates for the Republican Party's presidential nomination, one of them shared with the national television audience the thought (or theory, or rumor, or whatever) that vaccines cause autism. The candidate had encountered this factoid while wandering in the undergrowth of the internet and chose to share it with a national audience.

FOREWORD

In this difficult era, almost everything, from showerheads and stoves to pronouns and the teaching of arithmetic in grammar schools, gets swept up into the tornado of politics. It was perhaps dismally predictable that autism would not be an exception. Fortunately, Leland, whose business is journalism, knows a thing or two about how to sort sense from nonsense. And how to distinguish between a reliable source and someone pretending to be one.

He is a reliable source of wisdom about life "on the spectrum" of a disability, and off. After a psychologist examined Leland and explained the ominous implications of some startling test results, Leland's father asked, "Is there anything we can do? I mean anything?" The psychologist replied, "Generally not." Well.

"Generally" is often synonymous with "usually." Leland's father, however, is, to put it mildly, unusual. A businessman of substantial success, he decided that his most gratifying achievement could come in another sector: his family. Leland tells well the remarkable story of how, with paternal devotion and pressure, he soared out of college, into broadcasting, through wars, arriving at election night 2020. He was then with Fox News, and Fox News was conflicted about reporting the news that Joe Biden had carried Arizona, thereby winning the White House.

This book is a wonderful read from the first chapter ("Discovering I'm Weird") to its last ("Afterword from Dad."). It will inform everyone about health, health policy, the profession of journalism, and recent history. And it will hearten parents who are understandably unnerved by discovering that they must navigate on their child's behalf a labyrinthine tangle of medical and legal institutions, and complex social beliefs, expectations, and mores.

Leland's story is one of adventure, exploration, and discovery. First and foremost, from beginning to end, it is about the mountain-moving power of parental love.

—George F. Will

Chapter One

DISCOVERING I'M WEIRD

The call from the teacher at Ethical Society Nursery School made my parents nervous. For the first four years of my life, they had convinced themselves my quirks and delays were just part of what made me unique. I was a little awkward, but every kid is, right? I just needed some time to break out of my shell.

The nursery school was an inviting place, just down the street from our home in St. Louis. It was the end of the school year at the Ethical Society, a time when parents looked forward to celebrating their children's growth and achievements. Instead, my parents, Mark and Carol, walked through the neighborhood toward the school with uncertainty. Why did my teacher want them to visit the classroom to talk?

Everything changed that spring day in 1986. As Mom and Dad walked down the bright, artwork-lined hallway, they were anxious. From the serious look on my teacher's face, they could tell something was off. This meeting wasn't about celebrating my progress or getting ready for kindergarten.

The classroom was its usual mess when they walked in. Drawings covered the walls, shelves overflowed with toys, and round tables with little chairs were scattered throughout the room. My teacher offered Mom and Dad seats across from her at one of those kid-sized tables. She took a deep breath and began. "Thank you for coming. I wanted to talk to you about Lucky."

My parents exchanged worried glances. Growing up, there were always little signs that I was "different" from other kids. I didn't speak until I was three. Not a word. The pediatrician never said anything about my behavior; they just recommended Mom and Dad take me to a speech therapist. But there, the therapist told Mom and Dad not to worry. I didn't have a speech impediment or anything. I just didn't talk. So everybody figured I was a late bloomer who would eventually catch up.

But there were other signs. When I was two, Mom took me to an early childhood education playgroup to help me socialize. Each session began with a group activity, and for the first fifteen minutes, the moms would leave the room. While the other kids played and interacted with the teachers, I ignored the activity entirely, standing by the door, waiting. I wouldn't move until the moms returned. My mom remembers the look I gave her when she walked back in—relieved but stern, as if to say, *Don't do that again.* After that, everyone would sit in a circle to sing songs, kids on their moms' laps. Except for me. I walked past Mom and sat in the teacher's lap instead. I didn't look at or speak to Mom until we got home for lunch.

When I finally started talking, it was in complete sentences, as if I had been storing them up for years. I talked all the time. I could go on endlessly about topics beyond my years. But socializing never came naturally—in fact, it was a disaster. I couldn't make friends or relate to kids my age. On the playground, I was lost in my own world. While the other kids played tag or built towers with blocks, I preferred hanging around adults. I couldn't connect with my peers, plus the adults didn't bully me.

Back at the meeting with my parents, my teacher was gentle as she got to her point. "You need to have Lucky evaluated," she finally said.

Those words hung in the air. Mom and Dad sat in stunned silence, taking it in. This was the first time someone had suggested my differences might be more significant than my parents had thought.

DISCOVERING I'M WEIRD

My teacher explained how my struggles went beyond being a shy kid. The way I interacted—or, more precisely, didn't—with peers. How basic instructions somehow got lost on me.

Dad sat quietly, but inside he was angry at what he heard. *Evaluated for what?* he thought. *There's nothing wrong with our child. I know he has a hard time playing with other kids. But, you know, that's kids!* At the same time, he could tell that my teacher was reluctant to share the news. It was clear: For the first time, there might be a real problem. Mom and Dad finally had to reckon with the fact that their son was different—not just an introvert. I needed to be "evaluated." Which meant something was officially "wrong."

Not long after that meeting, I found myself at St. John's Hospital for an evaluation—aka testing—with an occupational therapist and psychologist. Mom volunteered with kids who had disabilities and knew a therapist there who helped arrange the testing. At that age, I didn't think much of it. Dad told me, "You're going to go meet with these people," and that was that.

The therapist tested my motor skills, spatial awareness, and ability to follow multistep instructions. But the most impactful part of that evaluation wasn't about motor skills—it was about how I learned. The therapist explained to my parents that remediation, or my ability to overcome challenges, would depend on two key things: my intelligence and my will. If I was smart enough and wanted to change badly enough, I could adapt.

As I got older, the challenges only became more apparent. In fourth grade, Community School brought in a specialist to administer the Wechsler Intelligence Scale for Children (WISC), a standard IQ test used to assess cognitive ability. At the time, IQ tests measured verbal abilities like vocabulary, comprehension, and reasoning, as well as nonverbal skills like spatial reasoning, visual perception, and problem-solving. It all seemed silly to me. Little did I know, those evaluations would shatter my parents' understanding of who I was. Because the results were unlike anything the evaluators had ever seen.

They explained to my parents—and me, since I was sort of a mini adult—that a learning disability was usually represented by a 20-point spread between the two halves of the IQ test. When I finished, the evaluator sat my parents down to review the results.

My spread was *68 points*.

On one end of the spectrum, I was a genius. On the other, I was considered, in the medical jargon of the time, mildly retarded.

"We've seen kids who score higher, and we've seen kids who score lower," she said, "but we have never seen a spread this big. It's hard to imagine what's going on in his mind."

She wasn't kidding.

Simple things, like forming a basic sentence with a noun and a verb, baffled me. I couldn't write a sentence to save my life. I still can't spell. I remember one time when Dad tried to help me write a story about Abraham Lincoln. We focused on the often-attributed quote, "Do I not destroy my enemies when I make them my friends?" He wanted me to build a story around that idea. In reality, he basically wrote it while trying to teach me what writing was.

Meanwhile, things like math and science came easily. In third grade, we had something called McDonald's Multiplication Day. If you learned your multiplication tables, you'd get a McDonald's lunch based on how far you got. Single digits earned you a Happy Meal. If you made it through the teens multiplied by teens, you got a hot fudge sundae. Most kids took months to memorize the tables. I finished in four days. That's just how my mind worked. Plus the task had a definable goal with a real reward; I liked that.

It was social reasoning—reading cues, interpreting context, communication—where I was hopelessly lost. If the IQ test could have measured my EQ, it would have been near freezing levels.

Shocked by the assessment, Mom and Dad sent the results to another clinical psychologist who specialized in childhood development for a second opinion. They were looking for reassurance. Instead, they got the opposite. "You've got a very serious situation here," she said. "I have never seen this disparity to this degree."

The experts didn't have a name for what I had. Asperger's wasn't a term until the 1990s, and now it's no longer a diagnosis. Autism wasn't understood to be a spectrum disorder; either you were autistic or you weren't. The idea that there were high-functioning autistic children wasn't understood. Nobody back then considered that there were kids between what was considered *normal* and what people saw as nonverbal drooling. In those days, autism was often thought of as a condition where kids banged their heads against the wall and screamed—what would now be called "profound autism." That wasn't me. The only diagnosis experts could offer to explain the gap between my intellectual capacity and social capacity was "social blindness."

At the time, pervasive developmental disorder was often attributed to a cold, distant mother—an indifferent figure who failed to teach her child warmth and love. Mom was anything but that. She showed me kindness, patience, and unwavering love, doing everything in her power to connect with me even when the world struggled to understand.

As my parents wrestled to process the psychologist's grim prognosis, Dad asked her one thing before leaving. "Is there anything we can do? I mean, anything? Is there any way out of this? Is there any maturation out of this?"

Anything? His desperation was palpable.

Her answer was gentle but firm, blunt yet tinged with hope.

"Generally not," she said. "But there are circumstances where if you have two things, you can have a much better life. Number one is something you can't control—you have to be highly intelligent. You either are or you're not." The message was reassuring. "And he clearly is that."

Hallelujah! Dad thought.

"The second thing," she continued, "is that he has to want to do it. He has to want to be better. He has to want to be part of society. Lucky has to *want* it."

Born Lucky

Looking back, there was a third part—one the psychologist didn't mention. For years, I would have to trust Dad when he told me that what I felt was wrong and what he was telling me was right. It meant trusting that his way would eventually help me find my place in the world.

That was all Dad needed to hear. Those five words—*Lucky has to want it*—guided Dad for the next fifteen years. He never told me that, but everything he did from that moment on was geared toward me wanting to be better. If I could just look at things a certain way, he thought, I did not have to be defined by my diagnosis.

The Silent Label

I always knew I was weird.

After one evaluation, I remember asking Mom and Dad, "How did I do on the test?"

"Great!" they tried to reassure me.

My parents, especially Dad, were determined not to let the results define me. But no matter what they said, it was clear to me that they knew I was different. And I did too.

I could relate well in conversation with adults because I could talk about adult things. It was sort of like a party trick—there weren't many seven-year-olds who could hold a conversation about Reagan and Gorbachev. But while I impressed adults, I was completely out of sync with kids my own age. I never had friends who were peers. They just didn't understand me, and I didn't understand them. I didn't play, and I couldn't comprehend "kid stuff" like cartoons and comics. Instead, I was fascinated by things most kids wouldn't even think about. In fourth grade, I carried around huge books about aeronautics and bridge building, completely engrossed in their diagrams and engineering concepts. My teacher eventually asked Mom to make sure I stopped bringing them to school. Understandably, reading about suspension bridges at recess did nothing to help me fit in—in fact, it opened me up to even more ridicule.

I moved to a private school around that time, which only made the bullying worse. That's when I started to act out because I didn't understand what was happening. All the touching and noise were overwhelming. If another kid touched me in the lunch line, it felt painful, purposeful, and aggressive, and I would turn around and confront them. I didn't understand why no one was nice to me. I tried to make friends but couldn't because I was weird. The conversations were awkward. Everything I did was painfully awkward.

My parents didn't want me to know that I was different, but the signs were obvious. I looked different too. I was born severely cross-eyed—almost cartoon-character-like—and had surgery at six months to correct it. But the surgery wasn't entirely successful. My left eye still drifted up, and my right eye out to the side. "Lazy Eyes" became a frequent nickname. My lack of depth perception meant I couldn't play any sport involving a moving ball. Kids loved tossing a ball at me, laughing when I missed catching it or—worse—when it hit me in the head. There are baby pictures of me where you can tell I looked different, and the same was true when I was six, seven, or eight.

I was clearly on the autism spectrum, but Dad refused to allow psychologists to diagnose me with anything. My parents never said a word about it—to me or anybody else. I didn't present with the classic signs associated with autism. I struggled tremendously with social cues and age-appropriate behavior, and eye contact was impossible. But at a young age, I could engage with adults on their level so long as they forgave my "social blindness."

Dad believed the minute they said I had a problem, I'd have a label placed on me that would remain for the rest of my life. At the time, special classrooms and accommodations for kids like me were just beginning to emerge. But Dad didn't believe in that. He believed the world wasn't going to change for me, so I had to learn to adapt to the world. In his mind, if I had been given those accommodations, it might have softened the edges of my experience as a child, but it wouldn't have prepared me for the real world.

My parents feared that labeling me would put me in a box, and I'd be treated differently, not just by teachers and kids but by society. I'd be given special treatment, extra time on tests, and softer expectations for what I could achieve in life. Dad thought, *I don't know what he's gonna be like when he's twenty or thirty or forty or fifty. But for the rest of his life, he'll be that kid.* Mom and Dad wanted me to navigate life without the crutch of a label, believing that in the long run, I'd be better off for it.

My parents knew their decision to avoid a formal diagnosis came at a cost. They never outright said they regretted it, but as the years went on, I could tell they wrestled with the consequences. The decision meant that school would be much harder for me than it had to be. If I had been born five or ten years later, maybe things would have been different. Maybe teachers and classmates would have had a better understanding of kids like me. But in the 1980s and early '90s, no one really knew what to do with a kid who was socially lost yet intellectually capable.

In retrospect, I can see how this decision was both a blessing and a curse. On one hand, it meant I would grow thick skin and learn to navigate a world that often felt against me. On the other hand, it meant I wasn't defined by an autism diagnosis. *Autism, Asperger's, learning disabilities*—those words didn't exist in our family's vocabulary. I had to develop coping mechanisms and resilience that have served me well into adulthood. But during those early school years, it often felt like I was fighting a losing battle. I didn't understand why I was different and why making friends was so hard. I spent a lot of time in the principal's office, either because I was acting out or because I was getting bullied—and oftentimes both. My parents were there plenty too. During one meeting, they offered coffee, and Mom remembers looking down, surprised and appalled to see that she had broken her empty Styrofoam cup into a thousand tiny pieces.

DISCOVERING I'M WEIRD

It was a rough road, but looking back, my parents were preparing me for a world that wouldn't always be kind or accommodating. They believed in my ability to rise above my challenges without being defined by them. They believed in my potential, even when I didn't. They refused to let me use my differences as an excuse. They were determined that I would be seen for my abilities, not my disabilities.

But it wouldn't be easy.

My Path to Independence

When I was eight, Mom and Dad decided to take me on vacation to a "dude ranch" in Arizona. When we arrived, everybody there was with their kids on spring break. The big lawn in front of the lodge became a makeshift soccer field. The dads found a soccer ball and split up the boys and girls into teams of six for a friendly game on the lawn.

But for me, it was anything but friendly.

I could not do it. As the other kids played, I found myself bumping into others, getting hit, and not understanding why. Not only were the social interactions hard; just physically running was nearly impossible. Of the many enviable skills I inherited from Dad, hand-eye coordination wasn't one of them. Everybody else was having a great time, playing like little kids do, and I was distraught. Dad looked on incredulously.

"Whoa!" he blurted to my mom. "We got a problem here."

The evaluation had caught my parents' attention, but with time they thought I'd grow out of what I had. But it was becoming clear: This wasn't something that would magically change. It could no longer be ignored. This was who I was. *Period.*

That's when Dad turned to Mom.

"I think we have twelve years of a really bad road ahead of us," he said. Dad figured he repeated that to Mom a dozen times. "We just gotta buckle up," he added, "and see what happens."

Dad started paying closer attention after that vacation. He knew things were bad, but he didn't realize just *how* bad until he stopped by Community School one afternoon a few years later to check in. The real bullying had started in fourth grade—two boys who constantly pushed me around, called me names, and humiliated me in that relentless way kids do when they sense weakness and see someone different. What bothered me wasn't so much getting punched every day. It was the isolation, the taunts, the hourly reminders that I didn't belong.

One afternoon, Dad walked the short distance from our house to the school, determined to do something. He went looking for Jim Hoots, the PE teacher—a guy he knew from another school's football program. "Lucky's having a rough time," Dad told him. "He's coming home every day in terrible shape. Is there anything you can do to help him?"

Hoots hesitated. "Well, I'm trying," he said. "Today he's out playing soccer."

Dad was relieved. Finally, maybe things were turning around. "Let's go watch him for a minute," he suggested.

"I'm not sure we ought to do that," Hoots said.

Dad was confused. "Why not?"

"Well . . ." Hoots exhaled. "To protect him, I'm having him play with the girls."

Dad couldn't believe it. Hoots meant well—he was protecting me in his own way—but for my dad to see his son sent to play with the girls showed everything about my problem. It wasn't just that I struggled socially. It was that even the adults saw me as fundamentally different.

Dad stood there for a moment, letting the weight of it sink in. Finally, he managed: "I don't know what to say. Thanks for trying to help."

Then he turned around and walked home. His mind raced on the short walk.

Oh my gosh, he thought. *What can I do to help my son?*

Later I would come to understand that Dad shared some of the same personality traits I had growing up, though his weren't nearly as pronounced. But he'd had something I didn't: athletic talent. Being a gifted athlete through grade school, high school, and even college gave him a shield—protection from the kind of relentless isolation I faced. I didn't have that. And he knew it.

It wasn't that I wasn't trying. I wanted to fit in and to have friends. But the social world was foreign to me. Dad understood that now, in a way he hadn't fully before. No one was going to "fix" this for me—because there was no fix. There wasn't a teacher or therapist who could step in and suddenly make me fit in. If I was going to have any chance at a normal life—at making friends, at earning respect—something had to change. Dad knew the world wasn't going to change. It wasn't going to adapt to me. So he made a decision: If I was going to make it, he would have to adapt me to the world.

Dad figured if I could come out of it by the time I was twenty, I would be able to navigate life. If not, he feared I never would. This belief was underscored by what that woman had told him after my evaluation: I needed two things to have a chance at a normal life. First, I had to have the intelligence to understand, and second, I had to want it, to really desire to be part of the world around me. With that in mind, Dad decided to shape me his way.

He never explicitly told me his plan. It was more implied: *I need to teach you these things.*

For starters, Dad decided that push-ups would whip my eight-year-old body into shape so no schoolyard bully would dare mess with me. Soon he had me doing two hundred a day. But it was never just about the exercise; it was about goals. Dad always paired the physical challenges with a reward system: If I did a certain number of push-ups every day for three or four months, I'd earn something special, like a trip to Disney World with Mom. This discipline came with Dad's first lesson: "Self-esteem is earned, not given."

That lesson became a cornerstone of my upbringing. Dad's approach to building my self-esteem wasn't about shielding me from the world's harshness but about preparing me to face it head-on. This meant that I had to work for my sense of worth. It wasn't something that could be handed to me. It had to be built through real effort and achievement. For someone who struggled with social skills and relating to others, being told I should feel good about myself wasn't enough. I needed to develop the ability to interact successfully, and that required hard work. Every push-up, every small victory in overcoming a social hurdle, was a step toward earning my self-esteem.

Dad's honesty extended to all areas of my life. He never offered false encouragement. This tough-love approach meant I had to face my shortcomings and work hard to overcome them. Dad believed that my self-esteem should be grounded in real achievements, not empty affirmations.

The push-ups made me stronger, but I faced a different kind of struggle. At the private school I attended, physical bullying was rare but happened. What I faced was being completely ostracized in class. I never got invited to a birthday party or play date. I had no friends. People made fun of me about everything—my hair, the fact that I was chunky, even my socks. I often rolled them down because I didn't like the feeling of socks on my calves, but to the other kids, it was just one more thing that made me different. I was pushed around on the playground and humiliated constantly. I was easy to make fun of because I was weird. Walking around with a calculator at recess and wanting to talk to teachers about politics seemed normal to me but made me strange to others.

Dad understood that if I was going to have any chance at a normal, productive life—whatever that meant—I needed to learn social skills. If I didn't, I was doomed to always be different, friendless, and isolated. And I felt that isolation deeply. The loneliness was crushing at times, often bringing me to tears. But just as often, it made me angry. Frustration built inside me—and for years I would take that frustration out on Dad by yelling at him for hours.

I saw the relationships Dad had—real, meaningful friendships with people who respected and enjoyed being around him. I wanted that.

DISCOVERING I'M WEIRD

I watched other kids who had close friendships, who laughed easily together, and I desperately wanted those same connections. That longing became a motivating force, pushing me to try to understand the unspoken rules of social interaction. The constant bullying and awareness of my differences made the desire even stronger. The pain of being left out and picked on wasn't just hard—it was a powerful motivator.

Almost every parenting book is written from the parent's perspective, never the child's. Dad will tell you he believed helping me adapt was only possible because of my "intelligence." I would counter that it couldn't have happened without his love and determination.

Today, society wants to make accommodations for every perceived disability. My diagnosis, with an IQ spread from genius on one test to mentally impaired on others, would have gotten me significant special treatment as that became in vogue in the late '80s and '90s. But Dad believed that a cruel world would not make such accommodations after high school, and he was right. The lessons he taught through tough love, the drive he instilled in me to chase friendships and fight through the pain of loneliness—all of it led me to where I am today.

And yet, even now, when people think of autism, they don't picture someone like me. I talk on television every day and carry myself with confidence. I don't fit the stereotype of someone on the spectrum. If anything, I'm proof of how misunderstood autism still is. People are realizing that autism doesn't always look the way they once thought it did. Some of the most successful people in the world have been identified as being on the spectrum. Their autism hasn't gone away. Their success doesn't mean their struggles aren't real. It just means that for people like me, the road to success isn't as obvious, but it is possible. You're never "cured," but through a lot of hard work, you can learn to survive.

Looking back, I realize that this wasn't just a journey to independence. It was a journey to belonging. And, in the end, that's all I really wanted.

Chapter Two

BORN LUCKY

Some kids are born lucky. I was just lucky to be born.

That's how the story goes when my parents talk about the day I was born. I've heard it a hundred times, and it always starts the same: Dad sitting behind the blue hospital curtain at Barnes Hospital, holding Mom's hand, pretending to be calm for her sake. He wasn't thinking about me. He'll tell you that part without hesitation. "I was there for your mom," he says. Up until the moment I arrived, I was more of an abstract idea—a future Dad hadn't planned for, the kid he wasn't sure he wanted.

The curtain lying on Mom's chest was there to shield her from seeing the C-section—a thin, sterile blue wall between her and the doctor. She lay awake, the epidural blocking pain but not the sensation of pressure as they worked to get me out. Dad sat beside her bed, gripping her hand, unsure whether he was comforting her or himself. The hospital had done this same routine thousands of times for other parents. There was no reason to expect anything but a normal delivery. Dad felt helpless, watching the top half of Mom's body while the rest of her disappeared behind that curtain. Every so often, he'd lean around the edge to sneak a glance at whatever the doctor was doing on the other side.

And then, just as they were pulling me free, Mom and Dad heard commotion and whispers from behind the screen. Then came the pause. Then the fateful words.

"This is a very lucky baby!" the doctor said.

Mom tensed, alarmed by what she was hearing. Her hand gripped Dad's a little tighter.

"What's happening?" she asked. "What's wrong?"

Dad leaned forward, looking around the blue screen.

"Doc, is everything all right?" he asked.

The doctor didn't look up.

"Yep," he said. "Everything is fine."

Dad repeated it to Mom. "Doctor says it's okay."

But the room felt different now, heavier somehow. A nurse leaned in for a closer look, beginning to wipe me down. She gasped.

"Oh my God," she said. "This is a lucky baby."

Mom's voice broke the silence again.

"What's going on?" she asked. "What's happening?"

Dad leaned around again and was given another reassurance.

"He's fine," the doctor said. "Everything's fine."

This was my parents' worst nightmare. In 1982, waiting until thirty-five to have kids was considered a huge risk. They knew that. But they trusted the doctor, trusted the process. When they heard "everything's fine," they believed it. But those moments in the operating room—the whispers, the gasps, the repeated assurances—have stayed with them forever.

What they couldn't see then, what the doctor and nurses were discovering as they pulled me into the world, was just how close it had all come to going terribly wrong. The umbilical cord—my lifeline—had wrapped around my neck. There were also two knots in the cord, a potentially lethal combination. Had this been a natural birth, had Mom not agreed to a C-section, the pressure of the delivery would have tightened those knots and cinched the cord around my neck. I would have either died during delivery or, if I survived, been severely brain-damaged. But something had happened—a twist, a turn, a stroke of luck—that had kept those knots from tightening, cutting off oxygen, leaving me with cerebral palsy, or worse. If I hadn't turned exactly the way I did, if any single thing had gone differently . . . but it hadn't. I was here, I was breathing, I was alive.

The nurse took me to a small table in the back of the room, under bright lights, to clean me up and check my vital signs. Dad stayed with Mom, still holding her hand, still behind that blue curtain, both of them waiting to hear what would happen next. The nurse's voice carried across the room as she called out my weight: "Seven pounds, eleven ounces!"

"That's it!" the doctor said. "We're calling this kid Lucky."

And just like that, I had a nickname before I had a name.

No Kids, No House . . . and Then Me

If I was born lucky, my parents' love story—the one that led to my even existing—feels more like a gamble.

It started long before the blue curtain and the delivery room, back when Mom didn't have time for a guy who wore tennis shoes with no socks and ate a pint of ice cream for lunch. My parents met in high school in St. Louis, but life pulled them in different directions. Years later, they crossed paths again in Washington, DC. Dad, fresh off selling his first company, was working at the US Chamber of Commerce next to the White House. Mom, meanwhile, had plenty of suitors. After they went on one or two dates, she told him she was "busy"—not just busy for the next Saturday night but too busy for him, the guy who ate pints of ice cream for lunch.

"I am too busy," she said, standing on the steps of the chamber of commerce building as she dumped him. Evidently she was "busy" with lots of other dates. Years later, when I worked in DC, I'd walk past those same steps each day, picturing the moment she brushed him off.

Six months passed. Dad was in St. Louis, preparing to fly out for a meeting with Pedro Beltrán—the former prime minister of Ecuador and powerful owner of *La Prensa*, South America's most influential newspaper. But when he heard Mom was in town, he canceled the trip and convinced her to go out with him. The next day, a military coup erupted in Ecuador. Beltrán was arrested amid the chaos. In more ways than one, that date may have saved Dad's life.

Three dates. That's all it took.

Dad proposed to Mom at a rib joint—no ring, no grand gesture. Just barbecue sauce and, apparently, a whole lot of confidence. They were in their early twenties and perfectly content to keep things simple. They'd live in an apartment. No house. No kids. That was the deal.

But not everyone was thrilled. Mom's parents were the definition of old school, patrician, and they weren't exactly sold on Dad. They trace their lineage back to Jamestown, and Dad, in his tennis shoes and no socks, wasn't exactly fluent in the customs of high society. He was smart and driven, but table manners weren't his strong suit.

When Mom and Dad told her parents about their engagement in March 1972, my grandparents were too polite to object. But they didn't exactly scream, "Welcome to the family!" When they heard the news, my grandparents got up and walked to their respective desks on opposite sides of their grand living room and began flipping through their calendars.

"Well, when do you want to get married?" they asked.

"This week sounds okay," Dad answered.

They kept turning pages.

"We have dinner with the Smiths this night," my grandmother said.

"And Becky and Sam's anniversary is coming up," my grandfather added.

A few more page turns.

"The Browns' kids have a recital next month."

Before long, they had stretched the wedding out until June. That summer, Mom and Dad were married, but according to Mom, she almost didn't make it down the stairs. She stood at the top, crying, convinced she was making the worst decision of her life. It wasn't that she didn't want to marry Dad, but it all happened so quickly—suddenly the fun of marrying the guy from the rib joint got real. But, as Mom tells it, she wiped her tears, walked down the aisle, and married Dad.

For ten years, they stuck to the plan—no house, no kids.

But then Mom wanted to build a house. Dad didn't. He liked their apartment just fine—no gutters to clean, no lawn to mow. A house, to him, meant responsibilities he wasn't interested in. "I want nothing to do with a house," Dad told Mom. "When you build it, just tell me the day to come home."

But Dad did want one thing—a dog.

The dog thing was important to him. I didn't understand how much until I was older and he told me the story. When Dad was eight, all he wanted was a dog. His big brother, Bruce, was twelve years older and off at military school, leaving Dad more or less an only child. He begged and begged until my grandparents finally gave in. The dog came from a plumber who worked for the family business. His name was Rover. Dad loved him, right from the start. That whole first day, he stayed by Rover's side. When night came, he refused to leave him alone. My grandparents weren't the kind of people who let dogs inside the house. So Dad did the next best thing: He dragged a blanket out to the garage, where his mom made him a little bed on the cold concrete floor. The two of them—an eight-year-old boy and his new best friend—curled up together in the corner of the garage.

When Dad woke up in his bedroom the next morning, Rover was gone.

"He ran away," my grandfather told him.

"What?!" Dad was only eight, and the idea of Rover leaving him felt impossible. "Ran away?"

"He got out of the garage last night," my grandfather said.

That was it. No further explanation. No search party. Just an empty garage and a heartbroken kid. It wasn't until later that Dad pieced it together. The garage had been locked—it always was. My grandparents were impeccable about bolting every door. Rover didn't run away. My grandparents had decided they couldn't handle a dog, so they called the plumber that night, told him to come pick up Rover, and when Dad woke up, the dog was gone.

Dad always wanted a dog after that. So when Mom decided she wanted a house, Dad had one condition: He wanted a dog.

In preparation for building the house, Mom gave Dad a book of dog breeds. Every page showed a different breed, neatly laid out like a catalog. Mom had left it there like a contract waiting to be signed. Dad flipped through the pages, pausing when he landed on a Newfoundland. They were big, loyal, gentle dogs, independent enough to hold their own but loving enough to never leave your side. Not long after, Sally came home.

The house had happened. And shortly after, the dog showed up.

But a kid?

That wasn't part of the deal.

Mom and Dad had been married for ten years by then, and at thirty-five, Mom probably thought the whole "no kids" agreement was permanent. Having a first baby at that age wasn't the norm in 1982—most people were done having kids by then, not just getting started. And Dad wasn't exactly pushing to break the deal. He liked life without the extra responsibilities. Kids meant obligations, and Dad wasn't in the market for those. He wanted to work, build his businesses, and keep things simple.

But life doesn't always stick to the plan. One night, shortly after they moved into the new house, Mom dropped the bombshell. She was pregnant. Dad hugged her.

Dad never thought much about it after that. He probably figured Mom would handle everything, and he'd keep working, just like always. Whether they were having a boy or a girl, Dad didn't really see a child as his responsibility. At least, not yet.

Turning Points

By the time summer rolled around, Mom's pregnancy had gone as smoothly as anyone could hope for at thirty-five. She was healthy and there weren't any warnings or red flags—just routine appointments and waiting for me to come into the world.

Mom and Dad spent the summer up north at her parents' cottage in Leland, Michigan. The cool lake breeze, the quiet—it seemed like the perfect place to coast through the last few months of pregnancy.

A few weeks before I was due, Mom had her last appointment with her obstetrician in Traverse City, twenty miles north of the lake house. Dad drove her there, waiting outside in the car in keeping with his hands-off approach. It was a quick visit, nothing out of the ordinary. But when Mom came out, Dad noticed something was different.

"What's wrong, Carol?" he asked.

"Well," Mom said, "the baby is turned over."

I was upside down. Breech.

Mom, raised in Christian Science, grew up in a world where faith, not doctors, was the answer to healing. The church didn't outright forbid modern medicine, but it deeply discouraged reliance on it. She had gone to a Christian Science boarding school in St. Louis called Principia. When she was sixteen, she was stricken with a staph infection that nearly killed her. She overheard the school nurse telling her parents she might not make it. That's when she snuck out, hitchhiked to the nearest emergency room, and got antibiotics—saving her life. She left Christian Science after that, but by then the habit of trusting that everything would just work out had already taken root.

Mom didn't realize it at the time, but breech births come with complications. Being turned the wrong way increases the risk of the cord wrapping around the baby's neck or getting tangled in knots. But at that moment, Mom didn't see it as anything more than an inconvenience. She wanted a natural birth.

At the time, natural childbirth was the norm. There were articles everywhere about how C-sections were being scheduled for the convenience of doctors, not for necessity; delivering a baby at 9 a.m. on a Tuesday was preferable to delivering at 3 a.m. on a Saturday, and some believed doctors took advantage of that. So when her doctor advised she have a C-section, Mom thought about what to do. Maybe the baby would turn. Maybe she'd just go ahead and try for a natural delivery. But then she thought about something else—something she has always told me and I still live by to this day: "If you're not going to take your doctor's advice, you should get a new doctor." Mom figured if she wouldn't listen to the guy who went to medical school for this exact situation, what was the point?

That advice would later save my life, in the Middle East and other places. I've learned never to replace your judgment for those you have chosen to protect you. If you don't like someone's advice, go find someone else you trust. But if you choose them, you listen.

"I'm gonna have to have a cesarean," she told Dad from the passenger seat.

Mom and Dad returned to St. Louis for the birth. The doctors there confirmed the diagnosis: I was still breech. A few weeks later, on August 31, 1982, the doctors pulled me into the world and saw the truth of it. The umbilical cord was knotted around my neck. Twice.

Yet the knots hadn't tightened. I hadn't been deprived of oxygen. My Apgar score—a quick assessment done right after birth to check things like heart rate, breathing, muscle tone, reflexes, and skin color—was normal. That's what prompted the doctor to dub me "one lucky baby."

But if Mom hadn't taken the doctor's advice? If she'd decided to wait for a natural birth? That would have been a different story.

I wouldn't have been so lucky—I likely wouldn't have been alive.

Love at First Sight

The whiteboard hung just outside Mom's room at Barnes Hospital, a small rectangle of dry-erase smudges and medical charts, the kind every patient had for their newborn.

At the top, in neat handwriting, was my name: *Leland Holt Vittert.*

Leland for the town in Northern Michigan where my parents spent summers; Holt for my mother's maiden name; Vittert, of course, for my father. But sometime after I was born, the doctor came by with a marker, drew a small asterisk next to "Call this kid" and, in the space just below it, wrote, "Lucky."

For the next eighteen years, I was Lucky Vittert.

It wasn't a nickname. It was just who I was. When I walked into a room, I introduced myself that way. "Hi, I'm Lucky." No explanation. No backstory. My grandmother called me by my middle name—Holt—for a little while but gave up somewhere around middle school, maybe earlier. By the time I was old enough to write, it felt normal. I didn't question it, at least not until people started asking, "Is that your real name?" It wasn't something I explained back then, not like I do now. Lucky was just Lucky.

You already know that Dad wasn't in love with the idea of having a kid. But that changed the second he saw me. After the doctors untangled the cord, they carried me across the room and placed me under the warming lamp. Dad stayed where he was, hands in his pockets, watching from a few feet away. Up until that moment, I was a future he hadn't planned for. Then he walked over for a closer look. Dad told me once that, right until then, he felt almost nothing. "I went from zero to loving you in two seconds," he told me. From that point on, he never looked at me the same.

In the hours after I was born, everything felt simple to Dad. Maybe this fatherhood thing would be okay. I was healthy. Mom was resting. Dad was holding me in his arms, surprised by how quickly love had taken over. It was almost like an asteroid had missed. At first, no one really thought about how close it came to hitting. There wasn't much reason to. When you're standing in the hospital room, staring down at a baby who made it safely into the world, the sky feels too blue to think about the darkness. But as the doctors came in and out over the next few days, explaining more about what had happened—the breech birth, the umbilical cord wrapped twice around my neck, the knots that hadn't pulled tight—the asteroid's near-miss started to feel a little more real. The decision to schedule the C-section hadn't felt like a big deal at the time. Mom trusted the doctor's advice, took his advice, and that was that. But in hindsight, that decision was everything.

A few years later, Mom worked in a program with kids with disabilities. One of her closest friends had a son whose birth had been mismanaged. He was deprived of oxygen, and though he was cognitively alert, his body didn't follow. He could use his thumb and forefinger, but not much else. Mom had never known a child with severe disabilities before, and the more time she spent with him, the more she saw what I had escaped. It wasn't hard to picture how things might have turned out if the cord around my neck had tightened just a little more, if the doctors had waited too long, or if Mom had insisted on a natural birth. I could have been that boy.

It's strange how much can turn on a single decision—one image on an ultrasound altering my fate. I've thought about that more than I probably should. I made it out of that delivery room, but some days, surviving felt like the easy part. Being Lucky didn't mean being understood. It didn't make friends easier to find or teachers easier to impress. Sometimes, it felt like I'd used up all my luck before I even took my first breath.

Some kids are born lucky. I was just lucky to be born. I didn't know it yet, but the real fight wasn't behind me—it was just getting started. Maybe surviving day one made me lucky, but I've learned that luck can only carry you so far.

Chapter Three

THE MEASURE OF A MAN

I never met my dad's dad, my grandfather, but I feel like I know him.

I can picture him standing outside the family dry goods store in the Jewish Irish ghetto in St. Louis in the early 1900s, broom in hand, clearing the sidewalk. Not for customers—there weren't many of those left. But the snow didn't care if business was slow, and neither did he. My grandfather wasn't the kind of man who left things half done. I know because Dad told me, over and over.

My grandfather's neighborhood wasn't the kind of ghetto you see in movies, but the kind where your family ran a dry goods store and scraped by until the next generation could climb one rung higher. You wouldn't have known it looking at him. Even when times were tough, he dressed like a man who had already made it—pressed suit, vest, gold watch chain, tie pin, polished shoes. Dad always said he was the finest-dressed man in the room, no matter what was left in his pocket.

When the stock market crashed in 1929 and the real estate market collapsed soon after in the 1930s, my grandfather lost everything. He could've done what plenty of others did—declared bankruptcy and started over. But that wasn't who he was. Instead, he swept floors. He worked three jobs at once. He lived in the basement of a building he used to own. Because in his mind, debt wasn't just money you owed; it was proof of who you were as a person.

You didn't get out of the ghetto by being soft.

He was a hard, hard man.

That's how Dad described him.

"He wasn't mean," Dad would say. "But you didn't survive the Depression by playing golf on weekends."

Dad likes to tell the story of the day my grandfather fired a man who didn't even work for him. By the time Dad was old enough to notice, my grandfather had built a cleaning and waterproofing company from the ground up. He started as a window washer at seventeen and climbed his way into ownership. When you worked your way up like that, you didn't forget the value of keeping busy. Most days, my grandfather would visit his projects over lunch, still dressed in his suit with his gold watch chain, tie pin, and shined shoes. One afternoon, he stopped by a City Hall project where his crew was cleaning the building. Back then, the smoke from coal furnaces and power plants stained city buildings, thus the need for constant cleaning. The men were coming down from the scaffolding, getting ready for lunch, but one man was just standing there. A big guy, leaning against the railing, doing nothing. My grandfather walked up to him.

"What are you doing?" he asked.

"Nothing," the guy said. "Just waiting around."

That was enough.

"You're fired," my grandfather said flatly. "Nobody stands around on our projects! You're outta here. Take off."

Later that day, the foreman came into his office and said that so-and-so told him my grandfather had fired him.

"Absolutely!" my grandfather affirmed.

"He doesn't work for us!" the foreman shot back. "He was just coming over to have lunch."

Dad loved that story, not because of how tough my grandfather was but because of how clear the rules were. You worked hard, you didn't stand around, and you didn't test him. It wasn't just about work. Those rules applied at home too.

When Dad was about eight, he learned that the hard way—over something as small as brushing his teeth. One day my grandfather asked Dad, "Do you brush your teeth every morning?"

Without hesitation, Dad said, "Yeah, I brush my teeth once a day."

That was Dad's first lie. He hardly ever brushed his teeth then.

A few days later Dad went downstairs for breakfast. My grandfather looked at him from across the table. "Did you brush your teeth today?"

"Yep!" Dad said.

"Just before you came down?" my grandfather asked.

Dad nodded.

"Let's go upstairs for a minute," my grandfather said. Dad followed him, not thinking much of it. They walked into the bathroom. My grandfather pulled Dad's toothbrush from the cup by the sink and held it up. It was dry as a bone.

"What did you brush your teeth with?" he asked. Dad didn't have an answer.

There was no scolding, no raised voice. "Let's take a little ride," my grandfather said.

They got in the car, and Dad remembers thinking the whole thing felt almost fun, like an adventure. They drove through St. Louis as if nothing had happened. But after a while, they pulled up to a big brick building on a hill across the street from Forest Park. Dad remembers it being huge, but everything feels big when you're eight.

"I want to show you this place," my grandfather said as they climbed the steps and walked inside. "This is an orphanage." He walked Dad down the hall, and into the office of the man who ran the place. They didn't stay long. "I just wanted you to see what this was like," my grandfather said.

Dad was confused. When they left, my grandfather stopped at the top of the steps and turned to Dad.

"If you don't stop lying," he said, "this is where you're going to live from now on." Dad looked up at him, shocked. "You didn't brush your teeth, but you told me you did. You've told other lies before. I'm telling you now—you cannot lie."

And that was it. Dad learned his lesson.

Dad is adamant that my grandfather wasn't mean. He was just a hard man, made harder by the ghetto and the Depression. But tough didn't mean unloving. My grandfather may not have been the kind of dad who threw the ball around after work or took his kids to the movies, but there was no question he loved my dad and his older brother, Bruce. He just showed it differently.

My grandfather wasn't a "kids" kind of guy. He played catch with my dad once. *One time.* And he did it in his suit and tie. "I think he took his coat off," Dad told me. They never went to a baseball game. They did almost nothing together. That's why Dad says he can so vividly remember singular moments.

When Dad joined Little League, it never crossed his mind to expect his father to show up. My grandmother dropped him off for games, while the other dads gathered near the fence or watched from the stands. He never wondered where his dad was; he just knew he didn't care for sports and thought they were a waste of time. But one afternoon, as Dad stood on the pitcher's mound, he spotted a car through the trees. Parked way back, just off the road, was his dad's car. He never came down to the field. He stayed right there under the shade, watching from a distance. Dad said they never talked about it, but he was there. That mattered more than anything. Because even though my grandfather may not have said the words, his love showed up in singular moments. And those were the moments Dad held onto.

But the one memory that stayed with Dad the most wasn't a moment they shared—it was a letter his father left behind. Dad was sixteen the night he found out. He was standing in front of the mirror, combing his hair, getting ready for a date. My grandmother wasn't home. Dad hadn't thought much of it until he saw Bruce's reflection in the mirror behind him. His older brother was just standing there, quiet.

"Bruce?" Dad said. "What are you doing here?"

Bruce delivered the news: Their father had died suddenly that afternoon.

They drove downtown to my grandfather's office. It was a late, cold, rainy November night, but my grandfather had written a letter to Dad and Bruce and locked it away in the office safe. He had told Bruce about it, told him that one day, when the time came, it would be his responsibility to read it aloud to Dad. So in that office, sitting across from their father's desk in two big leather chairs, Bruce reached into the safe and pulled out the letter. It had been there for years. My grandfather had written it when Dad was four. It was about how to live a life that mattered.

The letter didn't talk about money or success. It wasn't about honors or titles. It was about character. Dad always said that was the part that stuck with him the most—the idea that who you are matters more than what you have or your position in life. My grandfather wrote that a man isn't measured by his net worth or a shelf full of awards. He's measured by his character.

Achievements, not accolades.
Tell the truth.
Keep your word.
Earn your self-esteem.

Simple things, but those were the lessons that shaped Dad long after his father was gone. The letter didn't just tell him how to live. It gave him something to measure himself against. Dad always believed in setting goals—articulable, achievable goals, as he called them. And once you set them, you worked like hell to reach them. Dad's famous line was, "I was never afraid of failure. I was always afraid of not succeeding."

That letter became more than just words on a piece of paper. Dad has carried it in his wallet ever since that day. It became the map Dad would follow for the rest of his life. And, whether he realized it or not, it became the map he passed down to me.

The 107th Call

Dad was twenty when he started his first company. He says he had no idea what he was doing. But he didn't want to go back to St. Louis after college and work for the family business or rely on anyone else's money. He wanted to make it on his own. So he did.

That mindset started long before his first company. The summer between his sophomore and junior year of college, Dad went door-to-door with a can of reflective spray paint and a set of stencils, offering to paint house numbers on curbs. He wanted to learn how to "sell." His pitch? Easily visible numbers could help the police or an ambulance find their address in an emergency.

He refined his pitch, adjusted his timing, and figured out that dense subdivisions—where he could move from one house to the next with minimal effort—were the most efficient. He studied what worked and what didn't. He made a game out of improving his numbers, setting a daily goal and trying to beat it. By the end of the summer, he was selling dozens of houses a day: his first real lesson in persistence, salesmanship, and, most importantly, goal-setting.

Years later, he would teach me that same lesson. If you don't have a goal, you don't know where you're going. And if you don't know where you're going, how will you ever get there? That summer, selling curb numbers for a dollar at a time, was where he first proved it to himself.

Not long after, Dad graduated from DePauw University and jumped right into building his first company on June 1, 1969. He secured an investment of $56,000 from John Burkhart, an insurance executive in Indianapolis, and rented a tiny headquarters—so small he said it felt like a men's room stall.

The idea was simple: Reach college students. Back then, companies had a hard time marketing to kids on campus. College students didn't read newspapers. They weren't glued to TV screens or radios. Cell phones and social media didn't exist. But if you could introduce them to a brand at eighteen or nineteen, there was a good chance they'd stay loyal for life. Razor blades, colognes, credit cards—small decisions that stuck around long after graduation. Dad saw an opening. He figured he could pitch big companies on the idea of letting his business represent their products on campuses across America.

Just after graduation, Dad opened that office in Indianapolis and hired five of his fellow college grads to work the office and sign up college students to work on campuses around the country. He was the lone salesperson dialing the phones. He started cold-calling company after company, asking if he could stop by for an appointment. That summer he traveled from Los Angeles to New York to Miami. Oil companies, airlines, consumer goods—you name it, he visited. Every time, the answer was the same: No.

By the end of August, the company had $1,000 left in the bank. There was no debt, but there was no future either. Dad had made 106 sales calls across the US without a single yes. He gathered the group at the office in Indianapolis on a Monday.

"I haven't made a sale," he told them. "I think we're going to close up on Friday."

Most of the crew were already set to leave. They had business school, law school, or other jobs lined up. By Wednesday, Dad was ready to shut it all down. He had two final appointments in Houston—one with Texaco in the morning and another with Humble Oil in the afternoon. Neither felt promising. But sitting in the office felt like attending a funeral. He just wanted to disappear. So he went—just to get out of town.

His first meeting, with Texaco, was at 9 a.m. He waited in the lobby, only to realize he'd been stood up. Outside, the Houston heat hit him—humid and suffocating. He sat on a low, brick wall near the office, staring at nothing, wondering what to do next.

The next meeting with Humble Oil was at 1 p.m. *Why bother?* Dad thought. It'd just be another polite no, he figured. He found a pay phone, hoping for an earlier flight home. The plane was full. He sat back down.

The weight of the disappointment hit. He felt like he'd let everyone down—his dad, the people in the office, and Mr. Burkhart. But with nothing else to lose except time, he kept the final appointment. Humble Oil's office tower felt a world away from the cramped little Indianapolis headquarters. He rode the elevator up, walked into the office, and sat down across from an executive named James A. Fite.

Dad gave the same pitch he'd given 106 times before. It didn't take long—four minutes, maybe.

Mr. Fite looked at Dad. "I think we'd like to do this."

Dad kept talking. He didn't process the words at first. He just kept rolling through the sales pitch.

"Son, do you understand me?" Mr. Fite asked. "I think we'd like to do this here at Humble Oil."

Humble Oil, which was part of what is now ExxonMobil, agreed to hire Dad's company to distribute credit card applications on college campuses. Mr. Fite asked his secretary to write up a memorandum. The agreement was a small marketing initiative for Humble Oil, a rounding error on their books. But to Dad, it meant survival. Mr. Fite brought the printed letter over and handed it to Dad. "Will this do as an understanding?" he asked.

Dad gets embarrassed when he tells this part of the story, but he put his head in his hands and started to cry. Mr. Fite came around his desk and pulled up a chair next to him.

"Are you okay?" he asked.

"You just saved me and saved my company," Dad said.

Then he admitted something he hadn't told anyone else except for the five employees back in Indianapolis.

"We're scheduled to close the company on Friday," he said.

Mr. Fite raised an eyebrow. "What? Well, do you want to do this or not?" he asked.

Dad called back to the office and got one of the guys on the phone. This was before speakerphones—or at least Dad's company didn't have one—so everybody gathered around the receiver and Dad told them what had just happened. One by one, the guys who were packing for law school or other jobs said they'd stay.

"Everyone is gonna stay," he said.

That 107th sales call saved Dad's company.

By the time he flew back to Indianapolis, everything had changed. The deal with Humble Oil opened doors Dad didn't even know were there. More companies followed—Sun Oil, Gulf, Standard of Indiana, and Trans World Airlines. Within one year, his company had marketing reps on *seven hundred* college campuses across the country. They were distributing credit card applications; running marketing polls for Miles Laboratories, Schlitz, and Levi Strauss; and even handling promotions for Hamm's Beer.

In early 1971, Dad sold the company, College Marketing & Research Corp., to Playboy Enterprises for $1.5 million. He was twenty-three years old. *Time* magazine wrote an article about him: "MILLIONAIRES: Campus Conquistador."

> He is a bachelor who does not drink, smoke or cuss and seldom dates. He drives a battered, four-year-old convertible, lives in a spartan one-room apartment and dislikes business entertaining to the point that he serves visitors sandwiches for lunch in his office. He professes little interest in making more money. "What can I do with it?" he asks, echoing the concern of the confused generation. "Eat four meals a day?"[1]

The article made him sound more like a college kid scraping by than one of America's youngest millionaires. But that was Dad. The money wasn't the point. It wasn't about the sale. It was about the 106 rejections that came before the first yes. I think that's what stuck with me the most. The way Dad always told the story—the victory wasn't in selling the company or becoming a millionaire. It was in not quitting before that 107th call. He never framed it as a business lesson. It was bigger than that. I don't even think Dad told me the full story growing up. I pieced it together over time, hearing it during speeches he gave. What I remember more than anything was the feeling that came with it: You don't give up. *Ever.* Later he applied the same work ethic to helping me.

After he sold the company, Dad didn't stop. By the time I was born, he had already revived and sold IBC Root Beer and developed a racquetball company that he partnered with Brown Shoe Co. to start. Then came the *Business Journals*. A friend brought him a chamber-of-commerce-style newsletter from Houston and suggested he start something like it in St. Louis. Dad sat on it for a year. It wasn't until he saw *Crain's Chicago Business* introduce their publication that he decided to give it a try. What started with one paper in St. Louis eventually grew to papers in six or seven cities—Baltimore, Cincinnati, Indianapolis, Philadelphia, Pittsburgh—and a number of other publications.

Alongside the business, Dad started writing a column for the paper—and he's still doing it forty-four years later. Out of everything he's written, there's one column people remember the most. It was about his dad. It opened with a line that has stayed with me for years. I must have read it a thousand times, hanging on the wall by his shelf at home.

The headline read: "I'd give every asset I have if I could just have him back for one day."

Dad wrote that he'd trade everything he'd ever earned to spend just twenty-four hours with his father. The column wasn't about regrets. It was about the questions he never got to ask—how his dad fell in love with my grandmother, how he built his career, why he was so tough, and why he loved so deeply even if he rarely showed it. "I know those twenty-four priceless hours would be worth it," Dad wrote in the final sentence, "if at our goodbye he said, 'I like the way you turned out, son.'"

For all the businesses Dad built and the hours he worked, he never let that get in the way when he was home. Mom would get me ready for bed, and then she'd sit me on the steps outside the garage, waiting for Dad to come home. It didn't matter how late it was or how long he'd been working—when he pulled into the driveway, he'd scoop me up, take me inside, and put me to bed.

Sometimes, I wouldn't let him leave. I'd throw my arm over him, refusing to let go until I fell asleep. That happened a lot during dinner parties. Dad would take me downstairs to put me to bed, but occasionally, he'd fall asleep beside me. I'd wake up later and wander back upstairs in my pajamas with my teddy bear. Guests would laugh, and Mom would have to go to my room, nudge Dad awake, and send him back upstairs.

Dad worked a phenomenal number of hours. But when he was home, he was exactly where he needed to be.

The Day Everything Changed

Bert Steppig was the kind of man you couldn't help but admire. Bert came from nothing in Columbia, Illinois, and was building a business empire brick by brick. They met when Bert wanted to open a discount grocery store and came to Dad for advice and financing. Bert had an unrelenting energy, two little boys at home, and a business on the rise.

One afternoon, Bert showed up at Dad's office with a wild idea. "I want to buy a professional baseball team," he said. Dad thought he was nuts. Baseball teams weren't the billion-dollar investments they are today—this was the early 1980s, and owning a team sounded more like a financial sinkhole than a smart business move. Dad wasn't interested.

"I want you to be my partner," Bert insisted.

Dad laughed it off. "You've got the wrong guy."

But Bert wouldn't take no for an answer. "You're my good luck charm," he told Dad. "I won't do it without you. I'm asking you if you would do this."

Eventually, Dad agreed to take a small stake. Bert needed connections. He had no way of knowing which teams might be for sale. Dad knew Dick Waters, the publisher of *The Sporting News*, and called him.

Born Lucky

"Dick, I know this is crazy for me," Dad said. "Are there any Major League Baseball teams for sale? A pal of mine came in and he really wants to buy a professional baseball team."

A day later, Waters called back. "The Pittsburgh Pirates are for sale," he said. The price: $11 million. Dad told Bert, and they set a lunch for the next day to go over the details.

Bert was never late. If Bert said noon, he'd be there at 11:50. That's why Dad was surprised when the clock hit 12:15 and Bert hadn't arrived. By 12:30, Dad was starting to worry. Bert must have been in an accident, he thought. He called Bert's house but got no answer. Finally, the phone rang. It was Bert.

"I'm sorry," Bert said. "I should've called earlier. My mind hasn't been clear. I'm at the airport."

He was flying to the Mayo Clinic. The night before, Bert had an insurance exam with someone from Washington University Medical School. Bert had been applying for a life insurance policy. As he took off his shirt, the guy noticed a bump on his back. "Have you been paying attention to this?" he asked.

Bert, surprised, replied, "I didn't even know it was there. Who looks at a bump on their back?"

The intern recommended Bert see his doctor as soon as possible. By the next morning, Bert had an appointment. His doctor confirmed the worst—it was melanoma. Within hours, Bert was waiting to board a plane to Minneapolis.

Dad wished Bert well. "Whatever happens," Dad told him, "we'll start fresh when you get back." But there was no fresh start.

Two years later, Dad visited Bert at his hospital bedside on a Friday night. The next morning was a quiet Saturday. Dad told Mom he was going to take a walk, just to think about things. I was little, barely three. Dad walked across the street to John Burroughs School, circling the high school running track a few times. When he returned home, Mom was waiting for him on the front steps.

"Bert died last night," Mom said softly.

"Carol," Dad said, "I'm going for another walk."

He wandered for hours, passing the country club and familiar streets, thinking about Bert's two little boys, about his own life, and about what really mattered. Bert died in 1985, within days of his fortieth birthday. Dad, who was thirty-eight at the time, felt the weight. It was a reminder that even the strongest, healthiest people aren't immune to life's unpredictability.

By the time he returned home, Dad's mind was made up.

"I'm selling everything," he told Mom.

"What are you talking about?" she said.

"Bert is leaving two boys behind," Dad said. "He didn't know what was going to happen to him. I don't know what's going to happen to me."

Dad had been working since he was twenty, pouring everything into his businesses, barely stopping to breathe. But after Bert's death, he saw things differently. Bert had everything ahead of him—a thriving business, two sons, and a future that should have stretched out for decades. And a bump on his back changed all of it. Dad wasn't going to risk one day regretting the hours he missed with his family. So he made the decision to step away.

"I'm selling," Dad told Mom. "I'm done. That's that."

Bert's death had underscored what my grandfather's letter had already made clear: Life's real scoreboard isn't tallied in bank accounts or accolades. It's measured in the time you spend with the people who matter most.

Chapter Four

MY FATHER'S PROMISE

Shorewood wasn't the biggest house on the lake. It wasn't the fanciest, either. But standing on that dock, it felt (and still feels) like an escape from whatever is wrong with the world.

The lake house sat at the edge of Lake Leelanau, in Leland, Michigan. It was a big home with six bedrooms in the main house and two more in the small cottage. Mom's grandfather built it during the Depression. My great-grandmother had heart disease, and her doctor recommended she spend summers out of the heat. Summers in the Mississippi Valley during the 1930s were unbearable—hot, humid, and sticky. Without air-conditioning, the only escape was to head north, as far as the car and a little disposable income could take you.

That's how my great-grandparents ended up by Lake Leelanau. They weren't looking for land; they were visiting their dear friends who had a small summer cottage by the lake. One afternoon, standing right where Shorewood sits today, my great-grandfather cast his line into the clear water and reeled in a "large" fish. That was all the reason he needed. By the end of the trip, he'd decided this was the spot to build something permanent: a house big enough for family, friends, and an escape from the heat.

By the time I sat on that dock, the house had passed from my great-grandparents to my grandparents and then to my parents. Mom and Dad didn't buy it because they needed more space—they bought it because they needed more space for *people*. Dad liked people. And people liked Shorewood. In the summers, they came in droves. Friends from St. Louis, old business partners, college buddies he hadn't seen in years. I didn't know most of their names, but I liked the company—generally adults were nicer to me—and their conversations. They were interesting people, and I, with my insatiable curiosity and questions, liked hearing about their lives.

In 1986, everything changed. Dad sold everything—the *Business Journals*, the real estate holdings, all of it. At four years old, I didn't understand what that meant. I just knew there were fewer phone calls and more mornings with Dad. Selling was the easy part. Companies had been circling, waiting for the chance. What came next was harder. Dad had been running at full speed for twenty years. He wasn't good at stopping.

The thought of sitting at home all day watching soap operas was unbearable for Dad. It wasn't about money. He didn't need to sell. His businesses had been rewarding, and by all accounts, he was financially secure. But after a while, success wasn't enough. He wanted to do something that mattered.

The famous Nazi hunter Simon Wiesenthal had long fascinated Dad. Wiesenthal had survived the Holocaust and made it his life's mission to hunt down the Nazis who orchestrated it. By the '80s, he'd already helped track and capture hundreds of war criminals. Most of the men he pursued were in their sixties or seventies by then, scattered across the world. Some had slipped into quiet lives in South America or the US, while others hid in plain sight in Europe. But Wiesenthal kept going, often working alongside the Office of Special Investigations in the US Justice Department. Wiesenthal's dogged determination to track down war criminals resonated with Dad. Maybe it was his Jewish background or the belief that injustice shouldn't go unanswered.

MY FATHER'S PROMISE

Dad decided he wanted to join Wiesenthal. Dad didn't speak German. He had no experience. But that didn't stop him. Once Dad made up his mind, that was usually the end of the discussion. The same persistence that got him through 107 sales calls when he started his first business out of college kicked in again. For six months, he worked every angle he could, eventually convincing Wiesenthal's lawyer, Marty Mendelson, to arrange a dinner in DC with the famed Nazi hunter himself. That dinner became an interview. Dad was there to pitch himself as Wiesenthal's assistant.

At the start of the meeting, Wiesenthal introduced himself in German. Dad looked at him like he was speaking gibberish.

"You know German, don't you?" Wiesenthal asked.

"No," Dad replied.

Wiesenthal paused, then continued in German.

Dad just stared at him.

Mendelson leaned in, clearly confused.

"Well . . . don't you know German?" he asked.

"I don't even know my name in German!" Dad said.

It turned out someone had misunderstood somewhere along the line. Mendelson must have thought he was hiring this unbelievable find, an entrepreneur who not only had built a successful company but also somehow spoke fluent German and wanted to track down war criminals. The dinner ended politely, but the message was clear: Wiesenthal needed someone who could translate, someone who could sift through Nazi records without needing to stop and ask what each word meant. That wasn't Dad.

But if there was one thing Dad was good at, it was knocking on the next door when one closed. Right after realizing the Wiesenthal job wouldn't work out, Dad started thinking about the United Nations. My Jewish grandmother had fled Ukraine during the pogroms, so the cause felt personal. He learned about a job (volunteer) opening at the UN working alongside the deputy high commissioner for refugees in Geneva.

And so in March 1987, we packed up and moved to Switzerland. I didn't understand why we left. All I knew was that Shorewood sat empty that summer, waiting for us to come back.

Ritz Crackers and Paddleboats

I was turning five when we moved. At that age, living at a hotel on Lake Geneva felt like stepping into a playground. We spent a few weeks in the hotel before moving into a small apartment nearby. Geneva in the 1980s was a combination of wealth and secrecy: Arab businessmen arriving with briefcases full of francs trying to buy watches, Swiss bankers who would take money from anyone, and an atmosphere that felt both luxurious and mysterious. To me, it was like Disney World with fewer lines and better chocolate.

Life beside the water felt like something out of a postcard. I remember learning to ride my bike on the path that circled Lake Geneva. It was the kind of place where even something as ordinary as riding a bike felt like part of a big adventure.

I went to the International School, where diplomats' kids were driven by their family's security detail. My mom took me. The diplomat kids showed up with French desserts and pastries—éclairs, pistachio cakes, things with fancy layers and powdered sugar. It was a competition between the mothers to see whose kid had the fanciest snack. I had Ritz crackers. But somehow, the crackers were like gold to the other kids. One Ritz cracker could get me four éclairs. The kids thought cheese crackers were exotic. I'd come home every day with my pockets full of desserts, and Mom couldn't figure out how I'd managed to trade up.

Dad said he didn't do much in Geneva besides drink coffee and twiddle his thumbs. He wasn't busy the way he had been back home, and that left time for experiences. I didn't have any friends there; not only was I a weird kid, but I didn't speak the language. Dad seemed to know that, and he made sure I didn't feel alone. Material things never meant much to Dad—he still owns only two pairs of pants—but experiences were everything. I was really into trains, so we spent days and weeks riding them and visiting train museums. Switzerland was the train capital of the world. One day, Dad called around and arranged for us to visit LGB, the famous model train company, for my birthday. I still have a photo of me sitting at the chairman's desk.

I don't remember much about Geneva. I was so young that most of it feels like a blur. But there are those little bits, those singular moments in life that stand out no matter how young you are.

One of those was the time Dad nearly died there. He caught a cold, something minor, and a doctor prescribed antibiotics. "Any allergies?" the doctor asked.

"No Sulfa," Dad replied.

But the doctor misunderstood, thinking Dad was saying, "No allergies, give me Sulfa." And the doctor gave him the antibiotic that basically was going to kill him. He kept getting sicker, almost to the point of death.

By the time Dad arrived at the hospital, things were serious. On the way there, he held the pill bottle in his hand and asked Mom, "Should I take this next one?"

Mom, who was alone in a foreign country with a toddler, told him, "Maybe don't take it." He didn't. Later, Dad described waking up in the ICU, convinced for a few moments he had died and ended up in the morgue. Not taking that last pill almost certainly saved his life.

My other Swiss memory sticks out not because it was extraordinary, but because looking back it was a first marker of how different I was from everyone else. One day, Dad and I took a paddleboat out onto Lake Geneva. It was one of those small boats with pedals and a little steering wheel in the middle that went left and right. We were about fifty yards off a fishing jetty when the paddle wheel snagged a fishing line. Dad called over to some fishermen for a knife. "Sit here and hold onto the steering wheel," Dad told me. "Don't move!"

He dove into the freezing lake and swam to the fishermen to retrieve the knife. I sat in that little paddleboat, hands gripping the wheel, waiting. When he got back, I was still holding on. I didn't know any better. When Dad said not to move, I took it literally.

When we paddled over to return the knife, next to the fishermen was a topless sunbather. She was a nightclub singer. I asked her, "Do you sing with your clothes on?" Dad thought it was hilarious. I didn't know any better.

Socially awkward would have been a generous description of me at that age. Honestly, I would have given anything to just be socially awkward. I was far beyond that—living in my own world, completely oblivious to how out of place I was.

When Dad sold his businesses, he wasn't thinking about problems or concerns with me. There had been small comments from Mom about how I never seemed to make friends or how I didn't talk. But Dad either brushed them aside or submerged them. He didn't have much to compare me to. He wasn't around many kids growing up. His brother, Bruce, was twelve years older, so to him, I was just a regular little boy. I didn't have friends, but Dad figured I'd grow into it.

Geneva began to change that.

As I mentioned, I was enrolled at the International School. I guess I remember pieces of it because the story has been told to me over the years. One day, the head of the school, a strict Swiss educator, pulled Mom aside at the end of the school day.

"He doesn't fit," she said. "We don't want him here anymore."

For a prestigious international school, filled with diplomats' kids from all over the world, to ask a five-year-old to leave—especially an American, especially the son of someone working with the UN—was significant. It wasn't just about me not fitting in. For them to say they couldn't have a little boy at the school was a big deal. Someone pleaded with the school to let me stay. Maybe it was Dad, maybe his boss at the UN, but someone convinced them I could stay. The school agreed that if Mom stayed with me during class, I could remain at the school.

That was a wake-up call to Dad that something might be really different about me, something that wouldn't just "smooth out" with time like he'd been hoping. The cracks were showing. He didn't understand, at least not at first. How could a five-year-old not "fit" into kindergarten? Dad had never heard of autism or Asperger's. To him, I was just . . . me. "You're you," he always used to say, as if that explained everything. But now he was starting to wonder if I wasn't just a little different. Or maybe I was something else entirely.

Not long after, Mom got pregnant—a surprise neither of them had planned for. The doctor said she either had to fly home to the US within the next month or stay in Switzerland until the baby was born. There were some complications in her pregnancy—nothing severe, but enough to make them nervous because of what had happened during my birth. Dad decided to cut the stay short, and we moved back to America.

A Leap of Trust

Late that summer, back at Shorewood, Dad taught me one of the most important lessons of my life from the branch of a tree. By this time, my parents owned Shorewood and my grandparents had moved next door on the lake. In the middle of my grandparents' yard next door stood this big tree with a limb cut out just right—like a little platform that I could stand on. It wasn't high, maybe five feet, about the height of Dad's shoulder, but to me, it felt enormous.

One afternoon, Dad lifted me onto that notch and held his hand against my tummy to steady me. "Do you trust me?" he asked, stepping back from the limb. I nodded. "Just jump into my arms," he said. It looked like a long way down. To a five-year-old, it might as well have been one hundred feet. I hesitated for a second, but then I dove forward. Dad caught me like he said he would.

"I'll always catch you," he said, holding me close. "You can trust me to always be there for you."

Years before, a friend of Dad's had tried to teach his own son a different lesson. He put his boy up on the mantle above the fireplace and told him to jump. When the boy jumped, the dad let him fall to the ground. "Never trust anyone," he told his son crying on the floor after the fall. Dad was horrified by that story. When he put me on that tree, he wanted me to know the world wasn't something to fear, at least not with him there. It was Dad's way of telling me, "I can help you. Trust me, and we'll figure things out together."

Looking back, that was one of those moments that shaped the bond between us. It wasn't just about catching me from a jump. It was about the kind of trust that would carry us through the years ahead. Trust would become the most important part of our relationship—I trusted Dad that things would get better, and I trusted that he would protect me.

My sister, Liberty, was born not long after we moved back to St. Louis. I was used to being the center of attention, and I didn't adjust well to sharing the spotlight. I'd had enough after about ten days. I asked Mom and Dad when we could take her back to the hospital and return her. I was five and a half.

Back in St. Louis, I started kindergarten at Rohan Woods, the same tiny, private grade school Dad had gone to growing up. I was the oldest kid in my class, partly because of my late birthday and partly because I was slow to catch on.

By 1989, Mom and Dad wanted to try living at Shorewood for a couple of winters, so we moved to Michigan. I went to first and second grade at Leland Public School, a tiny school with only about sixteen kids in my class. I had no friends and hated school. I was verbal by then—after not talking much for years—but I still didn't know how to interact with other kids. The year in Geneva probably didn't help. When you're that young and can't speak the language, it sets you even further apart. By the time we returned to the States, I was unable to communicate. Looking back, I realize how much that early isolation shaped me. It makes me think about the kids who went through the COVID-19 pandemic, missing out on years of social development.

Living in rural Michigan probably only made things more difficult. In the summer, it felt like paradise—tubing, fishing, and days on the lake. But winters were desolate. Leland was in one of the poorest counties in Michigan. I continued to get along with adults better than kids my age. I was sort of the fish out of water. At school, I was the weird kid from the summer family, the "fudgie." Locals called tourists *fudgies* because they bought fudge from the local shops in Northern Michigan. If you owned a summerhouse, you were *permafudge*—permanent tourists. That was me. I stood out, and not in a way that helped me make friends.

During one of those long, cold Michigan winters—in January 1991—the Gulf War began. I would sneak downstairs at night to watch CNN's coverage. The images of SCUD missiles and the so-called "SCUD Studs" reporting from Baghdad captivated me. Those quiet nights, watching the world unfold from a small Michigan town, sparked my first love for TV journalism. Years later, I would tell that story at every job interview I had with CNN—though they never bit.

Dad eventually got tired of the cold winters, and by December, we had packed up and hit the road. We traveled for months at a time during both first and second grade, probably five months out of the school year. We had a nanny who traveled with us, and I spent most of my time in the back of an RV reading or doing math. I loved reading and was good at math, which worked out because, in first and second grade, that's pretty much all you do. Writing, though, was another story. My handwriting was atrocious—it still is.

We drove down to Florida, across to Arizona. That's around when the incident at the dude ranch happened.

As we traveled, Dad began to take more of an interest in me. He'd always loved me, but until I started talking, I think I was sort of a blob to him. But as soon as I began talking, I was his. Dad saw how alone I was. When he was a kid, he'd had places to go—friends in the neighborhood, sports teams he played on. I didn't have any of that. And once Dad noticed that, he stepped in. "I thought maybe I could be your friend," he told me when we started talking about my childhood for this project. For many years, he would be my only friend.

In Leland, we developed a morning ritual. Every day before school, Dad would take me to breakfast at a little place called the Early Bird. It became our thing. I'd get French toast, and he'd have coffee. We'd sit there at 7:15 in the morning, talking politics—Reagan, Bush, Clinton—whatever was happening. Most kids talked about cartoons or sports, but I sat there dissecting elections like a mini adult. We talked current events, investing, and world news for an hour, and then I went to first grade at Leland.

Dad never treated me like a child. I was his little companion, his mini-me. When we moved back to St. Louis in third grade, the breakfast routine didn't stop. We'd go to the St. Louis Bread Company three or four times a week, grab a bagel, and talk. Those conversations with Dad were the only happy interactions I'd have all day; going to school was like going to battle.

Unfortunately, having Dad as a friend didn't make things easier at school. Third grade at Rohan Woods was a disaster. I was more interested in talking to teachers about presidential elections than playing kickball with other kids. I couldn't relate to them, and they couldn't relate to me. I didn't understand the social rules, and the gap between us only seemed to widen. I could tell they found me repulsive, but I didn't know why. I was a weird kid, and I felt it, even if I didn't fully understand it. Third grade was the first time I thought, *Oh my God, this is awful.* At that age, you start to notice things like how you fit in, or in my case, how you don't. Up until then, I hadn't really understood that I was different.

Around that time, Dad's focus on goals and toughness started to become part of my life. He had always been about setting and achieving goals. It didn't matter what the goals were, as long as there were goals. He never really cared if I got A's or C's or how I performed in school. To him, it was about discipline, about sticking to something until it was done.

Push-ups became part of that. They started in first grade. My grandfather had been an amateur boxer. He wanted Dad to fight, but Dad hated it. Still, my grandfather believed in physical toughness, and Dad did it to make him proud. When I was in first and second grade, Dad tried to teach me to box. He'd put up his hands, showing me jabs and crosses, teaching me combos like he had learned. It didn't take long for him to realize I would probably be the worst boxer ever. I hated it. I didn't like being touched, and I didn't like touching anyone else.

But Dad thought physical toughness mattered, especially for me. He could see what was coming—how I'd get bullied—and while he knew I wasn't cut out to be a fighter, maybe some physical strength would fend off the bullies, even if just a little. As I've mentioned, from a very early age, he'd set goals for me. "Do two hundred push-ups five days a week for three months," he'd say, "and you get to go to Disney World with your mom." We'd write it out like a contract, and I'd sign my name at the bottom. I still have some of those signed contracts tucked away somewhere.

I think Dad wanted me to have something I could succeed at. I was horribly uncoordinated, probably part of the autism, but push-ups didn't require coordination. Just effort. "Self-esteem is earned, not given," Dad would say. And with each push-up, I earned something. For Dad, the one thing he wanted me to know was that he was proud of me. I think that's because he never got to hear that from his own dad, who died before he could say it.

But no matter how many push-ups I did, it didn't change the fact that I didn't fit in at school. Looking back, "didn't fit in" doesn't really describe it. Some kids were magnets and attracted friends. I was the polar opposite; I *repelled* them. Try as I might, I was a square peg. Socially, I couldn't function. I was self-aware enough to know I was a weird kid. I knew that kids didn't want to be around me. I could feel it, but I didn't know how to *fix* it.

Again, Dad was my only friend.

He never forgot what the doctor had told him when my issues first surfaced: "The boy has to want it." That phrase stayed with him. Dad couldn't force me to change—I had to want it for myself. I had to realize it would be hard and believe it would be worth it. For Dad, the key was not being defined by the diagnosis. He wasn't going to let me be a victim. Victimhood is tempting—it gives you an excuse, a way out of hard work. But Dad wouldn't let me take the easy way out.

If I wanted a different life, I would have to fight for it.

Chapter Five

THE SOCIAL BLUEPRINT

Dad sat in a quiet corner booth of a little St. Louis deli the summer between his junior and senior years of college at DePauw. Across from him sat his high school classmate Terry Hess, who lived across the street from Dad growing up. Dad was the kind of guy people tolerated but didn't invite anywhere. After his dad passed away when he was in high school, his mom was in and out of institutions and hotels, and his older brother was already in his thirties. For all intents and purposes, Dad was alone.

Socially, Dad could never quite catch the rhythm. He was like me, the kid who missed the cues everyone else seemed to instinctively understand. But that summer, everything started to change.

Terry was different from Dad. He was the star of their high school class at John Burroughs—a great athlete, popular, the kind of guy everyone liked. But for whatever reason, Terry had taken a shine to Dad. "You have a good heart," he once told him. Maybe he saw something in Dad that others overlooked. Or maybe he just knew that someone like Dad needed a friend.

That afternoon in the deli, Terry changed Dad's life. He pulled out a paperback book and slid it across the table. "I want to give you something,"

Terry said. "I want you to promise me you'll read it." The book was *How to Win Friends and Influence People* by Dale Carnegie.

Dad stared at the cover. No one had ever pulled him aside to say, "Hey, you're really out of it." And Terry didn't frame it that way. He just said, "Don't tell anyone you've read it. If people know you're reading this, they'll think you're manipulative." Terry knew Dad so well he anticipated what might happen, that he would probably tell everyone, "Hey, I read this book." Terry was already looking out for him in ways he couldn't fully understand.

Dad went home that night to the little apartment he shared with his mom. After his dad's death, they'd left their home in St. Louis and moved to an apartment. Dad started reading, not expecting much. But within a few pages, it felt like somebody had opened the curtains and revealed the secrets. For the first time, Dad could see the patterns, the invisible rules of human connection that had always seemed out of reach.

Carnegie had a way of writing about two types of people in every situation—let's say, Jim and Bob. Jim always said the right thing, handled conversations gracefully, and made people feel important. Bob, on the other hand, stumbled. He interrupted, dominated conversations, and made everything about himself.

"I was always Bob," Dad said. "In every example, I was Bob." Every time Carnegie described Bob making the wrong move, Dad found himself shaking his head, thinking, *Oh my God, that's me!* It was like the book was written specifically for him.

He read through it that night, cover to cover. And the next morning, he woke up early and read it again. Reading the book felt like finding a gallon of water in the desert. Dad devoured the lessons, twice, within twenty-four hours.

It changed everything.

Dad wasn't magically transformed overnight, but for the first time, he understood why things felt "off." He was never a jerk or intentionally unpleasant; he was just out of sync, like someone marching to a different drummer than everybody else. If you had given Dad a sweatshirt that said "Clueless," he later joked, everyone would have said, "That's Mark." The book was his light bulb moment, explaining what he hadn't known needed explaining.

As Dad started to notice the same struggles in me during my early grade school years, he quickly realized the problems I faced were far more severe than anything he had experienced. He could see similarities to his own social awkwardness—the missteps, the inability to pick up on cues—but mine were magnified in ways that startled him. As I've said, Dad had sports to fall back on; he was a decent athlete, which gave him a certain level of protection. I had none of that. And the truth was, Dad wasn't quite as far on the spectrum as I was. If his social misalignment was subtle, mine was extreme. Whatever awkwardness Dad dealt with, mine felt amplified. What Dad saw in me wasn't just social awkwardness, either; it was something deeper, something that drew negative attention from classmates and, surprisingly, from teachers as well. I was an easy target. And Dad knew it.

I was like a pincushion, easy for others to poke and prod. I never wanted to fight anyone. But I had no sense of the moment. If kids were laughing at something, I didn't get the joke. If they were serious, I'd say the wrong thing. The frustration I felt started early and built up quickly. The harder I tried to fit in, the worse it got.

By the time I was in grade school, I had already begun building armor around myself. It formed naturally, layer by layer, out of necessity. Kids didn't dislike me because I looked different or because I was aggressive but because of how I acted—the way I missed social cues, the way I talked too much or at the wrong time. I quickly became defensive and withdrawn. I learned to keep my distance because getting too close meant opening myself up to teasing, or worse. I tried to stay away from other kids because I knew, sooner or later, they'd gang up on me. The armor was my best defense. But even that armor couldn't protect me from everything.

Dad eventually gave me my own copy of *How to Win Friends and*

Influence People around third grade. By then, I was already an active reader. I devoured books—big biographies about Paul Revere, George Washington, and Alexander Hamilton. There was a whole series of orange-covered nonfiction books for young readers that I couldn't get enough of. I read day and night. Books felt like friends when I didn't have any. They were my escape—and still are.

But Carnegie's book didn't click for me the way it had for Dad. I read the book a few times. *If it helped Dad*, I thought, *it certainly could help me, right?* But it didn't take. Then Dad tried to explain the lessons slowly. "Why do you think people don't want to be friends with you?" he would ask. I didn't know. I didn't understand. Dad had been able to absorb the messages instantly and put them into practice, but he couldn't get through to me. He'd try to explain it, gently walking me through scenarios, but I'd just look at him with a blank stare.

At one point, we took a trip to the Museum of Science and Industry in Chicago, which had several short videos about social interactions, all drawn from Carnegie's book. We watched them several times. But even with those examples, the lessons didn't sink in. They felt just out of reach, like there was a language everyone else spoke with ease that I couldn't understand, much less speak myself.

As he had since I was small, Dad realized the world wasn't going to adapt to me; I was going to have to adapt to it. He knew that while school environments had changed somewhat over the years—offering more resources and understanding than when he was a kid—those adjustments wouldn't last forever. Grade school and high school might bend to accommodate me, but eventually, I'd step into the same world he had, and there wouldn't be any exceptions. Dad understood this long before I did, and he quietly took on the responsibility of preparing me for the real world, no matter how frustrating or slow the process seemed.

I could sense that whatever I was doing wasn't working. I'd come home after school, crying because I had been bullied, not wanting to go back the next day.

Dad could see that I was trying, but I couldn't bridge the gap between knowing something was wrong and understanding how to change it. Maybe Dad's explanations weren't clear, or maybe I just couldn't grasp them the way he had.

Dad had Dale Carnegie, and I had Dad.

For Dad, it wasn't just about helping me survive school; it was about guiding me, step-by-step, until I could find my own way. Terry had helped Dad turn on the light switch, and now Dad was determined to do the same for me.

Summers at Shorewood

The happiest day of my childhood was always the last day of school. It meant escape—freedom from the daily hell of trying to survive. Summer was a break from the constant fight to fit in. When school ended, so did the exhausting and frightening effort to navigate the social world I couldn't understand.

From June 1 to September 1—roughly Memorial Day to Labor Day—we lived in Michigan. Three months in Shorewood; ninety days of freedom. It was like entering another life. In Michigan, there were no classmates to avoid, no recess to dread. I didn't have friends there either, but it didn't matter as much. If you're in a fire, fighting every day to survive, doing *nothing* feels like a relief.

With few exceptions, I'd given up on making friends my own age. Leland was a summer town where kids naturally gravitated toward one another—bonfires, swimming at the little white clapboard country club, junior golf, and tennis. I couldn't really participate in any of it. Saying I wasn't good at sports is like saying Alaskan winters are cold. I didn't fit in with the club crowd, and I definitely wasn't cool. The lake kids, the yacht club crowd, were everything I, a lump of permafudge, wasn't. Invitations to bonfires or cookouts didn't happen for me.

That was fine with me. I didn't have to try. I didn't have to feel the sting of exclusion every day. I could stay at the house with my parents' friends, who were like a ready-made social circle. They didn't expect me to act a certain way or pick up on subtle cues. Many of them just found me amusing, this unusual little kid sitting around listening in on adult conversations. In Shorewood, I could breathe.

Shorewood wasn't just a house. When Dad married Mom, he was drawn into its orbit, and before long, he fell in love with the place. At first, it belonged to my grandparents, but as my parents began to entertain more and more, they bought the house, and my grandparents moved next door. Shorewood became ours.

Summers at Shorewood felt like running a hotel. As I mentioned, we hosted all of Dad's old friends from college, business partners, and others who had become extended family. There were a zillion people. One summer, we racked up *three hundred* guest nights. One afternoon, a fill-in delivery driver knocked on the door, looked around, and asked Mom how to book a room. He thought Shorewood was some kind of lakeside inn and wanted to bring his wife up for their anniversary. As I got older and could drive, I found myself running back and forth to the airport. One day, I made five separate airport trips—an hour there, an hour back—driving Dad's friends in and out.

The steady stream of guests made up for the absence of friends my age. The house was always full, and I was content to sit among the adults, listening to their stories, and absorbing whatever I could from their conversations. I was so unusual, so off rhythm. I never shut up. I would badger guests endlessly with questions to the point I drove them crazy. As an adult I have a newfound respect for their patience.

One of Dad's closest friends, Rick Smith—who at the time was chairman and editor-in-chief of *Newsweek*—stayed with us for a couple weeks during the summers. He joked that for years, he thought my name was "Not Now, Lucky" because Dad said it so often when I would start asking questions. I'd hound Rick about everything from how *Newsweek* chose cover stories to how they handled mistakes, what the president was like, and who was likely to win the next election.

I was the same way with a lot of Dad's friends. They were all interesting people—CEOs, newspaper owners, doctors. It didn't matter what their professions were; I would badger them. If you were at Shorewood, you were fair game. Adults tolerated my quirks in ways kids never did. If someone wasn't paying attention to me at dinner, I'd grab their face and make them look at me. With adults, it was funny—a six-year-old demanding to know what they thought of the stock market. If I did the same thing to another kid, it was beyond just weird.

As much as I loved Shorewood, at night the world felt different. While my parents and their friends went out to some lakeside spot, I was often left behind with Liberty and the babysitter. The adults enjoyed drinks and long dinners, and I wasn't invited along. I didn't mind during the day when I could bug houseguests with questions, but evenings were quieter. I'd watch the cars leave the driveway, sit on the porch, and listen to the sounds of the lake or flip through one of my biographies until my parents returned.

I could see Dad had good friends. I wanted those kinds of relationships. I realized if I was ever going to have friendships like that, I had to figure out how to navigate the world of social interaction.

As the old saying goes, "You can lead a horse to water, but you can't make him drink." But I was ready to drink.

The Watch Tap

One summer night when I was eight, I really wanted to go with the adults. I begged Dad to let me join them. "I really want to come to dinner," I pleaded.

"Okay," Dad finally said. "You can come to dinner, but . . ."

That was when Dad taught me my first social cue.

"... when I tap my watch, you have to stop talking."

I nodded. "Okay, Dad."

That began a long process.

"I don't care what you're saying, who you're talking to, or if you think they're interested," Dad warned before we left. "When I tap my watch, you stop talking."

The stakes were high. Dinner that night was at Happy Hour Tavern, the local spot everyone in Leland frequented. Our crew took over a long table. The tavern served the best cheeseburgers and onion rings in the world. I sat down, thrilled to finally be allowed to come.

It didn't take long for me to start peppering the adults with questions. I'd ask about their businesses, their lives, anything I could think of. The first time I launched into one of my endless runs of questions, Dad tapped his watch. I stopped talking immediately. I sat quietly for ten, maybe fifteen minutes, until I forgot or glanced at Dad, who would give a small nod to signal I could speak again. I started back up, diving into my fifty-fourth question or story recounting what happened to me that day. Dad tapped his watch again. I stopped talking.

That night, I began to learn the rhythm. *Tap.* Stop. *Nod.* Go. At first, the watch tap was just about stopping my constant talking, but eventually, it signaled I was doing something off-putting. The watch tap became a universal symbol.

Dad wasn't done teaching. After dinners I attended, we'd sit down and he'd go over the evening like reviewing game film. "Do you remember when you were asking Mr. Smith the three-hundredth question and he was really trying to talk to somebody else at the table?" he'd ask. I'd think back and nod. "Well, that's when you needed to let him talk to somebody else," he'd explain. It just hadn't occurred to me. I'd tell jokes that didn't land, stories that went on too long, or interrupt people without realizing it. We'd walk through the moments, dissecting why my approach wasn't working. Dad never framed it as me being weird or wrong—it was always about "rhythm," like a song I hadn't learned to play yet.

THE SOCIAL BLUEPRINT

I had enough emotional understanding to realize how I interacted with people didn't work, but I didn't know *why*. I wasn't around kids enough, and the few I did meet didn't want much to do with me. I didn't understand the importance of letting someone else talk or the timing of a well-told joke. My issue was always the same: I talked too much. (Still do sometimes.) I've learned over time that it's hard to get into trouble when you're not talking. Very rarely does trouble come when your lips aren't moving—at least for me.

Dad believed he and Mom could help me through my issues, but, again, he wasn't interested in making life easier by shielding me from the world. It would have been simple to push for accommodations, to ask for extra time on tests, or to insulate me from challenges until adulthood. But that wasn't the route they chose. Dad said it sometimes felt like the wrong decision for the next ten years. If a child with Down syndrome is acting out, people instinctively show and feel sympathy because the condition is visible. There's an understanding, a recognition. But with me, there was no label. No diagnosis. No shield. They never let psychologists put a name on it. Dad and Mom thought if the school had labeled me, I'd become a "protected species"—set apart, handled differently, but never truly adapting.

If I was going to have a chance at a productive, meaningful life, I had to learn to navigate the world as it was. If I didn't, I'd always be different, isolated, without friends. That's how they saw it. The goal was to prepare me for a future where I'd stand on my own, even if that meant years of struggle. For the next ten years, there was no letting up. Every day felt like the one before, often worse. I'd come home from school frustrated, dreading the thought of going back the next day. Dad would explain, "Look, what you're going through now is going to make you much stronger for the future." I believed him because he had been through it, too, but also because I didn't have a choice—it was my only hope. Dad had faced the same social barriers, but without someone to guide him. It wasn't punishment; it was training. The world wasn't going to change for me. I had to change for the world.

I wanted to learn because I wanted to belong. The lessons—whether through the watch tap, role-playing conversations, or dissecting social missteps at home—became our routine. One time, I was in line at a movie theater when another kid bumped into me. I immediately thought he wanted to fight. Dad, who was watching, pulled me aside afterward and said, "Just because someone bumps into you doesn't mean they're being aggressive. Sometimes, people just bump into you." *Oh*, I thought.

Most kids didn't need to be taught that, but I did. Social interaction became something I studied, like math or reading. I learned to gauge when someone was interested in what I was saying or when I had overstayed my welcome in a conversation. This wasn't about intellect; it was about emotional intelligence. My EQ hovered near zero. As I grew older, I tried studying stand-up comedians like Jeff Foxworthy, watching their routines and mimicking their timing. It wasn't just about the jokes—it was about learning when to land a point, when to pause, and how to read an audience. For most people, that stuff comes naturally. For me, it was and still is a learned skill, a constant battle. For doctors or lawyers, lifelong study would be called "continuing education." It's no different for me; I need a constant reminder of the human equation.

There was no light bulb moment or instant transformation. I compare it to being an alcoholic: You're never cured, but you learn to manage it. Even today, when I meet someone new or get nervous, I catch myself talking too much or missing cues. I'll leave dinner and think, *Damn it! I missed that cue*, or *Lucky, why did you tell that third story?* But I recognize it now. Dad gave me the tools, and I'm still using them.

At its core, human connection relies on instinct—reading expressions, sensing tone shifts, picking up unspoken signals. But for me, those signals weren't hardwired; they had to be decoded, studied, practiced. The psychology of it, I've realized, is about pattern recognition. I *want* to connect with people. It's just that where others intuitively feel the rhythm of a conversation, I have to consciously track it, like following a script. That's why I sometimes overshoot, telling one story too many. And in some ways, that at times makes me *more* aware than most people. I don't take social interaction for granted. I analyze it, dissect it, think about what worked and what didn't. Sometimes, that means I see things others miss.

Dad helped me understand what the world could be like if I changed. I could have friends, I could do fun things, and I could engage in all these activities that I saw people do but couldn't do myself. I was so intent on not disappointing him, because he had given me this opportunity to step into the adult world—to come to dinner, to skip staying home with the babysitter. When he tapped his watch, I stopped talking. It was simple: If I learned the social blueprint, the world could open up to me.

And for me, that was everything. It felt like someone was unlocking a door to a happy place in a happy world I desperately wanted to be part of—a world where I wasn't just watching from the outside but sitting at the table.

Chapter Six

DO IT RIGHT THE FIRST TIME, EVERY TIME

I was about five or six years old, sitting on the floor at Shorewood one summer night watching the evening news like we did every night. The TV was small, one of those with knobs you had to twist, and out back was a giant antenna reaching into the sky to pull down whatever signal it could. Way up in Northern Michigan, the TV felt like our one connection to the rest of the world.

That night, there was a story about a ten-year-old boy who had flown across the country. I stared at the screen, watching this kid in the cockpit, and the moment the segment ended, I turned to Dad and said, "I want to beat him."

Dad didn't say much, but I meant it. Something about that kid being on TV for flying across the country felt like winning the lottery. At that age, I didn't understand why it mattered, but I knew I wanted to do something that set me apart. Dad was always drilling into me the importance of setting goals and achieving them. To him, life was defined by the goals you chased. When he was in college, his goal had been to start and sell a company for a million dollars, and he did it. Flying felt like a way to stand out, to prove I could achieve something no one else my age was doing. I didn't have friends my age. I wasn't on the soccer team or in Little League like the other kids back home in St. Louis. But this? This was something I could chase.

I don't have the first clue why I picked flying. I guess, in my mind, the fact that it was on the news felt important. This was a time when there was a thirty-minute national newscast every night. There was no cable news, no Twitter, no Facebook, or anything else. It was just a ninety-second spot on the news that sparked the idea, but I didn't let it go.

For the next three years, I incessantly asked Dad almost every day if I could take flying lessons. "I want to learn to fly," I'd say over and over again.

"No," he'd reply just as often. "You're too young."

By the time I was seven, I wore Dad down just enough that he bought me a pilot's guide. I read it front to back, memorizing diagrams of cockpit instruments, weather patterns, and airspace classifications. It became my obsession. Dad started buying VHS tapes from Sporty's Pilot Shop, ground school tutorials that I watched religiously. Christmases and birthdays brought new tapes, and I'd sit in front of the TV watching and rewatching them.

Finally, the summer after my third-grade year, Dad caved. "Look," he said, "I'm gonna take you to this little flying school." It was at the community college in Traverse City. "We'll go talk to the people." I think he hoped it would get me to stop asking. We drove out there and met a man named Bob Buttleman, the head of the program. Dad did everything he could for the guy to say I was too young and to come back when I was sixteen. Dad hoped Buttleman would give me a little logbook or a model plane to appease me, and that would be the end of it.

But Buttleman surprised him. "He should meet Stan Mick."

Buttleman led us back into the hangar. To me, everybody was old, but Mr. Mick looked ancient, though he wasn't more than late fifties or early sixties. He came from Mount Pleasant, Michigan, about five and a half hours south. Mr. Mick had been the head of advanced engineering at General Motors, where his claim to fame was inventing a mechanism that prevented cars from backfiring. At one point, he held more patents than anyone else at GM. He had always been a pilot, and after retiring, he and his wife moved to Northern Michigan, where he taught flying at the local college as a hobby. Mr. Mick was quiet, gentle, and devoutly religious.

"He wants to learn how to fly," Buttleman told Mr. Mick.

"I'll give you a lesson," he agreed.

When we got home, Dad told Mom, "Look, don't worry. He's going to go up once, throw up, and he's going to hate it. He'll never want to do it again." A week later, I showed up for my first flight lesson, in a Cessna 152. It was basically a sewing machine with wings. Dad was both right and wrong. I threw up all over the plane, but I loved every second of it.

Dad realized that this could be the outlet I needed. Flying gave me a sense of identity and purpose that existed outside the social structures I couldn't navigate. And Mr. Mick wasn't just a flight instructor; he became a pivotal figure in my life, a steady presence who provided something beyond lessons in flying.

Dad and Mr. Mick were polar opposites in many ways. Dad was charming, engaging, the consummate salesman and leader. Mr. Mick, on the other hand, was quiet and methodical, the kindest and strongest man I'd ever met. He approached everything with precision, and he had an incredible influence on me that endures to this day.

Flying lessons for an eight-year-old weren't cheap. At the time, it was about $50 an hour, which seems small today but was a lot of money in the early 1990s. But Dad believed in the value of what this meant to me. "I'm so happy we're able to do this for you," he said. "But if we couldn't, I'd go talk to everyone I know and find a sponsor for you." For Dad, this was about more than just flying. Once again, it was about teaching me the importance of setting a goal and working toward it. Flying became my training ground for life—where I learned that persistence and hard work paid off, even when things got tough.

I Won't Quit

I'm sure I let Mr. Mick know within the first thirty seconds of meeting him what my goal was. I wanted to be the youngest kid to fly across the country.

That goal didn't last long.

After my first lesson, I came home excited, only to find out someone had flown across the country at nine years old. I was eight. I remember sobbing like the world had ended. There was no way I could learn to fly and complete the trip before I turned nine. It was as if I hadn't gotten into the college I wanted or had been cut from the team I had worked so hard to make. I was never going to achieve my goal in life; I felt like a failure. It's funny now, but I was devastated.

Dad tried to calm me down. "Why don't we set a different goal?" he suggested. But I didn't want another goal. I wanted that one. Over the next few days, we talked more. If I couldn't be the youngest to fly across the country, maybe I could be the youngest to fly from Mexico to Canada. Or from Alaska to the Lower 48 states.

That summer, I started flying four times a week. I still have my logbook—I had nearly two hundred hours of flight time between the ages of eight and eleven. During the school year in St. Louis, I couldn't fly with Mr. Mick, but every summer, I was back in the cockpit in Northern Michigan.

There were times I'd throw up mid-flight, and Mr. Mick would calmly take over the controls while I dealt with the aftermath. After we landed, he'd clean the mess in the cockpit.

Dad wasn't a fan of flying; for nearly a decade, he had avoided even flying commercial after missing a flight that later crashed. My flying terrified Dad. He would ask me over and over why I wanted to keep doing it. But soon he realized how flying—specifically, my time with Mr. Mick—was the best "therapy" I could have.

One day, after another bout of motion sickness and throwing up, Dad pulled Mr. Mick aside. "Would you please just tell him he can't do this?" Dad pleaded.

Mr. Mick shook his head.

"If he won't quit, I can't," he said.

That moment stuck with me. Mr. Mick was the first person to believe in me other than Mom and Dad. He embodied the idea that you never give up. No matter how many times I threw up in the plane, he believed that if I was willing to keep going, he wouldn't stop me. It was the first time I felt like someone outside of my family believed in me as much as I believed in myself—or maybe believed in me *more* than I believed in myself.

Dad and Mr. Mick were clear: This wasn't a vanity project. I had to put in the work. Back home, that meant daily responsibilities. I had to make my bed, do my push-ups, and read twenty-five pages from those orange biographies written for kids. They weren't hard books, but I had to finish my pages by 5 p.m. each day.

One day, Dad asked if I had read my twenty-five pages, and I said, "Yes." I hadn't. He asked me which book I had read, and it was obvious I was lying. That was the first time I remember Dad catching me. He wasn't angry or loud. He just said, "Go to your room." I was grounded for two weeks, which in a Michigan summer felt like forever. But the worst part? Dad told me I had to call Mr. Mick and explain why I couldn't fly anymore. The thought of disappointing Mr. Mick, of having to confess my lie, felt unbearable. I sobbed in my room for hours.

After six hours, Dad came back. "Let's work this out," he said. I had to call Mr. Mick, explain what I had done, and why trust mattered so much. I promised I'd never lie again. We talked about honesty, and how telling the truth, even if it meant getting in trouble, was better than lying. I think I even had to write "I will always tell the truth" what felt like a thousand times. I learned then that nothing disappointed Dad more than lying. I could mess up my grades or forget chores, but the only thing that ever truly upset him was dishonesty. That lesson stayed with me longer than any flight or push-up ever did.

Mr. Mick taught lessons too. His most important one was simple and direct: "Do it right the first time, every time, or people die." He repeated it often, drilling it into me until it became second nature. It was a line I later saw in a Tom Clancy book, but I don't know where it came from. In aviation, the message rang true. Everything had to be done perfectly.

One of the ways Mr. Mick made sure I learned was by putting me "under the hood." He'd place a visor over my eyes that blocked the horizon, leaving me to rely solely on the instruments. It was disorienting. He'd tilt the plane into a dive or a sharp turn and cover the dials with stickers, asking me to figure out what was happening. When he peeled off the stickers, the reality often didn't match what I thought. I was convinced we were climbing to the right when we were actually dropping left. The lesson? Trust your instruments—your mind will lie to you. Now pilots have flight simulators, and learning to fly feels like playing a video game. But back then, we were using 1960s technology to fly the North Atlantic. Bad-weather landings, touching down with low fuel—all of it taught me how quickly things could go wrong.

I could never fly solo because of my age (you had to be sixteen), but Dad insisted Mr. Mick give me the full solo check ride experience. After about twenty hours of flying with him, Mr. Mick treated me like every other student. I went through the same checklist, emergency procedures, and drills, but he never touched the controls. It felt like flying solo, even if he was sitting next to me. After that, I planned my first cross-country flight. I mapped everything—routes, fuel consumption, and weight balance. This wasn't just flying; it was learning to be a real pilot. The technology was old—no digital displays, just round dials and gauges. By the time I was ready for the Mexico-to-Canada trip, I had gone through the full private-pilot check ride, even if I couldn't fly alone. Those were the standards that Dad and Mr. Mick set.

Learning to fly was about setting a goal and locking in on it until it became a reality. I had always had a capacity to work, to focus obsessively on one thing until it was finished. Maybe that is part of my autism, the ability to block out distractions and fixate on a single task until it was done. Dad always said if you set a long-term goal, life becomes simple. Every decision is either a step toward that goal or a step away from it. I learned early to be careful about the goals I set because once I set them, failure wasn't an option.

At nine years old, I completed the flight from the Mexico border to Canada. I flew commercially down to Texas, where I met Mr. Mick, and together we hopscotched our way up the country in that little Cessna with an engine that sounded like a sewing machine. With every mile north, I was proving to myself that I could set a goal and accomplish it. By the time we touched down in Canada, I was already thinking about what goal I would set next.

No Going Back

By the time I was ten, my next goal was to fly from Fairbanks, Alaska, to Traverse City, Michigan. I took several commercial flights to get to Fairbanks by myself—from Michigan to Minneapolis, then to Seattle, Anchorage, and finally Fairbanks. Mr. Mick had already flown the little Cessna up there to meet me.

The plan was simple: Fly from Alaska to the Lower 48. But simple didn't mean easy. Even after two years of flying, I kept getting sick, throwing up during flights. Right before I would throw up, Mr. Mick would take the controls. I'd throw up into a bag and then start flying again. The first legs on the trip down from Alaska were particularly bumpy legs filled with bad weather. We got stuck in a remote town along the Alaska highway in Canada, and cell phones didn't exist yet. I called Dad from the one phone in town and told him I wanted to come home. It was always the same message from Dad: "Lucky, you have to fly. Mr. Mick can't fly the plane." Finally, after two days and barely into Canada, I'd had enough.

"That's fine. You can come home," he said, "but you're coming home on that plane. Either Mr. Mick is gonna fly you home and you're gonna throw up all over the place, or you're gonna fly the plane and make it through." Dad wasn't yelling, but I could hear the starkness in his voice. Quitting wasn't an option. I had set the goal, and now I had to finish it.

I decided I wanted to go back to Fairbanks and fly. So we flew back and started over. This time, I made it all the way to Traverse City.

Eventually, the dream shifted. Inspired by Charles Lindbergh, my hero, I set my sights on crossing the Atlantic. From May 20 to 21, 1927, Lindbergh completed the first solo nonstop transatlantic flight, from Roosevelt Field in New York to Le Bourget Field near Paris, covering thirty-six hundred miles in thirty-three and a half hours in the Spirit of St. Louis, a custom-built, single-engine plane.[1] As a kid from St. Louis, that connection felt right. That was my new goal: I wanted to fly across the Atlantic to Paris.

I was eleven now, so I sort of understood what I was doing. The plane was now a Cessna 303, a twin-engine aircraft. We had the very first generation of GPS—the Garmin 100, which was state-of-the-art at the time but feels like an antique now. I flew the North Atlantic using NDBs (nondirectional beacons), which transmitted simple radio signals to help me stay on course, and DMEs (distance-measuring equipment), which told me how far I was from a ground station. I was flying across the Atlantic, wearing a survival suit, and trusting those instruments to guide me.

It was me in the pilot seat, Mr. Mick as the copilot, and a woman ferry pilot in the back. She had flown this route countless times. She was there in case anything happened to Mr. Mick. At age eleven, as capable as I felt, we needed someone experienced with Greenland's terrain and remote airstrips. This was the early '90s, before satellite phones. If we hit trouble, she knew the mechanics in Newfoundland and Greenland and had flown the approaches before. She was our guide in the sky.

The trip started in St. Louis. We hopscotched our way to Goose Bay, Canada, and then began our journey across the Atlantic. From Goose Bay we would fly over four and a half hours of open water to Narsarsuaq,

Greenland. I'll never forget our takeoff from Goose Bay. The control tower knew what we were attempting, and a couple of NATO pilots from the nearby base flew alongside us briefly and radioed, "We say good luck." It felt like something out of a movie. This was the critical "point of no return." Once we left Goose Bay, even if we had engine trouble, we had no choice but to continue. I remember the weight of the survival suit hanging around my waist during that leg because if we had to ditch, there wouldn't have been time to put it on otherwise. At my age, I felt how serious it was to fly twelve thousand feet over the frigid North Atlantic. We had no heat in the plane because heaters used fuel and lowered the gas mileage.

Back home, Dad was tracking our flight as best as he could. He had the phone numbers of radar centers and FAA stations, calling each one as we passed through checkpoints. But again, communication wasn't perfect. At one point, Dad called North Atlantic Control, asking for our location, and they had no record of us. "We haven't heard from that plane," they said. Dad was beside himself and frantically called the station that had passed us off. "We passed him off at 3:22," they told him. He worked his way down the chain, calling Gander Control and Reykjavík. No one could confirm our location. I later learned that through persuasion, Dad convinced the Canadian Coast Guard to put helicopters on standby, ready to begin a search-and-rescue mission over the Atlantic. He was told that if we didn't check in at the next waypoint within twenty minutes, they would launch the rescue. When we finally made contact, our voices crackled over the high-frequency radio. Dad called in so he could hear my voice.

As we approached Greenland, the weather began closing in. The landing at Narsarsuaq was one of the most intense experiences I had. The airport was wedged between fjords, with two-thousand-foot towering cliffs on both sides. The approach felt like threading a needle, flying through a mile-wide corridor at 130 miles an hour with cloud cover above and water below. There was no alternate airport. If we missed the landing, we wouldn't get another chance. You landed or you died. Our fuel was low, and Mr. Mick was more involved in that landing than any other I can remember.

After Greenland, we continued to Reykjavík, followed by the Faroe Islands, then Scotland. Each stop felt like another milestone on the journey. Finally, in May 1994, we landed in Paris, just weeks before the fiftieth anniversary of D-Day.

Mom, Dad, and Liberty were waiting for me at the airport. It felt like an incredible full-circle moment. We drove to Normandy, reflecting on the history and the accomplishment of my own journey. I remember visiting the American Cemetery, standing at the top of the hill overlooking Omaha Beach. I had read so much about D-Day and knew that my grandfather had been part of Eisenhower's company headquarters. As I stood there, I watched an older man with his family walk down toward the stone wall. He paused, letting his family wait behind him, and as he reached the edge, he broke down in tears, much like in the scene from *Saving Private Ryan*, which came out a few years later. Watching him, I felt the weight of history and sacrifice in a way I never had before. That juxtaposition—of completing my journey while standing in a place of such profound meaning—left a lasting impression.

Up until that trip, Dad had always said, "You can do all this flying, but there will be no publicity." I remembered how the ten-year-old who flew across the country had been on the news. But Dad insisted success is about you knowing you've had success, not about public recognition.

Mr. Mick and the ferry pilot flew the plane back to the States. While we were in Paris, Dad made one exception to his rule. "You can do one thing," he said. "You can do *Good Morning America*." One of Dad's friends had a connection with Bob Iger at ABC. He called Iger and said, "Hey, I have this kid who just flew to Paris at eleven years old." The next thing I knew, I was at the ABC bureau in Paris, doing a live shot with Charlie Gibson back in New York.

Dad had coached me for days beforehand. He was adamant I be upfront about not flying the entire way. Once, there had been a dangerous crosswind landing and another time I had to let Mr. Mick take over when I was throwing up during a landing. Other than that, I had flown the entire time. Dad rehearsed the answer with me. When Charlie asked, "Did you fly the plane the whole time?" I responded, "There were thirty minutes I didn't fly. Once when I was throwing up on landing, one time when there was a really dangerous situation, and a couple of times when I had to go to the bathroom when we were flying over the Atlantic, so it was about thirty minutes, Mr. Gibson." Those were my first-ever talking points.

I don't think anyone ever broke that record. Guinness didn't keep track of it, and neither did any official governing body. We submitted it to the National Aeronautic Association, and the Missouri Historical Society gave me an award for retracing Lindbergh's route. But the record wasn't about age—we filed it as a speed record for the size of the plane from St. Louis to Paris. It wasn't something anyone else was likely to attempt. Flying a small piston-engine plane from St. Louis to Paris wasn't exactly a common undertaking.

On that same Paris trip, Mr. Mick caught a cold he couldn't shake. When he got home, doctors diagnosed him with brain cancer. He was done flying. I tried to fly with other instructors, but no one else understood me the way Mr. Mick did. You couldn't re-create that magic.

Mr. Mick died five years later. I was sixteen. A few weeks before he passed, I drove down to see him. I sat with him and thanked him for everything he had done. It felt strange, being sixteen and making that drive alone, but I knew it was important. Mr. Mick was the first person outside of my family whose death really hit me.

At his wake, I saw the impact of what we had done together. Around his casket were articles and awards from our flights. His family and friends treated me almost like part of the receiving line. I didn't realize how much he had cherished our time flying.

The line he used to say—"If he won't quit, I can't"—stayed with me forever. Later in life another mentor, Thom Sehnert, would say something similar: "It's hard to beat a man who refuses to quit"—and that's a lesson I've carried ever since.

Chapter Seven

WALKING THROUGH HELL

There was never a singular moment I realized I was different, like some dramatic schoolyard incident or a heart-to-heart with my parents. My diagnosis happened gradually, like pieces of a puzzle I didn't know I was trying to solve.

Third grade was uncomfortable. I knew I was weird, but at that age, everyone was still figuring themselves out.

But by fourth grade, when I moved to Community School, the difference became stark. It wasn't subtle anymore. It was as if someone had flipped a switch and suddenly, everyone around me seemed to have silently agreed that I was on the outside looking in. The other kids had been together since kindergarten. They had their groups, their shared jokes, their social pecking order. I didn't fit into any of it. I was bright enough academically, but there's a big difference between being smart and being accepted.

The teachers started to notice it too. Each report card came with notes that stung more than the actual grades. Mom and Dad saved everything over the years, and looking back at those old report cards feels like flipping through chapters of a story I had lived but never fully understood at the time.

Two report cards from fourth grade at Community School stand out. Each had a list of items for "social development" and "work habits," with check marks indicating areas for improvement. In the "social development" section of the report, several boxes were marked *Needs Improvement*:

Demonstrates responsible behavior. *Needs Improvement.*
Thinks before speaking. *Needs Improvement.*
Contributes to the group. *Needs Improvement.*
Interacts with peers. *Needs Improvement.*
Assumes leadership. *Needs Improvement.*
Participates appropriately at lunch. *Needs Improvement.*

The pattern was clear. I wasn't behind in just one aspect of my development; social, emotional, and behavioral gaps appeared across the board. And the teachers spelled out my struggles further in the comments below those check marks.

Spring 1993: Lucky is still struggling to find ways to communicate with his peers in an accepting manner. We are encouraging him to approach situations with an open mind and appreciating that others have opinions that may differ from his.

May 1993: Lucky has had many adjustments to make this year. He has had difficulty interacting with the class. We believe Lucky would benefit from spending time with his classmates outside of the classroom.

The irony of that last line is hard to miss. None of my classmates wanted to spend time with me outside the classroom.

The tipping point came on October 28, 1993, at eleven years old. I remember being taken out of class to sit through what felt like endless exams at Community School. I didn't know it at the time, but they were assessing everything—IQ, adaptability, learning patterns. The results, as my parents later learned, were jarring. A verbal score of 145. A performance score of 77. I remember hearing that an average learning disability could involve a 20-point spread. Mine was nearly 70 points apart. A post-test report summarized the results:

> All sections in the verbal area were well above average. All sub-tests in the performance area, except one, were well below average. Block design and object assembly were both very low, indicating a possible visual perception problem. Lucky was very relaxed and confident during our one-hour testing session. His confidence may have gotten in the way of his ability to transfer information to the performance area. Due to the large gap between verbal and performance scores, I recommend a complete evaluation be done.

To an eleven-year-old, all I knew was that tests like that were long and boring. But for my parents, it was another reminder. They didn't explain much to me, but there were phrases like *social blindness* and *pervasive developmental disorder*. The term *autism* wasn't thrown around as commonly as it is today, but that was the implication.

The experts never put a neat label on it—my parents didn't let them—so they settled for what they knew: I was different, and it was going to make life harder.

One Day Closer

By the time I reached fifth grade, the situation at Community School had only worsened. I had been pulled out of Rohan Woods School after third grade because of bullying, and my parents thought moving me to a school with more resources might help. It didn't.

The teachers, perhaps intimidated by the social status of certain families, seemed unwilling to discipline the kids who made my life miserable. I was an easy target. Kids are mean, but here, the adults did little to stop it. They sort of just fed me to the wolves. I hated going to school every day. I begged Dad to let me stay home. I told him how awful it was, how relentless the teasing became, but I couldn't seem to articulate just how unbearable it felt. I trudged through the days, dreading every interaction. Two boys in particular were the worst; it's funny how you remember those names.

Everything came to a head one day in gym class. One of the boys shoved me, and I retaliated. We were fifth graders. It wasn't much, just another scuffle. But the next thing I knew, I was sent home, and the principal was talking about suspension. I told Dad everything: The other boy had pushed me first, and I had just reacted. But when the school called, their version of events was different. They claimed I had instigated the fight.

Dad wasn't one to take the school's word without question. He trusted me. And that trust wasn't built overnight. He had drilled honesty into me for years. This went back to when he made me write "I will always tell the truth" hundreds of times until I could practically see the words when I closed my eyes. I knew lying to Dad wasn't an option—and because of that, when I told him what had happened, he believed me.

The school warned Dad that I was on the verge of being suspended or even kicked out, so he was determined to get to the bottom of it. Dad called the gym teacher, and after a pause, the teacher lowered his voice and said, "I can't talk to you on the phone, but if you come around the back of the school—don't park in the main lot, come to the PE office through the back entrance—I'll talk to you."

When Dad showed up, the gym teacher confirmed my version of events. He admitted I hadn't started the fight and that the principal was covering for the bullies. "Your son is telling the truth," he said. "But I can't say that. I could lose my job. It'd be best if you took Lucky out."

The incident happened on a Tuesday, and I stayed home from school on Wednesday while Dad sorted things out. Dad came home that afternoon, and I'll never forget the way he sat me down.

He looked me in the eye.

"You don't ever have to go back there again," he said.

I started sobbing, I was so happy. The memory still brings tears to my eyes thirty years later.

Every day at that school felt like a nightmare, like there was no way out. And when you're in fifth grade, each day feels like a month. The relief I felt when Dad said I didn't have to go back was overwhelming. I had spent so long holding my breath that I didn't realize how suffocating it had become until I could finally exhale. I couldn't believe it—I was free. Dad says he can still see and feel that moment, how incalculably happy I was, and how he knew then he had made the right decision. It was like I was released from the torture chamber.

The next few weeks after Dad pulled me out of Community School were a hodgepodge of schooling. I stayed home while my parents figured out what to do next. I had already been working with an English tutor; my math and reading were fine, but I couldn't spell or write. Writing had always lagged behind for me, and I remember someone coming to the house to help me string sentences together. Even now, I still can't spell. In college, I scored 2 out of 20 on a freshman spelling test, which was supposed to weed out journalism students. It's funny to think back on getting gentleman's C's in English when I write a thousand words every day for a living now, plus most of my show scripts.

Mom and Dad decided to bring in more tutors for math and social studies. For most kids, leaving school might have felt isolating, but for me, it felt like freedom. I loved talking with the tutors and sitting across from adults who treated me like an equal. I remember diving into social studies, talking endlessly about politics with a teacher who probably didn't expect a fifth grader to care about the presidents. For a mini adult, it was heaven. I would wait impatiently by the front door every morning for the tutor to arrive. I actually loved to learn about things I was interested in.

It was a complete turnaround from the intense fear of what each day at school would bring.

I was homeschooled for the rest of fifth grade and all of sixth. My parents enrolled me in one science class at the local public school during sixth grade. I'd ride my bike there in the mornings and come home by 9 a.m. I think part of it was for legal purposes—something about needing a certain number of classroom hours—but they also wanted me to have some interaction with kids my age, even if just for an hour.

I think each day I made it through was a victory for Dad. There's a country song called "One Day Closer to You" about inching toward something better—one day closer to getting through the hard stuff. I think that's how he saw it. Every day that passed wasn't just survival; it was progress. One day closer to the finish line, one day closer to me making it to college, where he believed things would finally be okay.

Back to the Real World

Dad had gone to John Burroughs, so when it came time for middle school, that's where I was headed. I wasn't going to be shielded from the world forever. Burroughs was where I'd have to reenter the real world.

On the first day of seventh grade, Dad gave me some advice. "Look," he said, "just don't talk to anyone." His dad had given him different advice on his first day—to find the biggest kid there, punch him in the stomach, and stand over him telling him not to mess with him again. When Dad got home from his first day of seventh grade and admitted he hadn't followed through, my grandfather was furious. Dad's explanation? *He* was the biggest kid there. Dad took the opposite approach with me. "Just be mysterious," he said. And, of course, that day I invited a kid over to play. I so desperately wanted to fit in that I couldn't resist. The kid stayed for an hour, maybe less, before making an excuse to leave.

Dad not only attended Burroughs but had been on the school board and was close friends with the headmaster. They played cards every Sunday night. I think that connection gave Dad some peace of mind. He figured I'd have a hard time anywhere, but at least Burroughs was a place he could navigate, where he had the best chance to protect me.

A lot of the kids in seventh grade at Burroughs had gone to Community. St. Louis had—and still has—a massive private school culture, in part because of desegregation and busing. Public schools struggled, and families who could afford it fled to private schools. At one point, St. Louis had the highest percentage of private school enrollment in the country. Burroughs was part of that ecosystem.

One of the big traditions at Burroughs was Dryland, a kind of outdoor education trip for seventh graders. Half the class went at the beginning of the week, the other half at the end. They bused us down to a vast, one-hundred-acre area in the Ozarks, where we stayed in cabins and did nature hikes. One of the signature activities was called Solo. They'd take each of us out at night, sit us down alone in the woods, and leave us there for three hours. We were probably only twenty feet apart, but the idea was to make you feel isolated, to push you out of your comfort zone. I wasn't having it. I duct-taped a book and a flashlight to the inside of my leg and snuck them out with me. I thought the whole thing was profoundly stupid, and I had no intention of sitting alone in the dark. So I sat there and read for three hours. I guess even then, I had a knack for defying authority.

But despite moments of quiet rebellion, I was still an easy target. Earlier I mentioned rolling my socks down just above my shoes, a habit rooted in sensory issues, something common for kids on the spectrum. I couldn't stand the feeling of socks pulled up over my legs, so I rolled them. The problem was that it left this big, obvious roll on my ankles, and the other kids zeroed in on it.

It wasn't just the socks. Kids called me "retarded." I remember that word being used a lot. Later on, they even called me that to Liberty— "Your retarded brother," they'd say. Back then, the word wasn't as taboo as it is now, but hearing it over and over, especially from classmates, left a mark. I could deal with a lot, but eventually, I got tired of it. They mocked me endlessly. I don't remember exactly what the breaking point was, but the teasing built over weeks and months.

One kid in particular kept pushing me, both figuratively and literally. I told Dad about it. I'd come home and list the things this kid had done. "He knocked my books out of my hand," or "He told people I smell," or "He pushed me again in the hallway." Finally, I asked, "Can I hit him yet?"

Dad gave me his version of fighting back. "Next time he does it, don't hit him," he said. "Take his arm, pull it behind his back, push his head down, and tell him if he ever says anything again, you'll hit him in the nose."

The next time the kid mouthed off, we were in shop class. I was a fat little fella, but I was pretty strong, especially after years of doing push-ups. I walked past him, grabbed his arm, yanked it behind his back, and slammed his head down on the drafting table. I leaned in close. "If you ever say anything to me again," I said, "I'll break your nose." That was the first time I was physical with another kid. The teacher grabbed me and frog-marched me straight to the principal's office.

Dad got called in for a meeting. The headmaster, Dad's friend, shook his head and asked, "Where did Lucky get the idea to do this?"

Dad said, "Well, because I told him to."

The headmaster couldn't believe it. "You told him to do this?!"

Dad shrugged. "What do you want him to do? You're not protecting him."

The problem was, after that fight, all the bullies knew I was handcuffed. I couldn't follow through on any threat. It was a strange contradiction. I had finally stood up for myself, but now I couldn't defend myself further. The teasing didn't stop—it got worse. Dad told me I couldn't hit anyone or I'd be thrown out of school.

Tom Brokaw once gave a speech about how middle school is the best preparation for life. "Real life is not college; real life is not high school," he said. "Here is a secret that no one has told you: Real life is junior high."[1] I understand exactly what he meant. Later on in life, when I reported from the Middle East, I couldn't help but draw parallels between the sandbox politics of middle school and the delicate balancing acts of international relations. Weakness is provocative. Deterrence only holds for so long before someone tests the limits. Middle school, as strange as it sounds, is probably the closest many people will ever get to experiencing the dynamics of the Middle East. The constant testing of boundaries, the fragile alliances—it all played out in those hallways at Burroughs.

If getting bullied by other kids wasn't bad enough, even some of the teachers joined in. I thought I'd gotten used to the worst of it—then came eighth-grade art class. One day, the art teacher looked at me and said, "If my dog was as ugly as you, I'd shave its ass and make it walk backward." The whole class erupted in laughter. I cried the entire way home from school. That afternoon, Dad met me at the bottom of the driveway and asked me how school was.

"I got humiliated today."

The next day, Dad walked over to see the interim headmaster (his friend was on sabbatical). He didn't hesitate. "We'll suspend the art teacher if you want," he said. "You can't say that to a kid."

But Dad, true to his nature, said no. "If you punish him, the other teachers will take it out on Lucky," he said. "Let's make peace."

Dad's instinct has always been to de-escalate. I wanted the teacher fired. I recalled Dad's advice about bullies: Hit them in the nose and they won't mess with you again.

That moment highlights the biggest difference between Dad and me. I'm known for saying, "If I know there's a knife fight, I'm bringing an Abrams tank." Dad's approach? If there's a tank battle, he shows up trying to get everyone to shake hands on the battlefield. If it's a nuclear war, he'll bring a bomb—but only as a last resort.

I'm the opposite because when you've been humiliated like that—when you've felt small enough to disappear—you never forget the feeling.

You never forget the sound of laughter at your expense. So you make a decision. You decide that it will never happen again.

To this day, whether in business, journalism, or anywhere else, I'll bring a tank to a knife fight. I would never hit anyone, but I learned early on that in the real world, strength isn't just physical; it's perception. Sometimes you have to escalate to de-escalate. Projecting strength—metaphorical or not—matters. I'll never let anyone put me back in that eighth-grade art room again.

Chapter Eight

MY BEST AND ONLY FRIEND

It happened just weeks after I started at Burroughs—the kind of moment that sticks with you, even if you weren't in the room.

Burroughs was meant to give me a fresh start—or at least, that's what Mom and Dad hoped. But a few weeks into the school year, my parents were called into the office of the principal for seventh and eighth grade for the first time. No warm welcome. No gentle conversation about how I was adjusting. Instead, the principal got straight to the point.

"Well, Mark and Carol," she started, "the people here think Lucky is really pretty weird."

She paused, then added the part that hit the hardest.

"I guess I do too."

"Weird" went through my parents like an arrow. They sat there, stunned. They didn't push back. They didn't explain. They didn't mention the diagnosis. Back then, a label could follow you for life. It could change how everyone treated you. And they knew the world wouldn't make accommodations. So they left. They walked out of the principal's office, across the street to our house—a short walk that must have felt impossibly long.

They knew then what they had feared all along: The road ahead wouldn't just be hard. It would be lonely. The school year had barely begun, and already, I was "weird" in the eyes of the people who mattered—the people who were supposed to protect me. To the school administrators the bullying and isolation was *my fault*. But the hardest part wasn't that day in the principal's office. The hardest part came every afternoon when I got home.

The truth is, the principal wasn't the first to see it—just the first to say it out loud. Liberty saw it too. She's six years younger than me, but even she remembers. When I was in fifth grade at Community and she was in kindergarten, I'd pick her up every afternoon when school ended. One of her earliest memories were those walks home—me crying the entire way, *every single day*, and her holding my hand but not knowing what to say. Liberty instinctively knew I was weird; anybody could see it.

It didn't take long for Mom and Dad to notice. It became obvious that I wasn't just having a hard time at school; I was unraveling. Mom once told Dad, "I feel like he goes off to war in the morning trying to defend himself, and he's absolutely alone. He's helpless." She wasn't wrong. Mom described it as shoveling me into a jungle every morning, where I was tormented and left to fend for myself. By four o'clock, they'd see me coming up the driveway, head down, shoulders slumped. "We've got to be there to patch him up," she told Dad one day.

That's when Dad made up his mind. "I'm just going to be there for him," he said.

So almost every day, at 4:20 p.m., Dad stood at the end of the driveway, waiting to bandage me up. I'd walk toward him like a puzzle someone had dumped onto the floor and scattered. Piece by piece, he'd start putting me back together, knowing there was no one else to do it. I don't think he always knew exactly what to say, but he knew the right things to do.

He'd listen as I yelled. I'd come home angry—angry at the kids, at the teachers, at the whole system that let this happen. Furious at him, sometimes, for not making it stop. But he never fought back. He just let the anger and emotion pour out, understanding that it had to go somewhere.

MY BEST AND ONLY FRIEND

Looking back now, I understand the patience and grace Dad showed through those hundreds upon hundreds of hours. Maybe today, parents in his position would send their kid to therapy. But Dad was my therapist. He was the only person I trusted. The one person who made me believe I wasn't broken—that the world was wrong, not me.

Dad would spend a few hours each night helping me piece myself back together, often repeating the same reassurances. "The values that make you humiliated now are the same values that will make you strong and respected later," he'd say.

When I think back, I'm reminded of a Bible verse, Psalm 30:5.

> For his anger lasts only a moment,
> but his favor lasts a lifetime;
> weeping may stay for the night,
> but rejoicing comes in the morning.

Dad always promised it was going to get better. I didn't always believe him, and I think he knew that. It didn't stop him from saying it. He was determined to rebuild my confidence a little every day. He wanted to instill in me the belief that I was strong enough to survive, that this was a phase, and that the things making me an outcast in middle school would one day set me apart in the best way.

When Liberty started at Burroughs as a seventh grader, I was a senior. She was excited at first—thrilled to be at school with her big brother. That didn't last. My scarlet letter quickly became hers. Burroughs had a tradition: Each seventh grader was paired with a senior—a "big brother" or "big sister"—to look out for them and show them around. The school assigned three different girls from my class to be Liberty's "big sister." Every one of them refused. In the end, she didn't have one. That was day one, and things only got worse from there.

Kids in her class called her "the retarded kid's little sister." Some teachers weren't any better. One flat-out told her, "I hope you don't turn out like your brother." One claimed she couldn't do math and tried to fail her. That's how deep the resentment ran. That's how much hatred I stirred up—enough that teachers took it out on my little sister. She was caught in a brutal mix of trying to protect me, not knowing what was really happening, and trying to survive herself. I am lucky, because even then, and ever since, Liberty has always chosen to be my fiercest protector, even at great personal cost to her.

She remembers the bullying as catastrophic—the kind that leaves marks far deeper than a school year. Liberty went on to go to MIT and then got a PhD in math. She's a professor now, and she's told me she's never seen or heard of bullying like the kind I went through. Sometimes she reminds me of things I'd forgotten—or maybe things I chose to forget. When she brings them up, it feels like reopening wounds I didn't realize were still there.

Liberty remembers what Mom would tell her when Dad sat with me in my bedroom every night: "We have to put Lucky back together." That became a mantra, a quiet acknowledgment of the battle they fought each day. It was about slowly reassembling me, day by day.

Dad gave up a lot to be there every day. He didn't have to go to work—he'd already sold his businesses and didn't have to travel or make sales calls. But that's not why he was there. It wasn't because he had the time; it was because he *made* time. Even if he had worked twelve-hour shifts in a factory, he would have found a way to be there each night. His commitment wasn't only about being present. It was about his unwavering belief in me as someone who thought I was worth fighting for. That mattered more than the number of hours he spent. It didn't matter if he was there at 4:20 or two hours later. What mattered was that he showed up every day.

This is the same guy who was one of the founders of a hugely popular local television show called *Donnybrook*. Dad was successful and well-known, and he could have spent his time being social. But instead he chose to stand in the driveway, waiting for me. He and Mom could have been out every night around town, but instead, they decided I was more important.

As we began to work on this book, Mom and Dad both told me there were nights he'd sit in the living room and cry after I went to bed. The emotional courage, discipline, and strength he had all those years is incomprehensible. He felt the weight of knowing how hard life was for me and that there was little he could do to stop it. The next morning I was going to wake up, go back to school, and do it all again. But he could hold onto those small moments of comfort he provided at the end of each day, and he hoped they were enough to carry me through to adulthood.

I think he understood, better than most, what it felt like to be different. He knew I couldn't do it alone. He knew I needed him.

So every day, at 4:20, he waited.

A Dive into Trust

After years of flying with Mr. Mick, I found myself searching for the next challenge, something that could fill the void left by the skies. Flying had taught me discipline, precision, and how to handle high-stakes situations, and I needed something that could focus me on the next goal and offer that same challenge.

That's when I turned to scuba diving.

I immersed myself in the world of scuba diving, rising through certifications—PADI Advanced and deep dives. I loved the sense of freedom it gave me, and the way it demanded focus and calm under pressure. I was the only one in my family who dove, but I always tried to get Dad to go diving with me. When I was fourteen, after a couple of years of diving, I convinced him to take a resort course—just enough training to get by—and then we headed out together for a two-tank dive in Islamorada, Florida.

On the boat, it was clear Dad wasn't doing well. The ride out had left him seasick, and he'd been sitting on the deck for a while, visibly ill and nervous. This was completely new territory for him, and the combination of sickness and anxiety was taking its toll. When he finally slipped into the water, I stayed close.

As we took off swimming, Dad started porpoising—up and down from twenty feet below the surface to the top—unable to stay stable in the water. He couldn't figure out how to use his buoyancy control (BC) vest properly, a skill they'd barely covered in the resort course. He'd done only one hour in a calm pool, not this rough, open water, where they should have started him. He was being churned like a washing machine by the waves at the surface, adding to his seasickness and fear.

I could see how angry and frustrated he was, shoving me away to insist he didn't need help. But I refused to leave him. I was his buddy, and the rule was clear: You never leave your buddy. Watching from a few feet behind him, I could see he was scared and disoriented. Despite his efforts to push me back, I stayed close, knowing he might need me at any moment.

Then, it happened. In a moment of panic, he went to the surface and ripped out his mouthpiece. Without air in his BC and with his weight belt still strapped on, he then sank like a rock. I watched in horror as he plummeted past me, flailing and gasping. *I'm watching my dad die*, I thought as he descended into about fifty feet of water.

There wasn't time to think, only to act. I was fourteen, but years of flying had taught me a different sense of responsibility—and how to slow down when the world got sped up. I dove after him, going down to about forty feet, grabbed the back of his BC, and yanked as hard as I could to slow his descent. He was heavy—much bigger than me—and nearly unconscious by the time I caught him. You could see the air escaping from his regulator as he sank, and I knew once panic sets in, it's over. I couldn't shove the regulator back in his mouth, so I focused on the basics. I dropped his weight belt and hit the inflator on his BC, rocketing us toward the surface.

We broke the surface and Dad sputtered and gagged as he came to, panicked and disoriented. He fought me at first, but I held on with a bear hug, floating on my back. Then I towed him a couple hundred yards to the boat.

The instructor stormed over, yelling, "You shouldn't have taken your regulator out!"

I cut the instructor off. "Why don't you just leave us for a minute?" The instructor backed off, and I turned my attention back to Dad.

He was still coughing and catching his breath when he looked at me and said, "How did you know to stay with me?"

"The rules are the rules," I said. "You never leave your buddy."

Flying taught me more than how to handle a plane. If you've had enough bad landings and bad weather, you learn to control that sense of panic and fear and to trust your instincts, trust your training, and trust your instruments. That discipline to stay calm in chaos and rely on preparation saved us that day. Dad was as good as gone, and he'll tell you I brought him back. My experience with flying ended up saving Dad's life.

Even now, I think back to the lessons flying taught me—repetition, discipline, and trust in the process—and I realize how much they've shaped me. I quit diving after the accident with Dad, but those concepts stayed with me.

Not long after that incident, I found myself on the other side of that trust dynamic, thousands of miles from home in the wilderness of British Columbia. This time, it was me who had to place all my trust in Dad.

Counting on Dad

For as bad as things were at school, I still wanted to be a kid. I wanted friends. There were all these camp salespeople that came through St. Louis—sleepaway camps in Minnesota and Wisconsin where you learned to canoe, sailing camps in the Caribbean, backpacking camps, you name it. In Michigan, all the kids my age had their summer plans at the country club and sailing school. For obvious reasons these weren't options for me—they were just another chance to get bullied.

I started talking to Dad about camp. He'd gone to Camp Wah-Kon-Dah when he was seven. He has memories of how terrible and wonderful it had been at the same time. I wanted to go to camp too. It felt like a place where, maybe, I could finally make some friends. Camp directors came to our house and pitched different programs. I was determined. It was eighth grade, and I had my eyes set on a three-week backpacking trip in British Columbia for that summer before freshman year.

I think Dad knew this was a high-risk, low-reward proposition. But I lobbied hard for it. Most parents push their kids to try new things; I was the one nagging him. Long hikes with a heavy pack and white water rafting—I wanted that physical challenge. I thought it might help with rowing, which I was just getting into. Eventually, Dad agreed. The camp sent a packing list, and we went to the outdoor store. I bought everything. I loaded my backpack with pots, pans, and sandbags, then hiked around our neighborhood in Michigan trying to get in shape and prepare for what was ahead.

I flew out to British Columbia and landed in Vancouver, where a fifteen-passenger van picked up me and the other kids. We drove to a campsite for the first night, and they laid out the rules during orientation. No toilet paper. We'd hike for hours each day, sleep under the stars, and rely on nature for almost everything. I wasn't thrilled by the thought of using leaves to wipe. That wasn't in the brochure.

There were no cell phones back then, and the next chance to call home was five days away. That night, I found a pay phone at a small corner store near the first night campsite and called Dad. I told him I wasn't interested in this.

He listened, paused, and said, "Why don't you just go on the first trek? See how it goes." I wasn't convinced, but I agreed.

A counselor pulled me aside and said, "Don't worry, we have toilet paper if you need it." That was enough to get me through the night.

The next day we drove a few hours to a trailhead and hiked into the stunning beauty. I had never done outdoor adventures before. This was great! The group was six girls and six guys. I was one of the younger kids, but also the biggest. At 160 pounds, I carried a seventy-pound pack, loaded with heavy gear. We hiked eight to ten miles a day, and every step felt like a marathon. In my eyes, the mountains around British Columbia looked like Everest. This camp was supposed to be an adventure, a fun escape. But it felt more like a test. Two of the boys were bad kids. There's something called Outward Bound, which is the last stop before reform school, and these kids' parents thought they were signing them up for something like that.

One day during a hike, these two boys threatened to throw me off a sheer cliff ledge along the trail if I talked to one of the girls. To me, it seemed like the drop was a few hundred feet or more, and with a heavy backpack strapped to me, the threat felt real. Up until that point, the camp had felt like a fresh start, and boy, did I need it. A couple of the girls had been nice to me, and for the first time, I thought, *These are people who don't know me.* But these two boys were threatening me. It was scary. I remembered what I had learned from flying: You don't quit. No matter what, you keep going. I was the kid who threw up every day but kept climbing back into the cockpit. But standing there on that trail, staring down the ledge, I saw the juxtaposition. It was a hard thing to reconcile. Dad had always said, "Never let them see they got to you." But at some point, you have to draw the line.

After a few days of threats, I realized I needed to get out. I waited until we reached Whistler, British Columbia, a little village with a ski resort north of Vancouver, where we had a few hours to do laundry and maybe make a quick call home. I found a pay phone in a laundromat and called the house, but Dad was out golfing, so I called the golf club.

"Go get my dad," I told them. "Tell him I need to talk to him in fifteen minutes." I hung up the pay phone and called back exactly fifteen minutes later. Dad answered.

"How's the trip going?" he asked.

"Dad, you've got to get me out of here," I said. "These guys are threatening to kill me."

At first, he tried to calm me down. "Let's talk this out," he said. "You don't want to quit things."

"I'm not quitting," I said. "I'm scared."

We went back and forth like that for a few minutes.

"Dad, I don't know what else to say," I told him, reaching my breaking point. "You're my best friend. You're my only friend."

Those were the magic words. I don't think I had ever told Dad that before. I certainly felt it, but actually saying it out loud made it more real. "You're my best friend" wasn't just something I said to get out of camp; it was the truth. The other half of that sentence, "You're my only friend," was just as true. At that time, Dad really was my only friend. I think he knew he had to be because I didn't have anyone else.

Dad called the camp director, who tried to explain how disruptive it would be to pull me out. "Mr. Vittert, there are no refunds," he warned, "for any reason." The camp brochure had been clear about that, and he wanted to remind my dad. "We'd have to rearrange the whole trip."

Dad didn't hesitate. "I don't care. My kid needs to come home."

They packed up the fifteen-passenger white van, hitched the U-Haul full of gear to the back, and drove to the Vancouver Airport. It was a long, two-hour slog from Whistler to Vancouver. I sat quietly the whole way. This was supposed to be the trip where I broke free from the loneliness of school, where I could prove I wasn't the kid everyone thought I was. I felt like a failure.

When we pulled up to the terminal, the counselors—a guy and a girl, probably in college—stepped out with me. The male counselor shook my hand. "We're sorry to see you go," he said. "Are you sure?"

I nodded, grabbed my backpack, waved goodbye, and walked inside alone.

I handed over my passport at the counter, watching as the agent printed out my boarding pass.

"Okay, son, you're fourteen," the agent said. "You can fly by yourself."

It was eight o'clock at night when I boarded the flight out of Vancouver. I flew to Seattle, then to Minneapolis, and finally back to Michigan the next afternoon. By the time I arrived, it felt like I had been in the air forever.

Weeks later, in early September, Dad got a call from the camp director. "Mr. Vittert, I need to know where to send your refund," he said.

Dad paused. "Refund?" he asked.

"Yes," the director said. "It turns out your son was right about those two boys. We almost had to end the trip early."

Dad didn't need the validation. He had believed me from the start. The camp director's words only reinforced what Dad had always trusted: me.

The foundation for that trust had been built long before British Columbia, in small moments, like the time I jumped from a tree limb into his arms and he told me, "I'll always catch you," or the time he made me write "I will always tell the truth" a hundred times over. It wasn't just about camp. Our relationship became an unbreakable circle of trust. If I told Dad something, he believed it because he knew I wouldn't lie to him. And if he told me something, I trusted him without question. I think if I had said the sun was going to rise in the west, Dad would look west the next morning. And if he told me to jump from a window, I would do it, trusting there'd be something to catch me.

You Can't Hurt Me

After years of crying and being hurt, I felt something shift. I realized letting something hurt me was a decision.

When you have dealt with bullying and abuse for as long as I had, you eventually reach a point where you decide you can't be hurt anymore. You stop being a victim. It's not easy, but at some point, you stop letting other people's words, their bullying, and their attempts to tear you down define you. You become numb to it.

I think about what David Goggins wrote. He's a former Navy SEAL who basically made suffering his closest companion. The guy went from being overweight and stuck in a dead-end job to being one of the toughest endurance athletes on the planet. His book *Can't Hurt Me* is like a master class in mental resilience. Goggins talks a lot about how pain, both physical and emotional, is inevitable, but staying down is a choice. Life is like a series of mental battles, and the people who win aren't the smartest or the strongest. They're just the ones who refuse to quit.

I didn't have SEAL training to rely on, but I started to recognize that letting someone hurt me was optional. It didn't happen overnight. I went through the cycles—the crying, the feeling sorry for myself—but at some point, I got tired of giving people control over how I felt.

It's strange how the human mind forgets pain over time. Dad always told me that would happen. He was right. Ask someone who's been through it—for example, ask a Navy SEAL about Hell Week—and they'll tell you it wasn't so bad. Most women will only remember the magic of childbirth and holding their baby; the pain of labor fades away. It's funny how we rewrite our suffering into memories of resilience.

I've forgotten a lot—funny how the brain blanks out trauma—but some painful moments do resurface. I remember the teachers who tried to fail me, the ones who set traps, and the ones who accused me of cheating when I hadn't. There were teachers who could have been disciplined. The interim headmaster even asked if I wanted that. I said yes, but Dad said no. He believed in second chances, and maybe he thought kindness would eventually win. It didn't. He also worried that getting the art teacher suspended would unleash the wrath of the other teachers on me. Well, some of them made my life harder anyway, just because my dad had come in to address the issue. I used to think if we'd had the teacher disciplined things might've been different.

And it wasn't just at school. One of Dad's friends humiliated me during a dinner party, calling out something I had said in front of everyone. He was older, successful, the kind of man who had everything. I remember looking at him and asking, "Why are you doing this to me? What does it matter to you?" No bully, no matter their age, likes being exposed for what they are. He didn't answer, just shifted uncomfortably in his chair.

Even one of my uncles found ways to make fun of me, for how I looked, the things I said, or the fact that I didn't fit in. Entire summers passed without a single visit from my uncle and his family. My parents distanced me from people to protect me, even if it strained relationships. I think it cost them in ways they didn't always talk about, but they thought protecting me was worth it. Those moments left marks.

Even so, for as many people who hurt me, there were adults who saw an odd kid who needed a little guidance and kindness. I don't think it was pity, but they recognized they could make a difference.

At John Burroughs, Skippy Kiefer, the athletic director, gave me a refuge when I needed it most. I could go sit in her office when I needed a break. Sandra Mueller, my chemistry teacher, was always quite lovely to me. And Todd Small always did what he could to protect me, especially when an English teacher tried to get me expelled.

Dad's friends introduced me to a world I wouldn't have experienced otherwise. Thom Sehnert was the consummate restaurateur, an Irishman with a knack for business and storytelling. He lived by the famous saying, "It's hard to beat a man who won't quit." Thom lost everything in a flood but rebuilt his life and his restaurant with determination. He understood me in a way few adults did. There was Jackie Smith, the Hall of Fame tight end. My dad presented him at his Hall of Fame induction. Jackie would take me to work out, patiently trying to teach me to run; it was hopeless, but boy, did he try. And I'm still close with Dave Scanavino, one of my dad's best friends from college, whose quiet confidence I admire to this day.

My godparents Margie Susman and Louis Susman really understood me and were the most eminently kind human beings. Bert Walker, my other godfather, took me to the 1992 presidential debate when I was just ten, reinforcing the idea that even as a kid, I was worth bringing along.

I sat quietly in the audience as George H. W. Bush, Ross Perot, and Bill Clinton debated.

As great as those moments were, they felt like little islands. Maybe it was just fifteen minutes here and there, a quick conversation, or a single afternoon when I didn't feel like I was under attack. They didn't make the rest of it go away, but for a short time, I could breathe.

There was one other constant presence in my life that gave me that same sense of relief: Sally, our family dog. She was already part of the mix when I came home from the hospital, a Newfoundland who seemed to instinctively understand I needed her protection. Sally was there through every rough day, offering unconditional love. She helped me learn to walk, letting me tug on her ears to pull myself up. I've always believed that kids who grow up with big dogs are better for it. They understand life and loss in a way that's hard to teach otherwise. I remember the night before we put Sally down. I was in third grade, and we sat together reading to her, knowing it was our way of saying goodbye.

We lost Sally in April. That summer, Dad found a Newfoundland breeder in Northern Michigan and swore me to secrecy. He took me to meet Bessie, a tiny four-week-old puppy meant to surprise Mom. She filled the space Sally left behind, and once again, I had that quiet, unconditional love by my side. In a strange way, the dogs understood me when kids didn't.

Dad could stand at the end of the driveway, Sally (and later Bessie) could sit beside me, and in those two moments, I found enough strength to keep moving forward.

Over time, I realized the best revenge wasn't retaliation. Letting other people see that I was still standing, still moving forward, became enough. I started to believe that the greatest way to win wasn't through bitterness, but by focusing on the people who were there—like Dad waiting at the end of the driveway. In the end, success and love were the best ways to show the world I hadn't been broken.

Chapter Nine

WHAT WILL YOU BE GREAT AT?

The student-parent handbook at Burroughs said I needed to take music only in seventh grade. So when eighth grade rolled around and the school tried to make me sign up for chorus again, I already had my defense ready. I walked right up to the office, flipped open the handbook to the right page, and pointed.

"Well, actually, I don't," I said, "because the student-parent handbook says you only have to take it in seventh grade."

The school didn't take it well.

"Yes, but everyone takes music," an administrator at the school told me like I was supposed to care about what everyone else did.

I shrugged. "That's not what the handbook says."

I probably wouldn't have fought so hard to get out of music if it hadn't been for the choir teacher. He was just another insecure bully. During rehearsal for the Christmas pageant the year before, in front of two hundred kids, he'd stopped the music, pointed at me, and said, "Mr. Vittert, your off-note singing is quite noticeable. Sing softly. As a matter of fact, don't sing at all. Just mouth the words."

Born Lucky

Think about it: What kind of person singles out a seventh grader in front of two hundred kids—middle school and high school—and tells them to stop singing? You don't forget that. The idea of another year under his direction wasn't just unappealing; it felt like willingly signing up for more public embarrassment.

When we signed up for classes for the next year, the whole chorus lined up to get his signature. When I walked past, he looked at me and said, "Mr. Vittert, you haven't signed up for chorus next year."

"And I'm not going to," I told him.

The handbook was my ticket out, and I knew it better than anyone else. It was the one thing I could rely on to be fair, to say exactly what it meant. One of the signs of being on the autism spectrum is taking things literally—and I did. If the handbook said I didn't have to take music again, then I wasn't taking music again. And when I was told I had to take five academic classes, I said, "Well, the handbook said we only have to take four."

When you're a kid who doesn't fit in, and you know you're not going to charm your way out of things, you learn to use whatever you can. For me, standing up for myself wasn't optional; it was survival. The world often felt uncertain, but the handbook was predictable, and that made it powerful. And the funny thing is, when I pushed back hard enough, the bullies—whether they were kids or teachers—usually backed down.

Not every fight was about music class. Many battles felt like they were for self-preservation, like the time I ended up in the principal's office with my junior-year English teacher towering over me, ready to throw a punch.

This teacher had it out for me from the start. I never saw the world the way he wanted me to. To me, a river in a book was just a river, not a metaphor for life's winding journey. When Huckleberry Finn floated down the Mississippi, I figured he was just floating down the river. *How do we know Mark Twain meant anything deeper? Did he leave a note?* I openly challenged the idea that literature had to have hidden meanings beyond what was on the page. That alone made me a problem. But what really set him off was when I pushed back on the school's rule against using CliffsNotes.

I wasn't trying to avoid work; I just had different priorities. I didn't understand *The Iliad* and *The Odyssey* and didn't care. I wanted to read *The Wall Street Journal*. I wanted books about Eisenhower, the Revolution, World War II—things that I felt actually changed the world. But that wasn't what the curriculum valued. Burroughs had a strict rule: no CliffsNotes. I thought that was ridiculous. *You can't tell me what I can and can't read outside of school. If I can pass the reading quizzes, what does it matter?* But to my teacher, my refusal to fall in line wasn't just defiance—it was a personal challenge.

Then came the blue slip. At Burroughs, blue slips carried real weight. There were good blue slips: *Lucky scored a 98 on this test. Great job!* And bad ones: *We need to have a conversation about Lucky.* A "bad" blue slip triggered a whole process: a meeting with the teacher and principal, a signature from your parents.

The one from the English teacher was bad—a formal accusation that I had cheated.

My advisor at the time was Todd Small, who was also the principal. He was a nice guy who believed in me and protected me as much as he could at Burroughs. When I found out the meeting with the teacher would be at noon, I called Mom. "I need you to sit by the phone for the next hour," I told her. "If it rings, answer."

She hesitated. "Why?"

"I'm going to this meeting with my English teacher," I told her. "I may need you to come over here. Just stay near the phone, don't leave."

She didn't ask any more questions. Sure enough, the meeting was an ambush. The teacher accused me, I denied. He escalated, I stayed calm. When he realized he wasn't winning, he snapped. "You did this!" he shouted, his face turning red with anger.

"If it makes you feel like a big man to yell at a seventeen-year-old, go ahead," I said. That's when he got out of his chair, fists clenched. For a split second, I thought he might actually hit me.

Principal Small, seeing where this was headed, stepped in. "Sit down. Now!" he said to the teacher, almost rising from behind his desk.

I turned to him and said, "I don't feel safe. Call my mother." At that moment, the dynamic shifted. Mom arrived, I explained my side, and by the end of it, we reached a compromise: I'd finish the class with a B, and my grade wouldn't be left to chance.

I wasn't proud of the situation, but I had learned how to stand my ground. I had built a shell to protect myself, and I would get angry when I thought people were attacking me. I wasn't going to just roll over. If someone was coming for me, I had to hit back—not with fists, but with strategy. I escalated to de-escalate, fought back when I felt cornered, and made sure I was never the one left defenseless. That instinct would serve me well later in life, though sometimes it worked against me. There's no question I could be obnoxious. And when I got uncomfortable, I got even more obnoxious. Over time, I learned to harness my anger, but at seventeen, it felt like survival. It felt like the only option.

Burroughs prided itself on preparing students for the real world, but the truth was, I was already living in it. If they could try to expel me over a book summary, what else was fair game? The only way to make it through was to play the game better than they did. Some people fight fair, but some don't. By high school, I had learned to navigate the system.

Playing by Their Rules

Burroughs was also big on what college you got into, and they wanted your transcript to have club memberships on it. Everyone was in a club except for me. There wasn't a club I wanted to join, and I doubted there was a club that wanted me as a member.

In eleventh grade, they told me I had to have a club. So I pulled out the handbook. I flipped to the section on clubs and found my answer. All I had to do was hold one meeting a year, take attendance, and get a faculty sponsor. Easy enough.

I convinced one of Dad's golf buddies, the head football coach and a good man named Jim Lemen, to be the sponsor for a Young Republicans Club. I grabbed a couple of guys I knew and said, "You're founding members. We're going to have an officers' meeting. Elect me president. Ready? One, two, three . . ." The next morning, at the daily all-school assembly, I stood up and announced, "Tomorrow will be the first meeting of the Young Republicans Club." There were raucous boos. It was 1999, and Burroughs wasn't exactly a conservative-leaning school. They were doing "privilege walks" and "diversity days" before it was cool. "Our first meeting will be tomorrow at 8:05," I said. The bell rang at 8:10, so it was going to be a short meeting. "Attendance will be taken and donuts will be served."

I went to Krispy Kreme and bought twenty dozen donuts. I set them up outside the assembly hall with a legal pad. If you wanted a donut, you signed up for the club. By the end of the day, I was president of the largest club on campus.

The handbook was like my personal get-out-of-jail-free card. The school could push, but if it wasn't in the handbook, I wasn't doing it. I remember one time getting out of a parking ticket at school because the handbook said no-parking spots shall be designated by "No Parking" signs. I had parked exactly where I shouldn't have, right in front of the school, in the faculty lot. The ticket meant a one-hour detention.

I walked into the principal's office, ticket in hand. "You can't give me this," I said.

"Yes, I can," he said.

We went back and forth until I pointed out the exact line in the handbook. "There's no 'No Parking' sign there," I told him. He followed me out to the lot, stared at the spot, and muttered, "God damn it," before ripping up the ticket. A No Parking sign went up the next day.

It wasn't just about getting out of things I didn't want to do. It was about learning how to survive. When you're a kid who feels embattled—whether it's against classmates, teachers, or just the system itself—you figure out pretty quickly that standing up for yourself is the only option. A lot of people who end up successful later in life don't have it easy as kids. They had to fight through something. And their success comes not because life gets easier for them, but because they learn how to navigate their challenges. The handbook taught me how to make the rules work for me, how to turn them into an advantage instead of an obstacle. It was the one thing I could control.

There's this trend nowadays to make things easier for kids who struggle and to smooth the road for them. The problem is that life isn't that simple. If you don't learn how to get back up when you're knocked down or push through uncomfortable situations, you end up unprepared when the world doesn't bend for you. Mom and Dad could have pulled me out of school and homeschooled me for the rest of my school years to avoid the fights and the embarrassment. But they didn't. They knew keeping me in school would be tough, but that it was necessary. At times, I think Dad worried I'd become too hardened by it all and get angry, but even then, he understood that sometimes the best way to survive the world is to live in it.

Still, for all my maneuvering, there was one thing I couldn't get around: sports. The handbook said I had to participate in one, and trust me—I tried everything to find a loophole.

Finding My Sport

Sports at Burroughs were everything. It was the currency that mattered, especially for the boys. If you were good at sports, you had status. If you weren't, the sports field became the place you tried to avoid because that's where the bullies found you.

WHAT WILL YOU BE GREAT AT?

Seventh and eighth grade had sports baked into the schedule—PE from 1:30 to 2:45, then back to class. But starting in ninth grade, things changed. School ended at 3 p.m., and sports were mandatory. You had to play a sport every season. For me, just the thought was absolute hell. I tried to become an "athletic trainer in training" to avoid playing. No dice.

Dad had been a fairly successful athlete at Burroughs. Sports came naturally to him. He had great hand-eye coordination and was an amateur racquetball player in St. Louis. He picked up golf in his mid-thirties and became a near scratch player. He played college football and baseball at Ripon as a freshman. I inherited precisely none of his ability.

Football was the big fall sport at Burroughs, but I had no interest in playing. Dad used to ask if I was competitive, and I'd tell him, "Yeah, I'm highly competitive. I just don't like touching the person I'm competing against." I've always been sensitive to touch. One of the things about being on the autism spectrum is that sensory issues make things like getting hit feel overwhelming. Football was a sensory overload waiting to happen. Getting hit, hitting others—it wasn't for me.

I love watching football now. When I was living in the Middle East, the NFL streamed games with commercials for people overseas. Watching the full game, ads and all, made Sundays feel like I was home in America. But playing? No thanks.

I never had depth perception because my eyes didn't fuse properly, which made anything involving a moving ball nearly impossible. As you'll recall, I was cross-eyed as a kid, and my right eye still drifted off to the side as if I was staring somewhere else entirely. I've had three surgeries to tighten the muscles around my eyes: at six months old, then again in fourth grade, and the last one in 2016. But even with these procedures, balls that moved through space were practically impossible for me to track. I'd try to catch pop flies or field grounders, but I can't tell you how many baseballs hit me in the head or rolled right past me because I just couldn't judge where they were going to land. Suffice it to say that wasn't a recipe for making friends as a kid.

And so, of course, at one point I decided to try tennis, where the ball moved and you had to run to it. What could go wrong?

In reality, I opted for tennis because there was a girl I liked who played. It seemed like a good enough reason to pick up a racket.

One summer afternoon before eighth grade, Dad came to watch one of my lessons. Afterward, he looked at me and said, "I will pay for every tennis lesson you want, I'll come to every practice, but you will never be able to play tennis. Ever. You can't play tennis. No one can teach you."

He wasn't being mean. He was just brutally honest, which was standard in our house. There was unconditional love, but there was also no sugarcoating reality. Other parents might say, "Oh Lucky, you can be president," or "You can be an astronaut if you just put your mind to it." But Mom and Dad were brutally realistic. Dad thought it was important for me to find something I could be successful at, but I was horribly uncoordinated—part of being on the spectrum—and tennis was never going to be it.

Dad encouraged me in his own way. "Lucky, go have fun and try, but you can't play tennis," he said.

I asked that girl to play one afternoon in seventh grade. About three minutes in, she looked at me and said, "What are we doing here?" That was the end of tennis—and any chance with the girl.

I was desperate to find something before ninth grade. The idea of playing sports at Burroughs terrified me. Dad knew how much it weighed on me. That winter, he kept asking if there was any sport I wanted to try or anything else I might be interested in. Around that time, I talked to Kelsey Lentz, a girl in my eighth-grade class. She had already started rowing as a coxswain, the person who steers the boat and yells directions. Coxswains were supposed to be as light as possible since every extra pound was just another the rowers had to move through the water for free. Kelsey was petite—she probably weighed ninety pounds soaking wet—and someone had recruited her for the team.

There were kids at Burroughs who trained for things like horseback riding or other specialized sports, and the school made exceptions for them to train year-round with their club team instead of joining a team at Burroughs.

Rowing caught my attention.

Over Christmas break, Dad found the St. Louis Rowing Club. This was before Google, so I don't even know how we tracked it down. We drove out to a man-made lake near St. Louis and signed up.

Effort Equals Results

Rowing can be miserable. Early mornings, freezing water, and the constant burning in your legs. But I loved it. I took to it like peanut butter to bread.

Rowing was simple: The more effort you put in, the more you got out. There were no tricks, shortcuts, or special skills. You worked hard, and the results showed. It was my first taste at the kind of work ethic Dad talked about.

That had never been the case for me before. School was frustrating. I wasn't good at writing or academics, and on top of the social struggles that came with my diagnosis, I almost certainly had undiagnosed learning disabilities. I didn't understand why working harder in school never seemed to make a difference. Plus, Dad used to say, "The world is run by C students." Dad did fine without being a great student, so why should I care about my English grade?

Burroughs pushed me to take honors math and science, but I said no. I figured it was better to get a solid grade in the regular track than struggle and fail in the honors track. They argued I was supposed to be placed in the harder classes, but I just pulled out—you guessed it—the handbook again. "Well, it's not in the student-parent handbook," I said. I opted for the easier classes.

Rowing was different. There was no handbook, no loophole—just hard work. And for the first time, I could see the results directly. Effort in equals results out. It was my first taste of the lesson Dad had taught me about the 107th sales call.

As you know by now, I was a big kid for eighth grade. I was strong, and I was pretty good at rowing. There's not much to it—you go back and forth at the same speed as everyone else. It's slightly more complicated than running, but not by much. Rowing was the first sport that felt natural, the first I could actually do well. Many sports rely on innate skill, on things like fast-twitch muscles, but rowing was different. Rowing was about 80 percent legs and 20 percent upper body. It was more about strength and determination than coordination or finesse, which worked to my advantage.

The Burroughs sports program didn't include rowing, but I had a plan. I could say, "This is my sport," and the school would have to make an exception. But to pull that off, I had to make varsity. That became my goal starting in ninth grade.

I rowed a little in eighth grade at the St. Louis Rowing Club, a citywide club open to students from all over. The novice team's coach my eighth-grade year was a successful rower from Canada who worked as an engineer at Boeing. By the time I hit ninth grade, he was moving up to coach the varsity team. I made my pitch. "Look, I'm pretty good," I told him, and I wasn't lying. "I want to row varsity."

I think he understood me. He wasn't much older than thirty at the time, and he got that I was a good kid, just awkward socially. But when I was rowing, I worked insanely hard, and to certain people, that currency mattered. I made the varsity eight, a crew of eight rowers plus the coxswain who steers and calls the race. I was eighth on the depth chart, but I was there. The bowman isn't the powerhouse of the boat, but it still matters. Being part of the eight meant I was in. I could finally get out of Burroughs sports.

As a freshman starting on the varsity rowing team, I was already behind. My coach thought I was good enough, but the rest of the team did not. A few weeks before the biggest and last race of the season, on a cold, windy day in late April, I saw my varsity coach, the head coach, and the novice men's coach all talking when I got back from a six-mile run. As I was putting on a pullover, my coach called me over. He told me they wanted me to row not only in the varsity boat but that the novice coach wanted me to row in his boat, too, because he felt that it would give him an advantage at the race.

Over the next couple of days, I practiced with both the novice and varsity crews, and everything was going according to plan. The next week, as I was walking to the parking lot, the coaches yelled for me to come back.

The novice coach said, "When you're up at the race, don't tell anyone what you're doing."

I guess it comes from Dad, but when people tell me not to say something about what I'm doing, it makes me wonder why. "Is there a problem?" I asked, my body stiffening. I was starting to not like the sound of this.

"No, no real problem," he said. "It's technically against the rules for you to row as a novice, but we agree that it's okay and not a big deal."

"If it's not a big deal," I questioned, "why can't I tell people?"

"Well," he hesitated, "people might be upset and feel that it is against the rules."

"It is against the rules," I replied. This seemed painfully obvious to me.

"Yeah," he said, "but it's not against the spirit of the rules."

"But it's against what the rulebook says, right?" I challenged.

"Well, technically, it is, but we think it's okay," he said. "We've been around rowing for a long time, and our professional judgment says it's okay."

"No problem," I said. "I'll row the race, but when I get done, I'll go up to the referee's tent and tell him that I wasn't allowed to row in the race. If it's not a big deal, then he won't disqualify me. After all, he'll be able to interpret the 'spirit' of the rules."

I was starting to get scared. My coach had taken a real chance on me, and he had been involved in the sport since I was in preschool. The head coach came over. To rowers on the team, he was god. He'd had an amazing college career at MIT before coaching college rowing, and he was the father of junior rowing in St. Louis. After he produced ten junior national team athletes, nobody argued with him, much less a freshman. He was never one for words, but when they came, everybody listened.

"Lucky," he said, "in the end, you row for me, and you're insulting both my professional judgment and my personal integrity by questioning if you should row. Now, you're going to row, and you're going to keep your mouth shut, and if that can't happen, I don't have athletes who question their coach on my team."

I was fearful about what he might do to me, but I was more scared of what my parents would say if they learned that I had talked back to a coach. I lowered my head and replied, "Sir, I do not question either of those two things, but I have to live with the decision I make right now, and I am not going to do something that my own code says is wrong. Good day."

I turned and walked to the parking lot and got in Mom's car.

Without saying much, we drove home, and later that night, I explained the situation to Dad, who called my coach to talk about it. Through the night, cooler heads prevailed. The varsity coach came over to the house, apologized, and asked me to row for him. I was relieved. The next day at practice, the head coach came over and shook my hand—that was it, no words, nothing else, just a handshake. About a month later, he told Dad, "You have to admire that little kid. He stood up against the three of us—and, most of all, a lot of pressure from me—for what he believed in."

Most of the time, when you stand up to somebody and you're right, after they get over the ego bruise, they respect you more. That lesson stuck with me, and it came in handy later—both on and off the water. Rowing wasn't just about endurance and technique; it was about navigating team dynamics, earning respect, and proving myself with every stroke. And with rowing being a three-season sport, there were plenty of opportunities to be away from Burroughs.

WHAT WILL YOU BE GREAT AT?

Throughout the year, we traveled all over the country for regattas. We'd go to Atlanta, Cincinnati, Philadelphia, and Madison, Wisconsin, to compete against schools and clubs from across the country. Regattas meant long trips. We'd leave on a Thursday or Friday night, travel to whatever city by bus, sleep four to a room, and spend the weekend racing. I was the youngest and weakest link in the varsity eight, but once I was in the boat, I held my own.

I was terrified of the social aspect. Two varsity rowers, who were both talented and later rowed for the US junior national team, were the big guys on the crew. I was just a little ninth grader. Before our first long trip, they came up to me and said, "Hey, do you have a problem sharing a room with us? We're gay." I panicked. I had no idea how to handle it. I called Dad, completely freaked out. Eventually, he called my coach and asked if they could meet. They sat down at a little diner near the Boeing plant, and Dad laid out the whole story.

My coach listened, then burst out laughing. "They're just messing with him," he said. Rowing didn't stop the teasing, but it gave me a place on a team and some social currency.

Rowing was probably one of the best things that happened to me. I'd come back to school on Mondays wearing my rowing jacket, fresh off a win from the weekend. Kids heard about it. Since the rowing team pulled students from across the city, people from other schools knew me. It became my thing. Plus, I went from being this big, blobby kid to becoming strong and fit. Rowers develop a different physique. For the first time, I sort of felt like I looked the part and fit in.

I worked out in the mornings before school and then went to crew practice in the afternoons. A lot of mornings, I worked out until I made myself throw up. To me, that meant you knew you'd worked hard. A guy at the gym once told Dad, "I've never seen anything like it. Lucky will work out on the StairMaster or the rowing machine until he pukes. He actually gets sick, throws up, and then comes out and gets back on the machine. I'm betting on that kid." Rowing wasn't just something I did. It was *everything*.

Dad was relentless. "Find a goal, find a goal, find a goal," he'd say. And rowing, like a lot of other things throughout my life, became all about goals. He pushed me to measure everything. If I could shave a second off here or a meter more there, I was making progress.

I always thought it was just about trying to get faster, stronger, better. But later, I realized Dad saw something I didn't.

Rowing as a team was about synchronization, but individually, the goal became mastering what rowers call ERG times. The ergometer, or rowing machine, measured everything. There were three benchmarks: the 20-minute test, the 10,000-meter row, and the all-important 2,000-meter (2K) sprint. How far could you row in 20 minutes? How quickly could you cover 10,000 meters? How fast could you finish 2,000 meters? These times weren't just numbers. They were the ultimate measure of where I stacked up. I obsessed over them. I set goals, and Dad and I talked about them constantly. By the end of freshman year, breaking seven minutes for my 2K became the singular goal. And once I did that, the goal shifted to trying to make the national team.

Between my sophomore and junior year, I got invited to the national team development camp. But during camp, I hurt my back. I kept rowing into my senior year, but between the injury, burnout, and the realization that I wasn't tall enough to row in college, rowing competitively started to run its course.

As I've said, rowing is simple—work hard and pull hard. But the taller you are, the more power you apply to each stroke. At five foot eleven, I could keep up in high school by outworking guys who were six foot one. But in college, everyone worked just as hard, and the entire Princeton rowing team was six foot five. Every stroke they take, there's six more inches of oar in the water, six more inches of power applied for that same stroke.

I tried to explain that to Dad. "You can work harder than everyone else," he said.

But I told him, "No, I can't, because they're working just as hard—and they have six more inches of reach."

Sometimes, no matter how hard you work, there are limits you can't push past. No amount of hard work could overcome the law of physics. And that was okay. Rowing had given me the lessons I needed—not just about effort, but about recognizing when to pivot and find the next goal.

Chapter Ten

PRACTICE YOUR CRAFT

The summer before my senior year of high school I was ready for freedom. For the first time, I had a girlfriend and I wasn't ready to spend another summer at Shorewood in Michigan, hundreds of miles away from her. I had it all worked out: I'd stay in St. Louis, practice rowing, and live at the house.

Easy, I thought. Convincing Dad? Not so much.

"If you're staying here, you need a job," Dad said in his no-room-for-argument tone when I told him the plan.

I tried to sell him on the rowing idea, but he wasn't buying it. "No," he said adamantly, "you have got to get a job."

I hadn't thought that far ahead. But Dad's insistence turned out to be a blessing. Dad was involved in the media world through the *Business Journals* and the pilot for the show *Donnybrook* was shot at our dining room table. It was the St. Louis version of Fox News's *The Five* before *The Five* even existed. I remembered a conversation from a dinner years earlier. Charlie Brennan, the big AM talk radio guy in St. Louis, was a fill-in host on *Donnybrook* and had told me once, "Hey kid, if you ever want an internship, give me a call." I didn't know if he was serious, but I figured I had nothing to lose. So I called.

To my surprise, Charlie was serious. That summer, I became his intern at KMOX, the fifty-thousand watt clear channel AM station. Talk radio isn't a big thing now, but back then Charlie was one of the most influential people in town.

That summer wasn't about work, though—at least not at first. My parents trusted me to stay home, but they weren't going to leave a seventeen-year-old completely unsupervised. "You can't stay alone in St. Louis at our house," they said once I crossed the job barrier.

"No, you're right," I said. "I should have a babysitter."

I negotiated a deal with a former crew teammate a few years older than me who was now at the University of Wisconsin, convincing her to take the job with one condition: She'd get paid to keep an eye on me and keep Mom and Dad's rules in theory, but let me live my summer the way I wanted in practice.

I managed to hold up my end of the deal and show up at the station every day to work with Charlie on his 9 a.m. show. Talk radio always fascinated me. I wanted to have my own radio show when I was a little kid. I'd always loved politics, and I idolized Rush Limbaugh, forcing whoever was driving to listen to his show anywhere we went around St. Louis. KMOX in St. Louis was a big deal too. I grew up listening to local legends like Nan Wyatt, who hosted a morning informational show, and Jim White, known as "the Big Bumper," who bumped on the airwaves late at night. It wasn't journalism that drew me in so much as the chance to be controversial, to debate, and to push ideas—all things I loved in life. I was always a little bit conservative, a little bit libertarian, and it felt like talk radio was the perfect way to explore that perspective.

It was the summer of 2000, which was the perfect time to get an intro to political journalism. The Bush-Gore election was heating up, and the aftermath of Matt Drudge breaking the Monica Lewinsky scandal still lingered. Talk radio was thriving in what might have been its last heyday. There was no SiriusXM, no podcasts, no Twitter, and no streaming platforms. We still lived in a world where your cell phone was just a phone. It was the last time talk radio was a dominant force in American politics.

At KMOX, I got to experience the full scope of how a show got put together, from the editorial and booking guests to research and flow on air. It was a small team, just Charlie and a couple of producers, which meant I was involved in everything. It wasn't just an internship; it was an incredible crash course in how media was made during one of its most pivotal eras.

I got all the hands-on experience you could imagine. I booked guests, conducted pre-interviews, and even drove people to and from the studio. That's when I endeared myself to Charlie. One day, I had to pick up this lawyer, Chet Pleban, a prominent personal injury attorney in town. I picked Chet up at his house, and on the way to the studio, he spilled coffee all over himself. I had a clean white dress shirt hanging in my car. I handed it over. The moment became a running joke around the station—the seventeen-year-old intern who always came prepared. (Chet returned the shirt after getting it dry-cleaned.)

Working with Charlie that summer wasn't just a job—it was an education. Charlie's mentoring showed me how talk radio could turn ideas into action. For the first time, I could find my voice in a way that mattered. He gave me only one piece of advice: *Go practice your craft.* That would become a defining part of my young broadcast career. Later, while other kids chased internships at *ABC World News Tonight* or NBC's *TODAY*, I went to the smallest stations I could find—anywhere that would put me on the air. Charlie made me realize that getting better mattered more than looking good on a résumé.

By the time my parents returned from Michigan, Dad asked me, "What's next?" He was always pushing me to find the next challenge. Without knowing it, Dad's insistence on getting a job had set me on a path I never saw coming.

Fitting In and Falling Out

Looking back, I can see how much of high school felt like a crash course in belonging. Before that summer at KMOX, I thought maybe I could figure out my social voice too. By junior year, I was tired of being on the outside, tired of being the kid who didn't get invited to parties or have a place in the "cool" crowd.

At first, I tried to make subtle, small changes to fit in. For someone like me, understanding how to read people and navigate social dynamics wasn't second nature; it was a learned skill. That's the thing about EQ: When you have to work for it, you develop it more intentionally. While others who naturally fit in might take that for granted, I was focused on figuring out what made people tick. I started caring more about what people thought of me, chasing invitations to parties, and sucking up to the cool kids at school. I drove around on Friday nights, trying to figure out where everyone was. I wanted to be included, to belong.

For a while, it worked. I made inroads. People started noticing me. A couple of the cool kids' girlfriends liked me. I thought I'd cracked the code—until I hadn't.

The unraveling came one night when one of those girlfriends posted a message on AOL Instant Messenger saying she was going to kill herself after a fight with her boyfriend. Just a week earlier, the school had held a speech on suicide prevention—*If someone says they're going to hurt themselves, you must say something. Tell an adult.* Not long before that, a kid on the rowing team had taken his own life. So when she sent that message, I didn't hesitate. I called her. No answer. I called her dad. Nothing. He was a doctor, so I called his pager. No response. So I did the only thing I could think to do: I printed out the instant message thread, drove to the headmaster's house, and handed it to him. "Here you go," I said, thinking I was doing exactly what we'd just been told was the right thing.

What followed was the kind of backlash you don't forget. The girl's family blamed me for humiliating her, and her boyfriend, one of the most popular kids in school, turned the entire grade against me. All of Burroughs was told not to speak to me. I was ostracized overnight. No one at school would even talk to me, much less hang out. The teachers and administration—the people who were supposed to protect me—left

PRACTICE YOUR CRAFT

me to twist in the wind, defenseless. No one intervened. No one said I did the right thing. No one told the leader of the Leland Boycott to stop it. It was as though I'd simply disappeared, and everyone was fine pretending I had.

By April, near the end of my junior year, I'd had enough. I told the headmaster, "I'm not coming back next year." For my senior year, I was going to take classes at the local college instead.

The headmaster told me, "No one's ever done that before."

I responded, "Well, I'm going to, because you completely sold me out."

During my senior year, I took one or two morning classes at Burroughs four days a week but spent the rest of my day at Washington University. I was the only kid in fifteen years at Burroughs to do something like that. I didn't see it as quitting. For me, it was just a way of saying, "I've learned what I need to learn. Time to move on."

That was the moment I made a promise to myself and Dad: I would never change who I was for anyone else again.

That lesson stayed with me. Changing yourself to fit in is fleeting. It's not that the hurt disappeared—I've always wanted to belong and have those relationships—but after high school, I learned that trying to be someone you're not costs more than it's worth.

Today, I'm almost militant about it. I always say, "I don't dance unless there's music, and I don't eat unless I'm hungry." Even when it might be in my best interest to be nice or get along with someone whose values I don't respect, I won't do it, even to my detriment. I'm probably unreasonable in how high my bar is for trusting others, but I refuse to compromise.

Even as an adult, I've seen this lesson play out. When I got to Washington, DC, I saw my values didn't completely align, and I made a conscious effort not to change. Washington is just high school with fancier clothes and better cocktails. People chase invitations to parties, measure their worth by how many brunches they attend, and trade values for access. Here, the character traits that are celebrated are often transactional, shallow, and self-serving. As Churchill famously said, "Politics is almost as exciting as war, and quite as dangerous. In war you can only be killed once, but in politics many times."[1] It's a war I've chosen not to fight. I've decided to stay true to myself, even though it means I'm not on the "cool kids" list. I don't get invited to the pre-parties or the White House Correspondents' dinner after-parties. Not much has changed since high school. But I'm okay with that.

It's not always easy. On big weekends in Washington, when everyone else is out at the big parties that are good for their careers, it stings a little to know I'm not there. But then I remember the lesson I learned in eleventh grade: Changing yourself to fit in with people is never worth it. And I'd rather sit at the edges, true to myself, than dance to music I don't believe in.

Spinning Records

When Dad asked me, "What's next?" after the KMOX internship, I thought the answer was obvious: I'd go back to work for Charlie. But Charlie had other ideas.

"If you want to be on-air," he reiterated, "you've got to find a place to practice your craft." It wasn't the answer I wanted, but Charlie was right.

That winter of my senior year, I took his advice. I flew up to Northern Michigan, rented a car, and drove around. I went station to station, begging for a chance to get on-air. Finally, about an hour from the summer cabin, at a double-wide trailer on top of a hill, I found 92.3 WBNZ in Benzonia, Michigan. The owner, Mark, wasn't immediately sold, but I kept calling. Eventually, he gave in—not because I impressed him, but because I wore him down. As he later put it, "I gave him a chance so he would stop calling me."

That persistence is something I got from Dad. My first girlfriend used to say I'm more like my dad than he is—and she wasn't wrong. He's the kind of person who will call you a thousand times until you finally do the thing he's asking. I'd like to think I took his best qualities: his principles, his sense of right and wrong, and his relentless determination. That intensity and unwillingness to give up has always been a driving force in my life, and if I learned anything from him, it's that sheer determination can open doors.

Mark agreed to put me on-air from 7 p.m. to midnight, five nights a week. This not only ended my badgering but also saved him money. He didn't have to pay for syndicated programming when I was live. He paid me minimum wage and I spun records every night. My first night on-air, I nervously introduced myself: "Hi, I'm Lucky Vittert, and I hope you like this song."

The job itself wasn't a glamour gig. The station was old and run-down, with more cockroaches than CDs. Every night, I'd drive an hour from Shorewood to the station, open it up, spin records, and do the weather—"7:02 in Northern Michigan, 54 degrees in Traverse City, 58 inland in Gaylord"—then close up at midnight, put the station back on satellite, and drive the hour home, getting to bed around 1:30 a.m. It was repetitive and exhausting, but it didn't matter. I was on the air.

People still listened to the radio in the summer of 2001. There were no iPods, and Spotify and other streaming music services had yet to be invented. People in Northern Michigan tuned in while sitting around campfires or cruising on their boats. By the end of the summer, I was no longer just a nervous kid spinning records. I was telling stories, cracking jokes, and finding my rhythm. I wasn't just practicing my craft; I was discovering my voice.

Charlie was right: You don't learn how to be on-air by waiting for the perfect opportunity. You learn by showing up, night after night, and putting in the work, even when the booth is full of cockroaches. That summer on WBNZ taught me not just the mechanics of being on-air but the joy of connecting with an audience—even if it was just a few people listening from their docks in Northern Michigan. It wasn't the future I'd envisioned, but it was the start of something.

Stumbling into Journalism

If the person who had offered me my first internship had been a surgeon, I might have ended up in medicine. But it was Charlie Brennan, the king of AM talk radio in St. Louis, who gave me my first glimpse into a career. And because of him, journalism became my path—not by careful planning but through a series of unlikely events.

When I was younger, Dad always pushed me away from business. He had walked that road, and once you've walked through the valley of death, you don't want your kid to traverse it. He knew how hard it was—the struggles, the failures, the difficulty of making it. And he didn't want me to face the same. Instead, he encouraged me to pursue service, to give back in ways that mattered. For him, government officials and public servants were almost sacred. FBI agents were noble. Politicians were honorable. He saw journalism in the same light: a paragon of people trying to find the truth. He wanted me to live a life of consequence, a life bigger than myself.

Dad always talked about being of service and giving back. That stuck with me early on. When I was little, Mom helped me set up a lemonade stand to raise money for Save the Children. I still have the short blurb *Scholastic Reader* wrote about it. I was eight or so at the time, and one day, everyone at school got the *Scholastic Reader* and saw a picture of me in this "Help the People Club" or something. It was a small article, but moments like that shaped the way I saw the world; these were the things Dad always thought were important.

At one point, I thought the military might be my path. I was drawn to the discipline and sense of purpose it offered, and I seriously considered attending West Point or Annapolis. There was something about the idea of wearing a uniform and being an officer that had a cachet to me. The academies also appealed to me because they weren't like normal colleges, which terrified me after how socially difficult Burroughs had been.

The summer after my junior year I attended a weeklong program

PRACTICE YOUR CRAFT

at West Point. The kids who served as our counselors weren't trying to haze us; they wanted us to attend. But the counselor I was assigned to, who was supposed to represent the leadership of the US Army, came off as a dolt barking orders. I'd been expecting young Eisenhowers and Schwarzkopfs—larger-than-life leaders—not this dweeb. By the end of the week, I was disillusioned. There was one impressive leader who gave a speech on the final night, but I couldn't shake the idea of having to take orders from some doofus like my counselor. That wasn't something I could do.

I remember the conversation with Dad on the phone as I stood at West Point. I was leaving on Friday, knowing I was supposed to go to Annapolis for another weeklong program on Sunday. He asked the most obvious question: "Lucky, you get seasick. Why on earth would you join the navy?"

That sealed the deal. Kids make decisions for odd reasons, but I couldn't bring myself to give up the idea of a normal college experience, even if the social aspect scared me. With these military schools, you're not going to quit once you go.

As college application season rolled around, I wasn't sure what I wanted. I applied to Vanderbilt, Virginia, Ole Miss, and Washington University, but only Ole Miss accepted me. I wasn't sure about Northwestern until I visited my girlfriend, who was a year ahead of me and already enrolled there. When I told my college counselor I was visiting, he was brutally honest: "You're never going to get into Northwestern."

That October I drove to Evanston, Illinois, to see my girlfriend. It was a big football weekend, and the admissions office, housed in an old converted house, was packed with kids and their parents. As I walked in, I saw guided tours forming. I had no plan and no appointment. I made my way to the front of the line, where I saw a staff member standing on a chair.

"Hi, what are you here for?" he asked.

"What do you mean?" I asked.

"Are you here for the guided tour with an interview, the group tour, the special tour?" he said. "Do you have an appointment with an admissions officer? What are you here for?"

"I want to talk to somebody about coming to school here," I said.

He looked at me. "Fill out one of those cards over there." I filled it out and went to a fraternity party with my girlfriend.

When the application packet came in the mail, there were so many options to choose from. There was the School of Arts and Sciences, the School of this, the School of that. I noticed that the journalism school didn't require a foreign language, which was perfect for me. I'd struggled with Spanish at Burroughs, and my learning disabilities made picking up new languages nearly impossible. Other kids could get waivers for language requirements, but that never crossed my mind. It wasn't how we did things in my family. So I checked the box for the Medill School of Journalism.

When I told my college counselor I was applying to Medill, he laughed in my face. "You'll never get in," he said, pointing to my mediocre SAT scores and shaky grades. Medill, after all, was for the best of the best—editors-in-chief of high school newspapers, anchors of school TV stations, and journalism savants. I was none of those things.

I didn't apply to Medill because of some grand dream—I applied because it didn't require a foreign language. That, and I wanted to be near my girlfriend again.

Burroughs had a chart showing the colleges that students applied to and their respective SAT scores. Medill stood at the top of that chart, with sky-high requirements for verbal and writing scores. I didn't come close. I was a B-student with poor test scores, far from the mold of a Medill applicant.

Yet somehow, against all odds, I got in. Later, I learned why. Medill was looking for diversity—and at the time, I checked an unexpected box: a straight, white male from Missouri.

On my first day at Medill, about 160 of us packed into an auditorium for an orientation. It was 70 percent women, another reminder of how I'd made it.

"Look to your left, look to your right," the speaker said. "One of you won't be at graduation when we meet here again in four years." The statement felt over the top; this wasn't SEAL training. Then they continued, "If you were the editor of your high school newspaper, stand up." Seventy percent of the room stood up. "If you anchored your high school TV station, stand up." Another big group of kids rose to their feet. By the end, I was the only kid I could see still sitting.

I wasn't a journalism prodigy or a natural fit for Medill. I was just a kid from Missouri who hated foreign languages and followed his girlfriend to Northwestern. That moment was another stark reminder of everything I wasn't. It felt familiar, like all the other times I'd been the odd one out. But if I knew anything, it was how to keep pushing forward. Medill wasn't going to be easy, but neither was anything that mattered.

Chapter Eleven

IF YOU QUIT, THEY WIN

The day I graduated from Burroughs, one of the administrators told Dad, "We've had kids who've had it worse than Lucky, but nobody who survived." That stuck with me, not just because I survived high school but because, as I was about to learn, surviving doesn't mean the challenges are over.

Going to college felt like freedom, but it wasn't like everything magically got better. I thought Northwestern would be a fresh start, a chance to leave behind the isolation and awkwardness of high school. But when I got there, it was a lot of the same. I was the odd one out again, the kid who didn't quite fit in or pick up on the cues everyone else seemed to know instinctively. If high school was hell, college felt like purgatory.

I wasn't being tormented the same way, but I was still stuck—still watching from the outside, still waiting for some kind of transformation that never seemed to come. The freedom I was looking for wasn't the cure I thought it would be; it just meant I had more space to feel alone. In high school, I would sit and listen to speeches about how Burroughs was "the best years of your life" and think, *Well, sheesh, if that's true I'm in for a really rotten life.* College was just a bigger version of the same game, and I still didn't know the rules. And no one hands you a rulebook for belonging.

I had heard Dad's college story a dozen times growing up—he told it to me at my lowest moments—how he stood alone in his dorm at Ripon College on the night of fraternity bids, the only one out of 125 guys left without a bid. He had gone through the same isolation, and his success and friendships later in life proved that even if you don't change who you are, you still have options. But that didn't make it any easier in the moment.

The fraternity rush my freshman year was like déjà vu. I can still see myself standing on the corner outside the Kappa Sigma house, the last remaining fraternity on my list of houses I wanted to join, on a freezing January night. I'd been called upstairs and told, politely but bluntly, that they had no interest in me.

"Look, we think you're a great guy," one of the brothers said, "but you'd be better off trying somewhere that may want you." House after house had already handed me the same rejection. I was out of options, rejected from every frat I rushed.

I stood there in the bitter winter cold, tears freezing on my face, trying to catch my breath. It was getting late, close to 8 p.m., and I dialed Dad on my cell phone. He picked up immediately.

"Well, Dad," I said, "I'm just like you now. I didn't receive a bid from any of the fraternities."

He asked me where I was, and I told him—standing in the cold, in the snow, on some street corner in Evanston. He tried to reassure me. "You'll be okay, Lucky," he said. "It's gonna be okay."

But for the first time, I wasn't sure I believed it. In high school, I hadn't understood why people didn't like me. I just knew that they didn't. But by college, I had started to see it: the way I missed cues, talked too much, misread the moment. I understood why I was being rejected now. That didn't make it hurt any less. If anything, it made it worse. Loneliness with no explanation was painful. Loneliness with an explanation—one that pointed back at me—was gut-wrenching.

Still, that understanding gave me something I never had before: a road map. Dad had always known this, even before I did. He had spent years guiding me, shaping me, showing me how to navigate a world that didn't naturally make sense to me. That night, standing in the snow, I realized I wasn't just fighting for acceptance—I was learning how to adapt.

"Dad, you know something?" I said. "When these things keep happening, you have to just realize it may not be them, it just might be me. This is about me."

There had been a lot of low moments, but that might have been the lowest. Dad had heard me scared in British Columbia and sad after a long day at Burroughs, but he said this was one of the first times he ever actually heard me *truly* hurt. It was as if I had stopped trying to push through and just accepted that maybe I was the problem. That was the first time Dad ever heard me say something like that—something so raw. It hit him hard.

And for the first time, our lives overlapped in a way that neither of us could ignore. He had been there before. The details were different, but the feeling was the same. After he got rejected from every fraternity, he had picked up the phone, too, and called his brother. He had told him what happened, how much it hurt. His brother's response was blunt: *You can't let them win; just keep smiling.* And he did. For all the stories Dad had told me about resilience, about staying the course, about not letting them win, this was the first time I truly felt what he meant. The lesson wasn't just words anymore—it was real, and it stung. The whole experience hurt—even if I tried to show Dad I was strong—but it also taught me something about resilience. Dad always said, "If you quit, they win." It was a lesson he had learned thirty-five years earlier, standing outside a fraternity house just like I was now.

Little had either of us known that one day, I'd be the one making that call from Northwestern, standing in the cold, saying, "Boy, now I know what it's like."

"Listen, let's just talk this out," Dad said. "Is there anyplace that showed interest?"

I had a moment of inspiration. "There was one guy at Theta Chi who seemed kind of interested. I heard they're struggling to fill their pledge class. Maybe if I went over there..."

"Go up there, Lucky," Dad said. "Go talk to him. Don't give up."

Theta Chi wasn't really on my radar. It wasn't considered one of the top houses. The fraternity had lost a lot of members the previous year after a drinking incident, and they were reorganizing. I had met one of the leaders, a guy named Rob McLean, once before—at a club squash event, of all things. I couldn't hit a squash ball to save my life, but I went just to try to make friends. Rob was there, a senior when I was just a freshman, but he struck me as a remarkably good person—one of those guys who was forty years old at twenty-one. Mature, steady, reliable. More than that, he had the same kind of values I did. He had been friendly to me that day, and now, standing in the cold, I remembered that Theta Chi needed members.

When I walked up to the house the next night, Rob and another brother welcomed me immediately. "We'd love to have you," they said.

That was it. I showed up at 7:30 p.m., and not long after, I had a bid.

Theta Chi wasn't what I had pictured when I thought about joining a frat—it was just a landing spot. But to Dad, it was more. To him, I was a kid who, after a week filled with rejection, still had the courage to go up to one more fraternity and knock on the door.

But even after finding a place in Theta Chi, freshman year didn't become easier. My roommate situation at the dorm was a disaster. I had been assigned to a sophomore, which was odd enough, but the reason quickly became clear—no one wanted to live with him. He had severe OCD and mental health struggles, and when he mixed his psychiatric meds with alcohol, he would pass out on the top bunk for entire weekends. His arms, from fingertips to elbows, were raw from compulsive washing. The situation was uncomfortable at best and unsettling at worst.

By the end of the year, the tension had escalated. The roommate and some of his buddies ran a phone harassment ring—this was when dorm rooms still had landline phones—making obscene, threatening calls in the middle of the night. When he and his buddies would drink, get high, or both, I'd get calls. I felt so threatened that Mom came and stayed with me in a hotel. Finally, I had enough when they started calling my girlfriend too. I went to the campus police, who asked if I was willing to prosecute.

"Yeah," I said. "Let's stop this."

They put a tap on my dorm phone and my girlfriend's. That night, the harassing calls came in again, crueler than ever. That was it. I told the police to move forward. The case went to Cook County. The guy had to show up in court, his mom by his side, and a judge told him if it happened again, he was going to jail. Turns out, it wasn't just us receiving the calls. This group had targeted professors, girls across campus—anyone they could mess with. Nobody had ever stood up to them before. For all the bullying I endured, even I had my limits.

The hits kept coming. That spring, an older guy in Theta Chi decided he wanted me out of the fraternity. He was a drunk and a troublemaker, and, like a lot of other people, he didn't care for me. He rallied a group to try to get me blackballed—kicked out of the one place I had finally landed. Who gets blackballed after they've already joined? Unless you steal from the house or do something awful, that just doesn't happen. For a few days, it looked like it might happen to me. But then, out of nowhere, another guy in the house—a guy I barely knew—came to my room. He told me he thought it was unfair, and he was going to put a stop to it. And he did. Just like that, it was over. His name was Jonathan Feldheim. I haven't seen him since college, but much as with the bullies—maybe even more so—you never forget the people who stood up for you.

Theta Chi was not a perfect fit. It gave me a place to exist, but it didn't change the fact that I still felt like an outsider. The guys in the fraternity were friendly enough, but they weren't *really* my friends—except Rob and his roommate Andy Bauer. Other than that, I didn't make friends in college. Not real ones. Joining Theta Chi was a false sense of security, a temporary shield from the reality that I was still alone. But I also knew something else: Quitting wasn't an option.

Dad always said, "It's always easier to stay when you know you can leave." I had thought about quitting a thousand times. But Dad's other lesson stuck with me: "If you quit, they win." When I struggled in college, I reminded myself, *You can quit, you can come home, but you're letting them win.* I wasn't going to let them win. Not in high school, not in college, not ever. So I stayed through the ups and downs.

It wasn't easy. Dad was right when he told me that the qualities that make you popular in high school don't make you popular later in life. I said that in my speech when I went back to Burroughs years later. And I had learned that firsthand. Today I don't like anyone who says they like Washington, because the values that make you popular in DC don't mean you're a good person either.

Around that time, my godparents Margie and Louis began playing a larger role in my life. They were quite important figures in Chicago but made time for Sunday night dinner every few weeks. It was an incredible treat to come into Chicago and sit with them—they were like parents without judgment.

College wasn't the escape I had hoped for, but it became a proving ground. I was a freshman who wandered around and tried to make friends and become part of something. For all the rejection and isolation, I kept going, kept trying—because quitting would have meant letting them win.

Live from Anywhere

Everybody at Northwestern was chasing internships at *TODAY*, *World News Tonight*, and the biggest networks in the country. Me? I was heading back to St. Louis to a local TV station.

My strategy went back to that summer in high school at the radio station when Charlie told me, "Get on-air. Practice your craft." That advice shaped everything I did next. I took that lesson seriously. I called TV stations and offered to work for free if they would put me on-air, knowing that real experience was the key to getting ahead. I was focused on building a tape reel, something tangible that would allow me to skip smaller markets when I graduated. The only way to improve was to be on-air, making mistakes, learning from them, and refining my skills.

Between my freshman and sophomore years at Northwestern, that meant heading to KTVI, the FOX affiliate in St. Louis. Unlike my classmates, who were fetching coffee at network internships, I was getting my hands on real work. At KTVI, interns could go out with reporters, help put stories together, and even get a little time on camera. Of course, "getting time on camera" was easier said than done. My first attempt was at an ice cream stand, covering a story about the brutal St. Louis summer heat. It took me something like fifty tries just to get three sentences out. I'd start talking, stumble, restart—over and over. I'm sure the tape still exists somewhere, though nobody would ever want to see it.

Brad Remington, the news director, was the kind of boss who liked people who shook things up. He took the station from number three or four in the market to number one. He was a disrupter, and I think he kind of liked that I was too. Much as I had done to the first guy who gave me a job in radio just to get me to stop calling, I did the same thing to Remington to land my internship at KTVI. Once I was in, I was everywhere. A few reporters took me under their wing, letting me do stand-ups and test out my on-camera presence. And I guess I was pretty good; I could do it.

Not everyone at FOX 2 was as supportive. A few of the older reporters weren't thrilled with a kid jumping into their territory. At one point, people in the newsroom started putting up signs that read: "Interns should be seen, not heard." I didn't care. I logged sound bites even when I wasn't technically allowed to because of union rules. I made phone calls, stepping into conversations and sources that weren't mine. I probably worked harder than some of the full-time staff, and it made them look bad. But I was there to learn, and I wasn't about to waste the opportunity.

I've always gotten along with secure people, but insecure people have always been threatened by me. Newsrooms, especially local TV stations, were no different. In many ways, my first few internships and jobs felt like going back to middle school—full of cliques, jealousies, and petty drama. I had assumed that once I reached adulthood, once I was doing important things, all of that would fade. But if anything, it got worse. The stakes got higher, the backstabbing got sharper, and the knife wounds only added up. High school and college had prepared me for this. The cuts were brutal, but they also made me stronger. Anyone who reaches any level of success in television carries a lot of scars—most on their back, but some right in front too.

Remington, to his credit, became a mentor. I think for him, there was a certain satisfaction in seeing an intern shake things up in a newsroom resistant to change. For a boss trying to get everyone fired up, having someone challenge the status quo was kind of fun. He saw something in me and would give me the break of a lifetime when he hired me to work for him in Denver later in my career.

After that internship, I followed an important lesson from Dad: The shortest distance between two points is a straight line. If you set a goal way out in the future, every decision becomes simpler—you just ask yourself, *Is this move on the straight line to your goal?* Every opportunity, every choice, every setback can be measured against that line. If it wasn't taking me in the right direction, it wasn't worth my time. That straight-line focus didn't just shape my career; it defined how I approached everything from that point forward. The internships, the jobs, the moves—they all had to push me closer to that goal. And if they didn't? They weren't worth my time.

After my freshman year of college and that first internship, I set a goal: I wanted to be a network correspondent by the time I was thirty. I don't remember the exact moment the goal clicked into place, but it came from a conversation with someone in the KTVI newsroom who said, "Kid, you're pretty good at this. You could end up at the network one day."

Back then, network news was still the pinnacle. *TODAY* was flying Matt Lauer around the world on the GE jet. Tom Brokaw and Peter Jennings were near-mythical figures. I had grown up watching them, but in the early days of YouTube, I went deeper: I'd find clips of Brokaw and Jennings covering the fall of the Berlin Wall, then later, their voices guiding the country through 9/11. The idea of making it to a network was still a big deal. So naturally, I wondered, *What's the youngest anyone's ever made it?* The answer: thirty. That was it. That was the goal.

My determination wasn't really about journalism. It was about the way I was raised. Dad believed in setting extraordinarily specific goals. Remember: In 1970, he decided he was going to be the youngest person to start a company and sell it for a million dollars—and he did it. He expected me to set ambitious targets and chase them relentlessly. So I thought, *What's the biggest thing in TV?* Being a network correspondent. *And by when?* By thirty. *Simple.* Choosing journalism was almost secondary to the goal-setting itself. What mattered was having a clear direction.

To say the least, TV journalism wasn't the obvious path for someone like me. Autism probably made it harder. But when I flip that switch—when I decide to go all-in—I don't let up. People have said that I have this ability to just hammer someone with questions and never let up. Maybe that comes from the social deficit side of things. The natural human instinct is to back off when someone becomes uncomfortable. I don't have that instinct, either because I don't recognize it or because I just don't care. That ability to keep pushing, to keep pressing, turned out to be an asset in journalism, but it also made the road to get there even more challenging.

"I'm Not Leaving"

After my sophomore year, I landed an internship in Madison, Wisconsin, as part of a requirement to graduate. It was a disaster from the start.

The station didn't want me there, the reporters resented me, and I was completely out of my depth.

I was on-air as a cub reporter, and the people there didn't like me very much. I covered city council meetings, local building permit disputes, and whatever else they threw my way, but no matter how hard I worked, I felt like an outsider. One of my first-ever stand-ups on TV had me walking out of a cornfield to talk about a Walmart development—not exactly the hard-hitting journalism of *60 Minutes*. Another had me reporting from the beer garden of a minor league baseball game only to get drenched with thrown beer on live TV. It was an important lesson to a young reporter: Don't go live from beer gardens!

My professor from Northwestern, Joe Angotti—a former head of NBC Nightly News—came to check in on me, as he did with all the students on internships. Dad had come to visit the same day because I was having such a hard time. He stopped by the station briefly and saw me working for just a few minutes. The place was a little shack, not much to look at. As Dad walked outside, he met up with Joe, who was leaving the station.

"Well, how's it going?" Dad asked, still trying to be the supportive parent, hopeful that my early effort would pay off.

Joe really liked me, but he was a straight shooter.

"I've never had a kid not make it," he said, "but I'm not sure Lucky's gonna make it. This is right on the edge. There's a very reasonable chance he's not going to make it."

Dad told me later that hearing that felt like getting punched in the gut. It was always the same thing, over and over again. But he never got used to those moments. Joe didn't say why I might not make it, but he didn't need to. Dad knew why I was having such a hard time without anyone telling him. It wasn't just that I struggled to fit in—there was always someone, in every setting, who seemed to take issue with me, someone who didn't like me, who was nervous around me or maybe even jealous of me. In Madison, that person happened to be a reporter, a guy in his mid-twenties who clearly didn't want me there.

IF YOU QUIT, THEY WIN

I barely made it through that summer in Madison. I wasn't sure if I had proven myself or if I just survived long enough that they let me leave, but either way, I was still standing. By the time my junior year ended, I knew I needed one more internship, one more shot at getting on-air, getting better, and proving I belonged. That summer, I headed to Fayetteville, Arkansas, ready to take another step forward. What I didn't expect was to be assigned to a story that would force me to confront something far bigger than journalism, something that would make me see, for the first time, just how different my life could have been.

When the news director sent me to cover a baseball game for players with special needs, I didn't think much of it. I had covered plenty of community events before—city council meetings, county fairs, and parades. This was just another feel-good piece, a quick story to fill a slow news day. But when I got to the field, I realized this wasn't just another assignment.

I watched as kids with cerebral palsy, some who had full brain function but had bodies that refused to cooperate, played baseball. I saw parents cheering them on, beaming with pride over their children making it to first base or simply making contact with the ball. The kids smiled, fighting for every step, every swing, every moment on that field. I was so inspired. These kids, who had been dealt such a rough hand, had such a love of life; maybe I could too.

And then, suddenly, I wasn't just watching them; I was seeing myself. *That could have been me.*

The thought hit me, but I didn't fully understand why. It wasn't some grand revelation—I should have realized it before. But for the first time, the emotion of it overwhelmed me. And in that moment, I started to understand something else: Part of TV, part of storytelling, is connecting on an emotional level. Maybe this meant I was starting to open up.

I stood there, gripping my microphone, staring at the scene in front of me. My parents could have been those parents. My life could have been that life. And the truth was, that would have been the best-case scenario. The reality, more likely, is that I wouldn't have survived at all.

I swallowed hard and pushed through, conducting interviews with the parents, gathering video footage of the kids rounding bases and gripping bats with shaky hands. The weight of it all was suffocating. I told my photographer I needed a minute and walked away from the field. I kept walking, past the bleachers, until I was out of sight. And then, behind a tree, I broke. I bent over, threw up, and sobbed.

I don't remember how long I stood behind that tree, but eventually, I pulled myself together. I wiped my face, straightened my shirt, and walked back to my photographer as if nothing had happened. I had spent my whole life knowing I was "Lucky," but this was the first time I truly felt it.

When I was a kid, Mom had a friend whose son had cerebral palsy. Being around him always made me uncomfortable. I didn't know why at the time. But standing behind that tree, I understood. It wasn't discomfort; it was fear. Fear of what could have been, what almost was. I wasn't the kind of person who volunteered at disability charities or spent time around kids with special needs. Maybe I should have been, but I wasn't. And maybe that was because, deep down, I couldn't face it.

Watching those parents on the field, I thought of Mom and Dad, and for the first time, I grasped what that weight must have felt like for them. That was the beginning of my understanding of the sacrifices and difficulties my parents went through for me. Even though our struggles were different, seeing those parents cheering, worrying, hoping, made me realize what it meant to be the parent of a child who had to fight harder just to make it.

I don't think I ever told anyone about that moment. But I carried it with me. Twenty-plus years after that summer, I can still see the baseball diamond, the kids, and the parents. And even now, I find it incredibly difficult to be around kids with cerebral palsy. It's a reminder of what could have been, a reality I narrowly escaped, and one that still feels too close, too personal, too raw.

Back at the station, other challenges were waiting for me. As at the other internships, the Fayetteville office wasn't exactly welcoming.

Someone messed with my car. Someone tampered with my computer. It became clear that certain people didn't want me there, and they weren't being subtle about it.

Dad was worried. He told me to get out of there, to pack up and leave before something worse happened. I wasn't sure what to do. I only had about ten days left in the internship, but Dad warned me, "Things can happen in an hour. Just get out of there."

"I'm gonna think about it overnight," I said.

Rick Smith, our longtime family friend and former editor-in-chief of *Newsweek*, had been following my struggles closely—Dad had to tell someone. Rick had practically lived in our house during the summers and knew me as well as anyone. The morning after my call with Dad, I was sitting in my car outside the station, debating whether to walk in or drive away. Finally, I called him.

"I made my decision, Dad. I'm not leaving," I said. "I'm not gonna let them run me out of here."

Rick was driving with Dad on the way to the golf course when I called, and when Dad relayed the news, Rick slammed his fist on the dashboard so hard it nearly came unglued. "Yes!" he shouted. "That's it. This guy will go through anything."

In the TV world I'm in today, that moment looks like a tiny obstacle, but at the time, it was my whole life. That decision to stay meant something to Rick too. Rick had risen quickly at *Newsweek*, from driving a New York cab to put himself through journalism school to becoming chairman and editor-in-chief. Back then, *Newsweek* loomed larger than life. He had been through his own challenges—the jealousy, the meanness, the resistance in a different form. He saw something in me that day, something that couldn't be taught.

"A kid can't make that decision unless he's got 'it' inside," he told Dad, echoing one of the key necessities spoken about me when I was young: It would take toughness and passion to make it in an unwelcoming world. I had to *want* it.

Journalism rewards hard work and persistence. Many things in life are like that. If you have even a modicum of skill but are willing to outwork everyone else, you have an enormous advantage. I wasn't the most talented person in the room, but I could outwork anyone.

Those early experiences—being the intern people wanted to shut up, the kid who was stepping into spaces he "wasn't supposed to"—set the foundation for everything that came next. Getting picked on was almost proof that I was good.

Charlie's advice shaped the trajectory of my career. The only way to get better on-air was to practice, and that meant starting in small markets, putting in the work, and getting reps in places like St. Louis, Madison, and Fayetteville. I was out there actually doing the job.

Because of those summers, I skipped the usual four-year climb through tiny markets after graduation. Those early decisions saved me years and gave me a straight-line path forward. Getting on the air, no matter where, was the smartest move I ever made.

And in the long run, that made all the difference.

Chapter Twelve

CHOOSING MY PATH

It was the winter of my senior year at Northwestern, and I was aimlessly wandering around the career fair. I wasn't sure why I was even there—I knew I was going into TV. But as I walked around, I found myself standing fifty feet from the CIA booth, just staring. They were recruiting analysts, which sounded like the most soul-crushing job imaginable.

That's when a man walked up next to me and pointed at the booth. "Interesting, huh?"

"Yeah." I shrugged.

"Would you ever want to do something like that?" he asked.

"Be an analyst?" I said. "God, no. That sounds awful."

The man raised an eyebrow. "You got a résumé on you?"

I handed it over. It was a single page with a few sentences saying I was a TV reporter—nothing more. *Unconventional* might be an understatement. Everybody else had mission statements, bullet points, and long lists of qualifications. He asked me a few more questions—nothing I particularly remember now—but at the end of it, he handed me his card. "If you ever want to do something other than be an analyst, give me a call," he said. The card had the CIA seal, a phone number, and one name: Bob. No last name, no title, just Bob.

I took the card, slipped it into my pocket, and didn't think much of it. But something about it nagged at me. Maybe it was the simplicity of it. Maybe it was that Mom has always had the habit of changing the subject when asked about what she did in her twenties. She claimed she had just traveled the world, spent time in Southeast Asia and South America, and worked for the Department of Agriculture at one point. But to me, it always sounded like a pretty weird cover story. She never admitted to working for any other government agency. But the whole thing—her time between college and marrying Dad—was opaque. The fact that Bob found me? Maybe that wasn't entirely accidental.

At some point, I called Bob. Maybe we met for coffee—I don't remember—but I do remember him saying, "We're having a meeting at the Park Hyatt downtown in a few days. Tell them you're there for the Silicon Technology Conference."

So I showed up at the Park Hyatt, in the middle of a Chicago winter. There was a guy outside, dressed as a doorman. I walked up and said, "I'm here for the Silicon Technology Conference."

He smirked. "Oh, you mean the CIA?"

"No," I said nervously. "Silicon Technology Conference."

"Hi, Leland." He grinned. "Upstairs."

The CIA had all these little tests built into the recruitment process. The doorman, the fake conference names, these staged tests where they'd see if you could play along, if you got rattled, if you could think on your feet.

The cocktail reception was full of people from the directorate of operations—the ones who ran clandestine spy operations—and recruits like me. I was easily the youngest one there. Most were in their late twenties, already a few years into careers in law, finance, or the military. None of them looked like James Bond. They looked like your neighbor, your accountant, the guy sitting next to you at a baseball game.

We were given a basic current events test, which was easy stuff. Not long after that night, I got called back for a six-hour interview in downtown Chicago with a CIA recruiter named Penny. They always had me come in under a cover story: I was there to meet about an accounting job. They wanted to test if you could go along with it. Could you talk your way through an impromptu backstory? Could you stay in character? They threw scenarios at you, trying to see how you handled pressure. They wanted people who are risk-takers, who can think outside the box, who can live a different identity.

Eventually, I got invited to Washington for three days of psychological evaluations, role-playing, and intelligence tests. The whole thing was structured to see how you handled deception—both the giving and the receiving. The agency had two kinds of officers: those with official cover working at embassies under diplomatic immunity, and those with nonofficial cover, working overseas for Boeing, FedEx, or whatever else. The latter was riskier. No diplomatic protection. If you got caught, you were on your own. Naturally, that's what I was interested in.

This was post-9/11. The country was at war. Joining the agency seemed like a way to serve without the rigidity of the military. It was a world that rewarded risk-takers, people who could operate outside of normal structures, who could manipulate, deceive, and use people—but for the right reasons. Plus, growing up, service had always been important in my family. Dad believed that giving back, in whatever form, was a duty, and that the people who did it were worthy of admiration and respect. But the idea of joining the agency and going undercover terrified my parents.

I arrived at a nondescript office building in Virginia and stepped out of a taxi to find four heavily armed men stationed just past the front bushes. They checked my ID before gesturing me forward.

I had to fill out an SF-86, which is a background check form upon which they would base the security clearance polygraph. Right at the top, the form said something to the effect of, *This cannot be used against you in a court of law.* The agency's philosophy was simple: If you disclosed something, a foreign advisory couldn't use it to blackmail you later. So they asked: Have you ever committed a crime? Used drugs? Cheated on a partner? Looked at pornography?

One question on that form was: Have you ever committed a felony? I checked yes, wanting to be honest.

At my next interview, they said, "Tell us about that."

So I told them about my alcohol delivery service in college. Equipped with a great fake ID, I would stock up at Costco and charge a markup delivering booze to classmates. One day, ahead of a big party weekend, I had one of those orange flatbed Costco carts full of liquor, and when I went to check out, the system flagged my ID.

"Is there a problem?" I asked the cashier.

The manager came over and said, "What's with all this booze?"

I told him about the party.

"Well," he said, "you've bought so much liquor this month, we need you to sign an affidavit saying you're not wholesaling."

I was standing there, fake ID in one hand, real Costco card in the other, knowing that if I bolted, I'd look guilty. So I played it cool. The manager led me back to the office to fill out the affidavit, and I was sure the cops were going to burst in and bust me. But instead, he just started chatting. "Why do you buy so much liquor?" he asked.

I spun up a tale on the spot, told him my buddies and I had an apartment, we were all out of college—because my ID said I was twenty-five—and we threw a lot of parties. He nodded along as he photocopied the affidavit.

Just as I thought I was in the clear, he paused, looking at my ID, which had my fake address: 1865 Sherman Avenue, Mahwah, New Jersey.

"Mahwah?" he said. "I'm from Mahwah!"

My heart stopped. *Of all the towns in all the world, the Costco manager in Chicago is from Mahwah!* At that point running seemed out of the question; I was in far deeper than at the cashier. He started reminiscing about high school and local bars, asking if I knew them. I had picked 1865 Sherman Avenue because it was my dorm address—easy to remember, impossible to forget under pressure.

CHOOSING MY PATH

I quickly adjusted, lying the bare minimum—never add extra details you don't have to. It was January, so I told him my parents had just moved there for Dad's job and while I was there for Christmas I had to get a new ID. I barely knew the town, I told him. He gave me a few recommendations for bars I should check out and handed back my ID. I walked out, feeling like I had just barely escaped big trouble.

When I finished telling the story, the agency guy just smiled. "That won't be a problem." I think they actually liked it.

By the end of the three days in Washington—doing interviews, tests, and psych profiles—it seemed like I was going to get an offer. On the way to the airport, I called Dad from the cab. "I've got good news and bad news," I said, joking with him. "The good news is I passed. The bad news is I need to stay another couple of days. There's a next level they didn't tell me about."

There was silence on the other end. I could practically hear Dad's blood pressure rising through the phone. He really didn't want me to do this.

This was the last step before getting an offer of employment and then the polygraph. I'd been told to think it over, that they'd be in touch soon. Before I left, I received a reading list of books about the agency. Among them was *The Book of Honor*, which told the stories of CIA officers who had died in service, their names recorded on the Wall of Stars at headquarters. One story stuck with me. One of the first CIA officers killed in action was running a network in Shanghai when the communists took over. He was caught when Mao's government shot down his plane. For the next twenty years, Communist China held him there, and his mother visited him once a year throughout by going through Hong Kong into communist China until he died in a Chinese prison.

I could justify dying in the line of duty. But being captured and sitting in a cell for decades while my parents wondered if I was alive? That would destroy them. Especially Dad. This was the person whom I still, to this day, call every night to say good night. I knew the CIA life would be exciting. I knew I'd be good at the job. Autism—or the spectrum—lets you compartmentalize emotions. That was a useful skill. I could accept the fear, the danger, the worst-case scenarios of a life with the agency. But I knew what it would do to Dad. It would break him, and after everything that he had done, it didn't seem fair for him to be terrified every day and every night that I wasn't going to come home.

If he wasn't in the picture, I think I would have done it in a heartbeat. But I called the agency and said, "I'm out."

A week later, Penny called. "Are you sure?" she asked. "I just thought you'd be so good. Is there anything you want to talk about?"

I explained why. She listened, then said, "You're going to do interesting things. If you ever see something we should know about, give us a call."

And that was that.

Years later, I'd run into agency guys overseas. We stayed in the same hotels and worked in the same places. But for me, my path was set. I was going into TV.

Live from Little Rock

After being on the verge of joining the CIA I instead became a reporter in Little Rock, Arkansas. Could there be two more opposite ends of the world?

I turned down the CIA in March of my senior year. At that point, there was only one thing to do: get a job in TV. That was what I wanted to do and what I'd been training to do. The goal I had set after freshman year was to be a network correspondent by the time I was thirty. First step? A local news job. I had already done three internships and had been on-air in Fayetteville and Madison.

The TV industry is all about tape, and a guy in Orlando named Bob Jordan had seen mine. My tape had made its way to him through Sandra Connell, who ran a search firm in Dallas called Talent Dynamics that specialized in local television placements. She had passed it along to Bob in Orlando, a big market—top twenty at the time—which was a huge opportunity for a college grad. Bob called me and said, "I'd like to offer you a job working on the desk as a multimedia producer. You can report on the weekends. If in a year you're not a full-time reporter, you can leave."

"No, thanks," I told him. "I don't want to be a multimedia producer on your desk. I want to be a reporter."

"Well," he said, "stay in touch, young man."

I had worked for a guy in Fayetteville who had a connection with a news director in Little Rock at KATV, the biggest station in the state. He called and told them, "This kid's pretty good," which got me an interview. The station was one of the very few in the country that didn't make you sign contracts, which was a big deal for me—I didn't want to be locked into a two year deal, or more. It was my best option out of school. So I packed up my stuff in a little U-Haul rental truck and drove from Chicago down to Arkansas to start my first reporting job.

In Little Rock, I got an apartment close to the newsroom so I could be first on the scene for breaking news. I had learned early on that in local news if you were close, answered your phone, and always said yes, the newsroom assignment desk called you first, which meant you got the best stories. That was the game. One of the keys to whatever success I have enjoyed is always saying yes when asked, no matter how miserable the assignment or extra work. So in Little Rock, and every other city I'd work in after, I found a place as close to the station as possible. That's still the case in DC now, two decades later.

I worked nights, so my mornings were routine: I'd go for a run along the river—usually five miles—then grab breakfast at a small café in the River Market district, where a couple of old warehouses had been renovated and turned into a market. At night, it was a host to a busy bar scene, but in the morning, there were just a couple of little stands open, including my favorite breakfast place. Every morning after my run, I'd order my coffee and omelet, say hi to the people working there—Sarah,

Susan, and Kim—and then go about my day. I could never quite figure out their relationship, but the three seemed close. I did this for six weeks.

Then one day, Kim wasn't there. Or the next day. By midweek, I finally asked Susan, "Where's Kim?" expecting to hear she was on vacation.

Instead, Susan smirked. "That's funny!"

"Excuse me?" I said with a blank stare.

Susan was a hard Arkansas woman; all three of them were. She scoffed. "We know what you're doing."

I had no clue what she meant. It was like I was in an episode of *The Twilight Zone*.

"Susan, I have no idea what you're talking about," I finally said. "I hope Kim is doing well."

She looked at me for a long moment, then said, "You don't have any idea, do you? Have you heard of the Babysitter Killer?"

At the time, the Babysitter Killer case was the biggest story in Little Rock. A twenty-year-old woman had shot and killed the estranged father of the little girl she was babysitting. The babysitter had some developmental issues, and she had been told by the girl's mother that the father was dangerous. When he showed up, she panicked and killed him. The woman had been convicted but was out on bail for retrial. The conviction always seemed bogus to me.

It was a sensational case, and it was all anyone in town was talking about. But I wasn't covering it. I worked nights, and the trial was happening during the day shift. It was a huge story, but I had been completely disconnected from it. Now I was realizing just how out of the loop I had been.

"Sure, the trial is happening right now," I said.

"That's Kim!" Susan said.

While waiting for her new trial, Kim had picked up a job at the breakfast stand. The owner's daughter had met Kim in the women's prison. The other workers figured I, a local reporter, was undercover trying to befriend them to get a scoop. Meanwhile, I was just enjoying my omelet, completely oblivious. Kim was the Babysitter Killer, and I had no idea.

While in Little Rock, I met Governor Mike Huckabee. In a small state like Arkansas, if you were a reporter for one of the big stations, you spent a lot of time with the governor—sometimes enough that you could call him directly. I remember weekends when I'd head down to the governor's mansion, and Huckabee, in his running shorts, would throw on a jacket and tie so I could get my waist-up interview. "Just come to the back of the mansion, I'll come out," he'd say.

Then came Hurricane Katrina.

Little Rock was not quite a seven-hour drive north of New Orleans, but in the aftermath of the hurricane that made landfall on August 29, 2005, evacuees were being flown to a National Guard base outside Little Rock. KATV got word that planes carrying evacuees were incoming and that Governor Huckabee would be there to meet them. A photographer and I drove to the airport, figuring we'd interview a few evacuees, film some B-roll of Huckabee greeting the new arrivals, and leave. We were there when the first plane landed on the tarmac. These were people who had been bused out of the Superdome, put on National Guard transport planes, and flown to Little Rock without being told exactly where they were going. When they landed in Arkansas, many of them had no idea where they were, just that they were far from the devastation. C-17s would land one after another, unloading weary passengers who had nothing but the clothes on their backs. It was a surreal scene: families stepping onto the tarmac, completely disoriented, exhausted, and desperate for any sense of stability.

One person coming off the plane asked me if I knew where their kids were—they had lost them in the rescues. Another asked, "Where am I?"

Normally, the governor shakes a few hands, the TV camera catches it, and the governor leaves. But Huckabee stood in the simmering Arkansas heat, shaking every single person's hand. "Welcome to Arkansas," he'd say.

To someone who had grown up in a relatively privileged environment, the scene was completely foreign to me. This looked like TV news stories of refugee camps in Africa; things like this weren't supposed to

Born Lucky

happen in America. It was shocking to witness that level of desperation and suffering in this country.

After a few brief minutes filming in the heat and now dripping in sweat, the reporters retreated to our air-conditioned broadcast trucks to cut, write, and edit our pieces. We assumed Huckabee would leave shortly as well. But when we looked back out at the tarmac, he was still there. Plane after plane landed, and Huckabee continued shaking every person's hand, offering them a few words of comfort. He stayed until the very last evacuee had stepped off the final plane. It is still the most remarkable display of statesmanship, civility, humility, and humanity I have ever witnessed.

Huckabee was an old country preacher at heart, and before our final 10 p.m. live shots that night, he stuck around with a group of us reporters. The cameras were off, and we were all sitting around talking. "What do you think about today, Governor?" someone asked.

Huckabee paused and whimsically said something that has stuck with me ever since: "If you've got a roof over your head tonight, you know where your next meal is coming from, and, most importantly, you know where the people you love are—if you know those three things—get down on your knees tonight and thank God."

That night when I got back to my apartment, I did. It was the first time in my life I ever prayed like that.

But despite the eye-opening experiences, my time in Little Rock was short-lived. When Katrina was approaching the coast, I had repeatedly pitched covering it, but they sent a more experienced, not necessarily better, reporter. At that point, I knew I was leaving.

Two months into my job in Little Rock, I sent my tape to Bob Jordan, the news director of ABC 9 in Orlando. He called and said, "Didn't you tell me you were giving Little Rock a year?"

"They screwed me on Katrina," I said.

He asked when my next day off was. I told him.

"Great," he said. "There'll be a plane ticket waiting for you."

Chapter Thirteen

FINALLY HAVING FRIENDS

Not long after Katrina, I flew down to interview at ABC 9. It was by far the number one station in Orlando, a top-twenty market in the country. Bob Jordan really wanted to hire me—this time for a reporter job.

The station's general manger gave me the fraternity rush. Bill Hoffman would later go on to be a major media CEO, but at the time he was running Orlando. He brought me into his office and told me about the station, his vision, and why they needed me. For the first time, someone wanted me. I still remember the pitch and what that kind of leadership looks and feels like.

The assistant news director, however, was against it. She thought I was too young and inexperienced and had no business being in that role at twenty-two. To be fair, she was right; I had no business getting most of the jobs I got early on. But Bob hired me anyway.

When I got to Orlando, I again picked an apartment two blocks away. I could see the station from my window. When Bob asked why, I told him, "So I can be close for breaking news."

ABC 9 was the first place where my work ethic—just outworking everybody—paid off. That came from rowing, from my upbringing, from everything Dad instilled in me. The lessons he taught me weren't hard. If you had an insatiable ability to work, you were going to succeed. Orlando was where I started to prove that.

From day one, the assistant news director was hard on me. She didn't want me there and made sure I knew it. But that kind of pressure had never really bothered me. The hardest part of being a young reporter in local news is covering tragedies—car accidents, murders, senseless deaths. It almost always involves knocking on a grieving family's door.

I remember vividly that a couple of nights before Thanksgiving, a teenager had been killed by a driver while skateboarding in his neighborhood. I was sent to cover the story. One of the cops told me, "Hey, kid, the family's two streets over." I walked up to the house as Florida Highway Patrol troopers were leaving, having just notified the mother that her fifteen-year-old son was dead.

I knocked on the door. The mother opened it, and we locked eyes. I was just a kid myself. All I could say was, "I am so sorry." She fell into my arms, sobbing, wailing. The cameraman rolled tape, standing a few steps behind me. Looking into the house, I saw the dining table set for Thanksgiving dinner.

That image, that moment, never left me. Seeing parents who have just lost their kids has always haunted me. It always made me think of Mom and Dad and how unbearable it would be for them if something ever happened to me.

Bob was a tough boss. I worked nights and would sleep until ten the next morning. One morning, after I had screwed up an interview on live shot on the eleven o'clock news the night before, Bob called me at 8 a.m. while I was still asleep. I answered groggily, and he immediately started screaming. "You have any idea how badly you fucked up last night?"

"Yeah, Bob, I'm really sorry," I mumbled as I woke up. "You're right. It won't happen again. I'm really sorry."

"Don't be sorry!" he yelled. "I'm not done YELLING at you yet!"

That was Bob. But as tough as he was, he was also the kind of guy who drove around during hurricanes delivering food and water to his crews in the field. He was the kind of leader who backed his people.

Orlando news was competitive. Every interview, every exclusive mattered. There was a hotshot reporter from another station who had been there for years and was Mr. Orlando—he got all the exclusives. But that Thanksgiving story? The mother wanted to talk only to me.

"I love Channel 9," she said. "I don't want to talk to anybody else."

I told her she didn't have to. When reporters from other stations went to the house, she wouldn't talk to them.

Mr. Orlando came up to me later, trying to intimidate me. "Hey, kid," he said. "I don't know how you did things at other stations, but we don't play that way around here. We don't fuck each other over. You're gonna learn how this is done."

I looked at him and said, "Well, last time I checked, I don't work for you. I work for Bob Jordan. So if you have a problem, why don't you call him?"

I didn't think much of it. But the next day, Bob called me into his office. "Hey, I heard about last night," he said. "Great job getting the interview with the mom. Congratulations. Next time that asshole tells you something, you don't tell him to call me. You tell him to go fuck himself."

Bob missed his calling; he should have been a general or a football coach. Instead, he was a TV news director.

I had been in Orlando for a month. Out of college for less than six. But that moment, standing up for myself and knowing my boss had my back, was huge. It was a turning point in finding my voice. TV news could be brutal, but now I knew I could hold my own. I had a boss who believed in me.

For the first time, I had adults standing up for me because of my work. It was a revelation—proof of what Dad had always promised. The very values that made me a target in high school were now earning me respect.

I didn't have many friends yet, but something was shifting. The station's sports director and reporter nicknamed me "Rook," short for "the rookie." There was hazing, but then they would invite me out for beers after the newscast.

I was proving I could do this. Maybe I wasn't ready for the major leagues of Orlando right away, but I was learning fast. And I was learning something else: The newsroom had its own version of the bullies I'd faced in high school. Maybe that was normal—everywhere you go, there's always someone like that—but newsrooms could be especially brutal.

One reporter in particular made that clear. The station ran contests, dreamed up by Jordan. It was competitive but in good fun—best story, most exclusives, sharpest on-air presentation. I couldn't shy away from something like that. It became my goal to win. Even as "the rookie," I was determined. That didn't sit well with one of the veteran reporters.

One contest had an especially high-stakes prize: a flat-screen TV. Back then, those things were expensive, and given that my salary almost qualified me for food stamps, it might as well have been a luxury car. The challenge? Whoever did the most "active stand-ups" would win. In TV speak, that meant being dynamic on camera—not just standing in front of a scene but moving, showing the viewer something, making the story more alive. For example, instead of standing in front of a burning building, you walked from a fire hydrant to the building live on TV to show why it took firefighters so long to run their hoses. It took extra effort, extra creativity, and, most importantly, extra buy-in from the photographers, who weren't getting a TV out of the deal.

I came in second. The winner? The guy whose desk I faced in the newsroom—the one who already didn't like me. Losing didn't bother me too much; there would be other contests. But he wasn't done. Instead of taking the TV home, he left it on his desk, still in the box, in my direct line of sight. Just sitting there, like a trophy meant to remind me that he'd beaten me. And to make sure I got the message, he stuck a Post-it note on the side: "Mine."

It stayed there for a month, until even people in the newsroom started making fun of him for how petty this was. And maybe that was the real lesson. People were beginning to stand up for me—not because I had changed, but because suddenly I was in a world that valued my character and work ethic over being cool. The things that once made me an easy target were now making me stand out in the right way. Dad's lessons suddenly made sense. Hard work and character counted for something.

In the middle of all this—learning the ropes, holding my own, proving I belonged—I also started dating an older woman who worked as a main anchor at the NBC station across town. She gave me some of the best advice I ever got about being on-air: "When you're sitting there, when the camera is rolling, you're on. There's no place to hide. Thoughts will go through your head about what to say next. If a thought ever crosses your mind and for the slightest second you go, 'Maybe I shouldn't say that'—don't say it. It'll save your career."

"Really?" I said, thinking about it.

"It'll particularly save *your* career," she said.

Dad had his version of that lesson. He once told me, "Never try to be funny. You don't have timing. You don't have the funny gene. You don't know when to stop. You don't know when to start. Just put in your mind that you will *never* be funny." Later, after hearing that story, he refined his advice to, "Whenever you think you have a joke—don't say it!"

Journalism wasn't a calling as much as it was a learned skill. Just like flying a plane, it was something you could train yourself to do. The only real innate talent I had was controlling my emotions, slowing down the world around me, and staying focused under pressure. Everything else, I had to learn.

I wasn't great at the things journalists are traditionally good at. I failed grammar tests, I was terrible at spelling, and my first few on-air appearances were rough. If you watch the tape of me in Orlando, I was relentless—but not always in a good way. If a mayor wouldn't talk to me, I'd find him outside the city council office and badger him until he had no choice. I got in trouble for it more than once. Bob sat me down and said, "You can't do that to people." I nodded, said I understood, and then went out and did it again. Over time, I learned how to refine my approach, but it wasn't an instinct. Even now, if someone offends my sense of fairness—if they twist the truth or abuse power—I don't back off. I press harder.

As I got older, there was always someone in every newsroom who resented me, someone who had worked their way up and saw me as a snot-nosed kid who got opportunities too easily. To be fair, I had come from a family of means, but Dad never made a phone call for me or asked his friends to get me a job. In Madison, in Fayetteville, in Orlando—everywhere I went, someone was trying to undermine me. By the time I got to Orlando, I understood that this was just part of the job. The hostility became almost a source of pride. If people were trying to tear me down, it meant I was doing something right.

In Little Rock, I had no friends. In Orlando, I had no friends at first. But two years in, it felt like I was running the town. I was twenty-four, working in a city where local news was still a big deal. Reporters and anchors were minor celebrities. For the first time in my life, I was cool. Thursday nights after the 11 p.m. newscast, a bunch of us would go out together—reporters, anchors, producers. We'd walk into a bar, and people knew who we were. It's silly in hindsight, but when you'd never been invited to a party in high school, it felt pretty good.

A year after I started in Orlando, the assistant news director, the one who hadn't wanted to hire me, pulled me aside. She looked at me and said, "I want to apologize to you. I was wrong. Bob was right. You are a special talent, and I was a jerk to you. I'm sorry."

That felt good, and of course, it said a lot about her character. I was proving that I belonged.

Finally Finding Friends

Brad Remington, my first boss when I was an intern in St. Louis, always had a soft spot for me. He liked that I worked hard, and over the years, we stayed in touch. He had become something of a mentor to me, and I had always told him I wanted to come back and work for him one day.

While I was in Orlando, I became a good reporter. After starting as a news director in St. Louis, Brad had since moved to Denver to run the FOX station there. He wanted a young reporter to shake things up in the newsroom, so he called me with an opportunity.

I wasn't going to leave Orlando to be a reporter; it would have been a lateral move. But Brad had other ideas. "Come out and be a weekend anchor," he said.

At twenty-four, I had about as much business being a weekend anchor in Denver as I did being the quarterback of the Denver Broncos, but I took the job anyway. It was a chance to do something bigger, the next logical step in my career.

From the moment I arrived in Denver, my goal was to get to a network. But I was stepping into the job during a period of significant consolidation in the television industry. By 2008, the financial crisis was in full swing, and for the first time, major cuts and hiring freezes were hitting newsrooms hard. Up until then, local television stations had been one of the most profitable businesses in America, but things were changing fast. It was the first time I started to question if I was going to make my goal to get to a network by age thirty.

In Orlando, I had been a relentless reporter, pushing officials for answers and often forcing my way into stories. I still had that same tenacity, but I quickly realized the culture in Denver was different. One of my first days, I got into it with a local police chief who wouldn't do what I wanted. In Orlando, the police were used to being pushed around by reporters, but that wasn't the case in Denver. I was still learning, still a bull in a china shop, still breaking dishes.

Brad had to stand up for me a few times in Denver, just as he had in St. Louis when I was an intern. The woman assigned to be my co-anchor was much older and had worked her way up through all the local markets. She resented the fact that I was this young, awkward kid who had landed a major role. She did everything she could to make my life miserable. It was petty, sorority mean-girl stuff. Jealousy is a terrible disease, and I did not, in the words of the Bible, "suffer fools gladly" (2 Corinthians 11:9 KJV).

Eventually, Brad had enough. He told her, "If someone is going to leave, it's going to be you." Orlando and Denver were the first places I saw someone fight back for me in a way that made sense. And yet, when I left for the Middle East, she wrote me a card saying that she and I had grown together. It was another lesson from Dad put into action: Wear them down with quality.

During my three years in Denver, I worked on my craft and added tape to my reel. But more than anything, Denver was about coming of age—learning who I was beyond work.

When I arrived, I was scared and lonely. Dad's best friend, David Scanavino, lived in Denver, and we had dinner together often. He had been a close friend of Dad's since their fraternity days and was someone I had gone to for advice years earlier when I was considering the CIA.

I started dating. I started skiing during the week—when you work weekends, you get a few weekdays off. For the first time, I developed a real group of friends. Ron Neville, who ran a hotel in the mountains where I stayed a couple of times, invited me to go skiing with him. Then one day, Ron said, "I have a group of guys I ski with. You should meet them."

It all seemed a little weird to me at first. I had never really had friends before. It never happened that people liked me as a human and someone they could hang out with. And suddenly, I had a group—Ron, Scott Key, Chris Gersbach, and Jeff Luker—who skied together and just enjoyed each other's company. They were older than I—as you know, I had always connected better with older people—but these were real friends. It was like being invited to a birthday party for the first time.

As I grew personally and professionally in Denver, an offer came my way to be an anchor in Dallas. It was a big promotion. Dallas was a bigger market, and I would have more visibility. But the move didn't make sense for my ultimate goal; the job in Dallas didn't get me any closer to being a network correspondent. I reminded myself of the lesson Dad had taught me: The shortest distance between two points is a straight line. You could go from being an anchor in Denver or an anchor in Dallas to a network, so signing a two-year contract in Dallas didn't make sense.

Instead, I started going to New York, emailing every contact I could find, and begging for meetings with networks. I reached out to talent recruiters, producers—anyone who might listen. Most of the time, I got ignored. Other times, I got stood up. But I kept going. It may seem nuts, but I had a role model in Dad, my hero, who had made 106 straight unsuccessful sales calls before landing a sale. If he could persevere, why couldn't I?

John Stack, then VP of newsgathering at Fox News, finally agreed to meet with me—if only to get me to stop calling. It was an uphill battle for him to get a twenty-eight-year-old in the door, but he saw something in me. He recognized that while I might have been a little awkward and different, I had valuable skills. And he believed in me. I begged him for a shot as a network correspondent.

"The only job we have is in Jerusalem," he said. "And you're not ready for it."

Historically, Fox staffed Jerusalem with two correspondents, so if one was traveling or on home leave, the network always had a presence in case of breaking news. One of the two in Jerusalem had rotated back home, so they had an opening—an opening no one wanted. In fact, they offered the job to half a dozen people with no takers. At the time, President Barack Obama had gone to Cairo and given a speech about making peace with the Muslim world. Hillary Clinton was secretary of state and was working on a peace deal between the Israelis and Palestinians. In 2010, the situation in Jerusalem was—in a word—boring, so nobody wanted that job. But I kept telling them, "I want to go."

Finally, Stack relented. "All right," he said. "We're going to fly you over to Jerusalem to interview with the bureau chief."

Born Lucky

    Orlando and Denver had been valuable training stops along my progression. They had given me confidence, friends, and experience. But my eyes were always on the next step. And the next step was about to take me halfway around the world.

Chapter Fourteen

I'LL TELL MY KIDS ABOUT IT

As I said, the Fox News job in Jerusalem wasn't something people were fighting over. With major conflicts seemingly at a standstill, Jerusalem was uninteresting as far as news went. There weren't many stories, and correspondents weren't eager to relocate to a slow news bureau.

But I wanted it. I wanted it badly.

Ever since I was nineteen, I'd had that one goal: be a network correspondent by thirty. Peter Jennings was always my hero, and the idea of going overseas was the greatest thing ever. Fox had watched my tape and liked my work, but I was young for a foreign correspondent job—too young, they told me. The unspoken reality in TV at the time was that you had to pay your dues in a domestic bureau before getting an international assignment, but I wanted to be overseas, in the thick of it, and I wasn't going to take no for an answer.

So when John Stack agreed to fly me over to Israel for an interview with the bureau chief, Eli Fastman, I was thrilled. Fastman was a news legend, the kind of guy who carried an air of mystery with him wherever he went. He had known and covered Yasser Arafat, the longtime Palestinian leader, and Yitzhak Rabin, the former Israeli prime minister.

When I landed in Israel, I didn't know the difference between the Gaza Strip and the West Bank. Sitting across from Fastman, I felt completely out of my depth. Before the interview, I wrote a cheat sheet on my hand, a little map to remind myself of the basic geography—the Gaza strip versus the West Bank. Of course, between the brutal Middle Eastern heat and my nerves, the map melted into an ink-smeared mess. As I wiped my sweaty hands on my pants, I realized just how unprepared I was. Here I was, a weekend anchor in Denver, a kid from St. Louis, sitting across from a man who had been a CBS cameraman following the Mujahideen in Afghanistan and knew the region like the back of his hand. At one point, Fastman asked me what books I'd read. I don't remember what I said, but whatever the answer was, it worked.

After the interview, I flew back to the States, but Fox still wasn't sure if they were going to hire me. Then, reality forced their hand. The other correspondent, Reena Ninan, was pregnant and needed to return to the US. Suddenly, they needed someone—immediately. After months of being told no, I got the call: "Can you be there in three weeks?"

I was twenty-eight years old, and I had achieved my goal: I was about to become a network correspondent overseas. I hadn't taken the traditional route, but I had managed to skip a step, maybe two, just as I had hoped. I had been persistent, I had been in the right place at the right time, and, most importantly, I was young and cheap. Everything I had worked for, every rejection, every call pestering Fox to give me a shot—it had all led to this moment.

Before I accepted, I wanted to meet with my parents face-to-face. I called them from Denver and told them to meet me in Chicago at Joe's Stone Crab. Over lunch, I laid it out plainly: "If I take this job, I'm going to be doing some really dangerous things."

Dad is the most risk-averse person imaginable, especially when it comes to me. To him, walking the dog at night required caution. His protective instincts were one of the main reasons I had turned away from pursuing a career with the CIA. And now, here I was, about to move to the Middle East. Even if it was quiet there at the moment, who knew what might come?

But Dad didn't understand what I was telling him. To Dad, a foreign correspondent's job was covering diplomatic negotiations in Paris, not dodging bullets in a war zone. He imagined me sipping a martini in some elegant bar in Casablanca, not running toward explosions. It didn't help that one of his favorite movies was *Foreign Correspondent*, the 1940 Hitchcock thriller about a reporter who uncovers an international conspiracy—more intrigue than imminent danger.

Despite what I told him, he kept repeating the same things: "This is such a great opportunity. You're going to see the world. You're going to learn so much."

I accepted the job, and Mom flew with me to Jerusalem for a brief trip to find an apartment before I moved. We landed on a Friday evening and were taken to the American Colony Hotel in East Jerusalem. The hotel was a throwback to the golden era of foreign correspondents—a neutral zone where diplomats, spies, and journalists all gathered. It had a beautiful garden with bright lights and music. That night, having a drink with Mom under the glow of the lights, I felt like I had won the lottery. This would be my temporary home for six weeks until I moved into my apartment, and at that moment, I had made it.

Then the gunfire erupted.

There's no mistaking the sound of automatic weapons firing. Even if you've never heard it before—which I hadn't at that point—that sound is hardwired into the human brain as a signal of immediate danger. In terms of the sheer terror it causes, the only other sound I can compare it to is the distant whistle of incoming artillery shells.

Instinct kicked in. *Oh my God*, I thought, *the American Colony is under attack!* I grabbed Mom and threw her to the ground, covering her body with mine. My heart was pounding. *Had I just landed in a war zone?*

After a few seconds, I looked around. Nobody else had reacted. People kept drinking and chatting, unfazed.

A waiter walked over. "Sir, is everything okay?" he asked.

Still lying on top of Mom, I looked up at him.

"What do you mean, 'Is everything okay?' Gunfire!"

He smirked. "Just a wedding," he said. "Fire in the air!" He mimed shooting a rifle into the air. "Celebration!"

That was my welcome to Israel.

Mom and I spent a few days apartment hunting and then headed home so I could get ready for the move.

"My Dearest Lucky"

Mom and Dad dropped me off at the airport a few weeks after that incident. They were teary-eyed, watching their son fly off to the unknown. I moved to Israel in early August 2010 with three duffel bags, my passport, and a letter Dad wrote me.

As I sat in my seat on the flight to Tel Aviv, I pulled out the envelope, unfolded the letter, and began to read:

Mark Vittert

August 5, 2010

My dearest Lucky,

Tomorrow you are to embark on one of the great adventures of your life. As comes with any great step forward, there are accompanying challenges, opportunities, fears, excitement, and dangers. You are prepared for this nevertheless, possessing the rare blend of intellect and compassion in a most thoughtful manner.

The years have passed, and they have been in your favor. You have grown, not apart, but fully within the values and standards with which you adopted and set for yourself when you were young. You know that I am not a worldly person, but I do know that you will see and experience many things over the next 3 years which will disturb and disappoint you. Wherever you are, meet these with compassion and understanding.

As you know, we have friends who possess wonderful qualities. There is none that I know who combines the integrity, decency, loyalty, and kindness of you. These are life's finest traits and values, and certainly, due to an overabundance of your mother's genes, they are firmly set within you.

Lucky, you have had many tests already in your life. You and I know of that. And there was not one time, not one, that I wasn't proud of the manner in which you addressed those most difficult times.

Regardless of whatever may lie ahead for you, of whatever you choose or don't in life, your mother and I will support you, and feel so deeply within our hearts that you are the finest son any parents could wish for.

> With all my love,
> Your loving father

I carefully folded the letter and placed it in my passport. I would carry it with me through Israel, Egypt, Libya, Ukraine, and everywhere in between.

It was one thing to get a job as a foreign correspondent. It was quite another to land my happy self in Israel. The first few months in Jerusalem were uneventful. There was no war, no breaking news, just daily life. I covered a story about the Israelis dismantling a barrier wall, a symbolic gesture meant to signal peace was on the horizon. I rode alongside Israeli and American wounded warriors on a bike ride. These were meaningful events, but for obvious reasons, they didn't make for compelling television. Conflict sells, and Jerusalem was, for the moment, tranquil. I was lucky if I got on-air for the network once a week.

And the truth was, I wasn't just struggling for airtime—I was struggling, period. I had left behind a great life in Denver. Skiing every week, finally making real friends, enjoying myself in a way I never had before. For the first time, I felt like I belonged somewhere, and then, just like that, I was alone again. Jerusalem was fascinating, historic, and important—but it wasn't home. And in those early months, it certainly didn't feel like a great trade.

Much of those early months I spent adjusting to the culture shock of Israel. Jerusalem is a deeply religious city; the whole place shuts down for Shabbat, sundown Friday to sundown Saturday. Imagine a small town on Christmas—there was nothing to do! Israeli society took some adjusting to. Everything was foreign, and I was alone.

Then came the real shock. A month and a half into my time in Israel, Dad had a heart attack. Because it was Yom Kippur, the country had effectively shut down, and I couldn't get a flight home. I was stuck, helpless, relying on secondhand updates from Mom. I finally saw Dad briefly in November in Florida when I took my first home leave and met my parents and Liberty in Miami for Thanksgiving.

Leaving home again was different this time. When I first flew to Israel in August, Mom and Dad were the ones crying, and I smiled with excitement. But standing in the Miami airport, ready to board my return flight, I was the one sobbing. The loneliness I had tried to ignore came crashing down. I wasn't walking back into adventure—I was walking back into isolation. The job I had chased for so long had taken me far from everything familiar, and I finally understood what that truly meant. That was the moment I realized what I had signed up for. Being a foreign correspondent wasn't just about covering stories. It was about learning to exist in a world that often felt lonely—something I'd become all too familiar with.

And then, just as I was settling into my new normal back in Israel, the Middle East exploded. Cairo was burning. And my phone rang.

I'LL TELL MY KIDS ABOUT IT

The Call to Cairo

For six months as a foreign correspondent, nothing happened. The Middle East had been quiet. I watched the Arab Spring unfold from a distance that winter. It had started in Tunisia with a single act: Mohamed Bouazizi setting himself on fire in protest of government corruption. That "fire" spread across the region, toppling governments and igniting mass demonstrations. But in Jerusalem, it still felt like someone else's story, something happening outside of my world.

Then, literally overnight, everything changed. The protests reached Cairo on January 25, 2011, and within days, the streets were filled with demonstrators demanding Egyptian President Hosni Mubarak's resignation. I was sitting in my apartment in Jerusalem, watching the news at two o'clock in the morning. Reports were coming in of journalists being targeted, dragged from their reporting posts, beaten, and detained.

That's when my phone rang. It was the foreign desk in New York.

"You're heading to Egypt," I was told. "Somebody will pick you up in an hour."

"Aren't they telling all Americans to get out?" I asked.

"Yeah," they responded. "That's why you're going."

Click.

I didn't know yet that Fox News correspondent Greg Palkot and his cameraman, Olaf Wiig, had been grabbed in Tahrir Square by a pro-Mubarak mob. I just knew Egypt was on fire, and now, I was being asked to go into it. I called my parents. It was three in the morning for me, but back in the US, it was still 8 p.m.

"I'm going to Cairo," I told Dad when he answered the phone.

Silence. "Lucky, they are ordering Americans to leave Cairo. This is crazy."

Then came the questions. "Do you have to go? Will you have security? What happens if you get taken?"

All the fears a father has for his son poured out. At the time, Mubarak's

Born Lucky

government had declared that reporters were committing treason against Egypt and were openly targeting them. The US embassy had shut down operations. There were lines of Americans outside the Cairo airport, desperate to get onto evacuation flights. And I was heading in the opposite direction.

"I have to go," I told him. "This is what I signed up for."

You couldn't fly directly from Tel Aviv to Cairo, so my route would take me through Athens first. In the middle of the night, I grabbed my run bag—something every correspondent kept ready at all times—filled with clothes, a med kit, chargers, a satellite tracker, a sat phone, flak jackets, and, most importantly, a bunch of cash. I loaded my gear into the taxi out front and left for the Tel Aviv airport.

Dad was at a hotel in Florida, sitting in the small hotel room he and Mom had booked for their vacation. He later told me that night was the moment he realized just how wrong he had been. When I first left for Israel, he had imagined I would spend my time learning about different cultures and covering stories as a reporter in the classic sense—safe and structured. I had tried to tell him at lunch in Chicago, but he never fully grasped it.

Now, as he watched the chaos unfold on TV, it hit him all at once. The networks were filled with images of burning buildings, of furious crowds filling Tahrir Square, and of reporters being attacked in the streets. News had broken about Palkot and Wiig. Anderson Cooper was broadcasting on CNN from a darkened hotel room, talking quietly into a camera with only a flashlight illuminating his face. "I can't tell you where we are, frankly for our own safety . . ." Cooper told viewers at one point. Then later, "I don't mind telling you I am a little bit scared, because we frankly don't really know what the next few hours will hold. And I think there's a lot of people who are scared tonight in Egypt." This wasn't an assignment. This was a war zone.

I landed in Athens and called Dad. His voice was shaking.

"Please don't go," he pleaded. "This is really dangerous. We're seeing terrible things on the network. They're jailing reporters. There's a Fox reporter who got grabbed. They're kicking in doors. This is not part of the job."

Our conversation went on for probably thirty minutes.

"Dad, I don't have to go. I won't go," I said. "But then I quit, and I'm done in TV because this is my job. If I fly back to Israel, you'll see me in four days because I'll be flying home to the US. I'll never be able to show my face at Fox News again."

At that moment, I thought back to my decision not to join the CIA after college. I had turned down the opportunity largely because of my parents' concerns about the danger. In some ways, I regretted that decision. And yet, here I was, standing at the edge of another dangerous decision. Deep down, I had always wondered if I was tough enough. To me, backing out now would have been the ultimate cowardice. It sounds almost ridiculous in hindsight, given everything I would go on to experience in the Middle East, but at the time, it felt profound.

Time was running out before my flight to Cairo. Dad said, "I'll call you back." It was close to midnight back in the States. He called his friend and longtime St. Louis TV executive Allan Cohen at home and woke him up.

"Throw some water on your face. I need to talk to you," Dad told him.

Allan listened as Dad explained the situation. Allan said, "You've got to let him go. That's his job. Lucky knew what he was doing. He knew what he was getting into. You didn't. If he doesn't go on this flight, he's right, he's got to quit his job."

Dad called me back, crying.

"Go ahead and go," he said. "I understand."

"We talked about this at lunch ten months ago," I said.

"I know," he admitted. "But I didn't understand."

I hung up and made my way to the gate. Cairo was waiting.

A City in Chaos

Just months earlier, I had been in Sharm el-Sheikh, Egypt, for a high-profile peace conference. Hillary Clinton, Benjamin Netanyahu, Hosni

Mubarak—all the key players were there. The world believed that the Israeli-Palestinian conflict was the defining story of our time, and there was a sense that a breakthrough might happen. But in a matter of weeks, that optimism collapsed. The Arab Spring erupted. Tunisia fell. Protests swept through Egypt. Now Mubarak, the man I had seen standing confidently at that conference, was on the verge of being overthrown. The entire region was unraveling.

I boarded a near-empty Aegean Airlines flight from Athens to Cairo. The plane, a 757 built for two hundred passengers, held just a couple of handfuls of people. Four of us sat in first class: me, two members of Sweden's Special Forces—who were part of the Swedish Embassy's evacuation team—and the Aegean Airlines station chief, who was on board to clean out the company's safe in Cairo. There was a scattering of Egyptians sitting in coach. The US government had chartered the plane to bring Americans out of Egypt. I was one of the few going in.

During the two-hour flight, I started talking to the guy from Aegean Airlines. He looked at me and said, "You're a journalist. How are you going to get through customs with all that gear?"

I hadn't thought about that. Going into hostile environments wasn't something that had ever really occurred to me. If I had joined the CIA, I would have spent three years training at the CIA's massive complex known as "the Farm" before my first mission. Instead, I had just packed my bags, hopped on a plane, and landed in the middle of a crisis. My bags were loaded with satellite uplinks, gear, and a stack of cash—items that the Egyptian authorities would confiscate.

"I don't know," I said.

I had no preparation for this. No training for heading into a hostile environment. Yes, as I once explained to the CIA, I could talk my way past a Costco manager with my fake ID, but the Egyptian security services were a different story. If you joined the military, at least they put you through boot camp first. This felt like taking a high school quarterback and throwing him onto the field as the starting quarterback for the Kansas City Chiefs.

"Let me help you out," he said.

When we landed, his baggage handlers helped get my bags around security and customs. I walked through immigration without issue. The Cairo airport was chaos: miles-long lines of desperate people trying to get out. No one was trying to come in. My passport was stamped, and I stepped into the unknown.

The Fox foreign desk had given me the number of a security guy named Jock. "He'll meet you at the taxi stand," they had said. I walked outside. Pandemonium. Thousands of people trying to flee the country, shouting, pushing, panicked. And no Jock. The cell service was shaky. I sent a text to the number.

His reply was a single line instructing me to go a certain hotel.

Go to [this hotel], he replied.

That was it. No further details. No one coming to pick me up. I was a twenty-eight-year-old American journalist in a city where Americans were being ordered to leave, and I had to navigate my way to a hotel. I was terrified. I flagged a taxi and somehow got there. Only later did I find out that Jock was a little busy, evacuating Fox crews from the hotels around Tahrir Square as the situation worsened. He had sent me to a hotel Fox News had found near the airport, somewhere to hide from Mubarak's security forces. It had become a makeshift compound for the network after Palkot and his cameraman had been taken. I arrived around 1:00 p.m. local time and immediately started live shots. That was the true beginning of my time as a foreign correspondent—more than that, a war zone correspondent.

With the US embassy completely unwilling to help, Fox had flown in a bunch of former special forces operators and medics to evacuate Palkot, who had been grabbed less than twenty-four hours earlier. The US embassy was completely useless in finding him. They wouldn't leave their compound. Wiig, the cameraman, was from New Zealand, and the Kiwi ambassador, in nothing but a soft-skin car with no security detail, drove through Cairo, found the Egyptian secret police barracks where

Palkot and Wiig were being held, walked up, and demanded their release. Incredibly, the Egyptians handed them over.

That night, after the Fox paramedics had checked him out, I knocked on Palkot's hotel door. I had picked up a bottle of Johnnie Walker Black at the duty-free store in the Athens airport and smuggled it in. When he opened the door, his head was bandaged, his face bruised. The Egyptians had beaten him badly. I handed him the bottle. His eyes lit up. I thought he was going to kiss me. He was headed back to the UK the next day, but we sat down and had a drink. That was the start of a lifelong friendship.

The first few days were a blur. We worked our way down toward Tahrir Square—moving hotels early each morning, inching closer to the middle of the revolution. Mubarak's thugs had backed off, but he still hadn't resigned. By day, the protests swelled to a million people. Each night, we strategized, recalibrating our position, and the next morning we crept closer. It wasn't long before I was reporting live from Tahrir Square.

Six months earlier, I had been covering stories in Denver—things like bears stuck in trees or a fire chief getting a DUI. Now, I was at the center of a global revolution. Fox News put me on-air five times a day or more. We had a full security detail—about ten guys, mostly former British SAS operatives. Each reporting team had at least one or two professionals with them, plus local hires who were ex-Egyptian military.

It was the most exhilarating experience of my life. Back home, Mom was watching, jumping up and down on the living room floor, thrilled to see me on TV. I found out later that she had been glued to the screen, cheering every time I came on-air, as if I were scoring goals in a championship game instead of reporting from the middle of a revolution.

On February 11, 2011, just more than a week after I arrived, the situation came to a head. Around 6:00 p.m., Vice President Omar Suleiman announced on state television that Mubarak had resigned. Tahrir Square erupted. Tens of thousands of people cheered, waved flags, and chanted. Mubarak, who had ruled Egypt for longer than I had been alive, was gone, off to a hiding place. It was a defining moment of the Arab Spring and a

I'LL TELL MY KIDS ABOUT IT

turning point in modern Middle Eastern history. I was live on Fox News from the hotel balcony when the news broke.

"We're now hearing this unbelievable roar from the crowd at Tahrir Square. We don't know what that's about. Clearly, this is about as developing a situation as you can get. This is unbelievable. We can hear the screams coming out, the horns honking. It's unbelievable what's going on right now in the square. It's an electrifying moment in Cairo."

Most of the networks were covering it from their hotel balconies. But we had local security guys who knew how to get me onto the square. They set up a formation of three cars in a triangle, planning to put me in the middle, and told me, "We can get you down there." It was hard to imagine Mubarak leaving office—he had been in power for thirty years. And yet, here I was, about to step into a moment of history unfolding in real time. I was the rookie, barely understanding the magnitude of where I was and what I was about to do. I didn't hesitate.

The security team led me down into the square, weaving through the crowd. Protesters cheered and chanted, still in shock that they had done the impossible. Inside the makeshift barricade, people pressed in around me. I stood in front of a hand-painted sign that read Mission Accomplished. I barely had time to process it before my earpiece cracked to life. I was live on Fox News with Megyn Kelly.

"Leland, what a difference a week makes," Megyn said. "It was a week ago that our own Greg Palkot and photographer Olag Wiig were attacked by crowds. They were attacked by, we understand, pro-Mubarak thugs who were sent out there to intimidate journalists and others. Now look at you, a week later, right smack-dab in the middle of the crowds. What made you get down among them and how do you feel being there now?"

"I feel like I'm in something that I will remember for the rest of my life," I said. "There are very few moments you say you'll never forget. I feel like it's something I'm going to tell my kids about."

For eighteen days, the people of Egypt had poured into Tahrir Square, refusing to leave despite tear gas and rubber bullets. They camped out, sleeping on cardboard or bare concrete. They had faced unimaginable brutality. On the night Palkot and Wiig were taken, Mubarak supporters, some on camels and horses, stormed through the crowd throwing rocks and Molotov cocktails, turning the square into a war zone. Hundreds were injured, and at least ten people were killed. By the time Mubarak finally fell, the cost had been staggering. Across Egypt, at least 846 people had been killed.[1] Thousands more were wounded. Yet the people had done the impossible: They had toppled a man who had ruled for three decades, a dictator of unimaginable power. The people of Egypt had fought a revolution—and won. And I was there, standing in the middle of it all, microphone in hand, as history unfolded.

Across two hours, I reported live on Fox News from Tahrir Square, my voice occasionally drowned out by the crowd's chants. I could feel the weight of what had just happened, the enormity of what I was witnessing. These were people who had never voted, who had never imagined a world without Mubarak. And yet, here they were, standing on the other side of fear. Then, just as quickly as history had been made, the night began to turn as the crowd grew.

By 10 p.m., my security team advised us to leave. "We're gonna call this," one of the experienced ex–British Special Air Service guys told me. He had operated in North Africa, spoke the language, and understood the culture.

"What do you mean 'we're gonna call this'?" I said. "We're living on television. We're not leaving." Airtime is everything in cable news; the second we went upstairs, other correspondents would take over from the balcony. This was my breakout moment, and now I had to give it up.

"Look, my guys in the perimeter are starting to pick up chatter," he said. "People are getting agitated. We had a great night. I can't guarantee your safety anymore. My advice is to leave."

I asked what the other networks were doing. We were probably a hundred yards from the hotel, which, in a crowd like that, felt like miles if the mob attacked. By then, Lara Logan and her crew had made it down into Tahrir Square and they were staying put. But I thought of what Mom always used to say: "If you're not going to listen to the experts, find new experts."

"All right," I said. "If that's your advice, we're done."

We fought our way back through the crowd and returned to the hotel. An hour later, Lara was grabbed and brutally attacked by a mob just sixty yards from where I had been standing. At the moment, I hadn't thought much of the danger, but it hit me later.

A year and a half later, I returned to a different Tahrir Square—no longer filled with protesters but with a crowd celebrating the Muslim Brotherhood's rise to power as Mohamed Morsi was elected Egypt's new president. But the sentiment toward American media had further soured, and the crowd turned on me quickly. A mob started chasing us, shouting, "Fox News hates Muslims!" They were closing in fast, and we barely made it back to the hotel with ten yards to spare. I had come to the same square, the same streets—but they were now a reminder of how quickly everything could turn.

That first, historic stint in Egypt during the Arab Spring of 2011 lasted three weeks. When Mubarak was gone, the military took over, and the protests quieted—the story was over. It was time to leave. I boarded a plane back to Israel, exhausted but changed. I had arrived in Cairo as a young reporter, eager to prove myself. I left knowing I had what it took to be a foreign correspondent.

Back in Jerusalem, I planned to take a break—a ski trip with my friends in Denver, a chance to breathe. For the first time in weeks, it felt like the chaos had finally settled. But I wasn't the same person who had landed in Cairo three weeks earlier.

Chapter Fifteen

MOM, NO MATTER WHAT YOU SEE ON TV, I'M OKAY

I'd been back in Jerusalem for only a few days, ready to fly to Denver for the ski trip and step away from the chaos. I needed a break from war zones, explosions, and front lines. Just a moment to breathe. Then my phone rang.

It was the foreign desk. I figured they were checking in, maybe asking where I'd be in case they needed me while I was out.

Instead, I heard, "Hey, you need to book your tickets."

"What do you mean?" I asked, thinking they were talking about my ski trip. "My tickets are booked."

"Oh, nobody told you?" they said. "You're going to Libya."

The Arab Spring had started in Tunisia; swept through Egypt, where I covered Mubarak's fall; and now it had reached Libya. Muammar Gaddafi, the leader of Libya, was losing his grip, and the country was descending into civil war. So I was headed back to the front lines, my plans for a break erased as I packed my gear.

Getting into Libya wasn't straightforward. There were no flights and no safe roads. You couldn't just fly into Libya; Gaddafi was bombing everything. The only way in was on foot. I flew back into Cairo in mid-February and we drove up to the border, a group of four. With me were Mal James, a veteran war photographer; John Fiegener, my producer; and Shane Pataka, a Kiwi SAS guy built like a tank. We stayed overnight in a tiny flophouse near the Egypt-Libya border, waiting for sunrise. Then, we grabbed our bags and gear and hiked in.

Before crossing the border, Shane laid out the instructions. "If I yell, 'Run,'" he told us, "you drop your bags and run back to Egypt." That was our evacuation plan.

As we stepped over the border, chaos greeted us: men with guns, groups of refugees, no real security. One guy about my age waved at us and said, "Welcome to Free Libya!" They had all learned English from movies, and Fox movies were a favorite. That worked in our favor—when they saw our mic flags, they recognized Fox News.

We walked into Libya with four suitcases, a couple of Pelican cases of gear and satellite uplinks, and a whole lot of money. We had also brought in a stash of Johnnie Walker Black—normally the currency of choice for gifts in Arab countries. But instead of whiskey, the locals kept asking us about *Playboy* magazines. They didn't have the internet, but they had heard of *Playboy* and were convinced we could smuggle in a few copies.

A group of guys with pickups were just across the border, waiting for media crews to cross into Libya. You paid them a daily rate—$500 or so—and off you went.

The deeper we moved into Libya, the more I realized how exposed we were. I wasn't naive—I knew enough to be scared—but I don't think I had grasped just how dangerous it would be. Mal, who'd covered every major conflict for a few decades, told me later that he'd never been more terrified than he was in the beginning in Libya. There was no law. None. Anyone could have shot us, kidnapped us, or worse, and there wouldn't have been consequences.

We always had ex–Special Forces guys with us, but even they admitted this wasn't like Afghanistan or Iraq. There, if you were embedded

MOM, NO MATTER WHAT YOU SEE ON TV, I'M OKAY

with the US military, you had Black Hawk helicopters and medevac teams ready. Here, you were on your own. If something went wrong, the best-case scenario was bouncing in the back of a Toyota pickup for hours, trying to reach Egypt, then hoping to find a hospital and eventually evac out. We were seventy-two hours from medical care, with no cavalry coming to save us.

Our first stop was Tobruk, one of the first towns to fall to the rebels. The eastern clans had never been loyal to Gaddafi, so they kicked out his forces early. The atmosphere was surreal, celebrations mixed with terror. It's hard to imagine a society that had been repressed for so long. Years of fear, surveillance, and brutality had conditioned them to expect control. Now, faced with freedom, they weren't sure what to do.

In the town square, a ten-year-old boy approached me, holding a drawing of Gaddafi. Before the war, you couldn't draw Gaddafi or you'd get reported to the secret police. The boy had drawn the dictator as a butcher, holding a cleaver, blood dripping from his hands.

I asked him about the drawing.

"This is my dad," he said.

"Gaddafi?" I asked, confused.

"No," he said. "The blood. Gaddafi killed my dad."

Stories like that were a dime a dozen.

A couple of days in, we visited one of Gaddafi's secret-police prisons. A translator we'd hired—a local doctor's son who spoke English—took us inside. The place was a dungeon. This was where people had been tortured, broken, and disappeared.

My photographer set up his camera on a tripod inside one of the cells, a tiny, windowless, six-by-nine-foot box. He turned to me and said, "I'm going to close the door. Just talk. Say what you're feeling." I didn't realize he'd started filming. Before I could react, he walked out and slammed the door shut.

Suddenly, I was locked inside one of Gaddafi's torture cells. It was nearly pitch-black. I could hear my breathing, feel the silence. The walls had scratches—words and drawings left by desperate prisoners. It hit me as I started talking: the horror, the isolation, the agony of it all. People had died here, slowly, painfully. I started talking, not thinking about what I was saying, just trying to capture the feeling.

When the door opened, I stepped out, rattled. Seeing things explode and watching people die—these were no longer academic concepts. I wasn't a soldier, trained and prepared for war. I was a young reporter with a notepad, thrown into the fire. And I was realizing that war had a way of changing people. It was a pretty quick way to grow up.

"We're Leaving... Right Now"

Over the next several weeks in Libya, we ran with the rebels as they pushed west toward Tripoli. We were in the east, moving with them, trying to get closer to the action, then retreating as Gaddafi counterattacked. Without the NATO no-fly zone in place yet, his forces had complete air superiority, bombing rebel positions and strafing roads with machine-gun fire. On top of that, he had brought in African mercenaries, battle-hardened fighters who turned the tide in key battles.

We were in a town called Ajdabiya most of the time, staying one or two towns behind the front lines so we'd have some distance if things went south. That distance didn't always matter.

One day, at a checkpoint in the eastern Libyan town of Ras Lanuf, the last one before the front lines, we were filming and doing interviews, debating whether to push forward or not. Shane, the six-foot-six, 240-pound Māori SAS veteran with us, was always the first to sense danger. He looked at my photographer, then at me.

"We're leaving," he said. "Right Now."

"Let's get a couple more sho—" I started to protest.

"No!" he shouted. "Now!"

Before I could argue, Shane gripped the grab handles on the back of my

MOM, NO MATTER WHAT YOU SEE ON TV, I'M OKAY

flak jacket, lifted me and Mal off the ground, and started running. It wasn't so much us running as it was our feet skipping across the ground as he carried us toward the truck. He threw us in and yelled at the driver, "Drive!"

Forty-five seconds later,[1] we stopped about one hundred yards away and turned back. Mal set up the camera. A Libyan jet flew over and bombed the checkpoint. Many were injured; others lay dead.

We had the video. I knew Fox News was going to play it on a loop over and over: "Fox News crew bombed in Libya." And I knew my parents were going to see it. As we drove back to the hotel, I pulled out my sat phone and called home.

"Mom," I said, "no matter what you see on TV, I'm okay. Gotta go."

What I didn't know at the time was that Mom was sitting in a hospital room with Dad, who thought he'd had another heart attack from the stress of me being overseas. Meanwhile, my sister, Liberty, who was spending the year in Paris, was also in the hospital with an asthma attack. And now, Mom's son was calling from Libya, letting her know he had just survived a bombing.

I asked Shane that night, as we decompressed from the day, "Just so I understand, what did you see?"

"I just had a bad feeling," he said. "You do this long enough, sometimes you get bad feelings."

That bad feeling saved all our lives. The plane that attacked the checkpoint had been Gaddafi's forces bombing the rebels. I still have the ripped and torn Libyan flag from that checkpoint hanging on my wall. We went back the next day and retrieved it, a reminder of how close a call it had been.

War Calls, So Does Dad

Life in Libya meant long drives, front lines during the day, and hotels by night. We had satellite phones that looked like the old brick cell phones from the '90s. They had car antennas, so we'd get reception on the drive back from the front. We developed a routine: Leave in the morning local time, which was still the middle of the night back home, cover the battle, then head back to file our stories and do live shots late into the night for the shows on Fox seven hours behind us.

Dad had the number to my sat phone. And he used it.

"Hey, Dad, how are you doing?" I'd answer.

"Just checking in," he'd say. "You okay?"

"Yeah, I'm fine," I'd tell him, "but I'm a little busy."

Later, he'd call again.

"Hey," he said, "just making sure you're okay."

"Dad, first, I'm fine," I said, "but second, your calling is distracting, and me being distracted in a war zone is not what I need. If something is actually wrong, I need to be able to concentrate."

Then one day, on a long drive back, the sat phone rang again.

"Hey, Dad," I said. "How's it going?"

"Good, good," he responded. "Listen, I'm in St. Louis tonight. Is there any way you can call Annie Gunn's and get me a reservation?"

I was in Libya. And Dad wanted me to book a dinner reservation.

"What do you mean?" I asked.

"Well, I want to take some friends of ours to dinner, and they book up weeks in advance. You know the owner. Can you call?"

So, using my sat phone from a war zone, I called Annie Gunn's, got one of the owner's most trusted employees on the line, and said, "Hey, Vida, it's Lucky."

"Lucky! Oh my God, you're alive!" she screamed into the phone. "We've all been watching you on TV!"

"Yeah, yeah," I said. "Listen, I need a reservation tonight." I could hear the restaurant workers in the background.

"Lucky's coming," she yelled. "He's out of Libya. He's alive!"

"No, no, it's not for me," I told her. "It's for my dad. I'm still in Libya."

Pause. "Wait . . . you're calling from Libya?"

"Yeah, I'm calling you from Libya," I said. "My dad needs a reservation."

Longer pause. "What time does he want?"

Thousands of miles away, in a war zone, I was still Dad's little boy. Asked about it later, Dad told me, "Well, you weren't busy!"

Proving Ground

Eventually, Fox News rotated me out of Libya.

I had been there for nearly a month covering the civil war. They were smart about it—keeping people on the front lines too long wasn't sustainable. But I was incensed. I wanted to stay. The final battle for Libya was about to unfold, and I was going to miss it. Gaddafi's forces were making a desperate last stand, but the rebels, backed by NATO, were closing in, and I wanted to be there. But that was the deal: You rotate out so you don't burn out.

We left Benghazi one day in March, drove back to the Egyptian border, and crossed over. We spent the night at a hotel in Alexandria and had our first real meal in a month on the coastline. Then we drove another eight hours to Cairo before finally flying out. I went back to Jerusalem, dropped my gear, and finally, after two months in Egypt and Libya, I took a break. I flew to London to meet my parents.

I didn't realize how much I had changed. In ten weeks, I went from being a guy who had to write on his hand the difference between the Gaza Strip and the West Bank to a guy deeply embedded in the conflict. I reported on two revolutions, ran with rebels, and survived a bombing. I had become a war correspondent.

When my parents saw me at Heathrow Airport in London, they started sobbing. They had spent weeks terrified, watching me on TV, worried they'd never see me again. Parents of soldiers in war zones might get emails or sporadic updates, but mine had watched me get bombed on live television.

For a week, I stayed in London, decompressing. My godfather Louis Susman was the US ambassador to the United Kingdom, and I spent time at Winfield House, the American ambassador's residence. There is probably no greater change in life than going from the front lines of Libya to the Winfield House. As I walked the grounds, I kept thinking about how surreal it all felt. A week earlier, I had been in a war zone, barely surviving airstrikes, seeing death and evil up close—not just violence from gang fights or car crashes but war in its most brutal form. I had seen one of Gaddafi's torture cells up close and personal, for God's sake. Now, I was in one of the most exclusive residences in London, with some much-needed stiff martinis and good bottles of wine. I had seen the world in ways few ever do.

On one of my final days in Libya, an unexpected email landed in my inbox. In the Middle East, I started hearing from people back home in St. Louis—some I hadn't spoken to in years. One note stood out: A parent of a kid who had been especially cruel wrote to tell me how proud they were of what I had accomplished.

I grabbed my sat phone and called Dad.

"You aren't going to believe this . . ."

I still have that email. I forwarded it to Mom in the middle of the night from Libya and wrote: "Of all the events in the past two weeks—from being bombed and shot at, to seeing Gaddafi's torture chambers, to watching rebels march off to die for their cause—this has surprised me the most."

The world had come full circle. Nothing proved Dad's promise more: The currency of high school was now worthless, and the currency of life now mattered.

More than just surviving the Middle East, I had crossed a threshold, one that my parents had hoped for, one that had felt elusive for so many years. That was *the* moment. The inflection point. The proof that everything had changed. Not just through war, but through something deeper. For years, Mom and Dad had fought to get me to the point where I could stand on my own, where I could handle what life threw at me, and now I had proved it to them—and myself.

For so long, I had struggled to fit in, to navigate the social world of high school, of early jobs, of newsroom politics. Even in my first reporting jobs, the old challenges remained. The same things that made me an outsider as a kid—my intensity, my singular focus, my inability to read social cues—still caused friction. But in the Middle East, none of that mattered. No one cared about popularity or charisma in the heat of a firefight. What mattered was whether you could get the story, keep your team safe, and operate under extreme pressure. And I could.

For the first time, I felt the weight of real responsibility. In Libya, I had a team, but I was the one leading them. It reminded me of young officers in an infantry unit, responsible for older, more seasoned noncommissioned officers. I wasn't just a reporter. I was making decisions that impacted the safety of others. And I was succeeding. That gave me a confidence I had never had before.

It wasn't just that I had made it onto television or achieved my goal of being a network correspondent. It was the way I had done it. The Arab Spring was the most important global story at the time, and I was at the center. People back home, the ones who had last seen me as a socially awkward high schooler, were now watching me on TV, reporting live from the front lines of history. If you're in local news in Orlando or Denver, no one in St. Louis sees you. But now, people in St. Louis were seeing me as this different person. My old school, Burroughs, even invited me back to speak. The tables had turned. And that's the thing: What you're judged on in life changes. The skills that make you popular in high school are irrelevant in the real world. And the moment I stepped out of Libya, I knew I had survived.

No one could hand me the confidence I had now. It came from surviving, from setting hard goals and achieving them, and from refusing to let others define me. My parents never shielded me from struggle; they forced me to face it. They never handed out participation trophies or softened challenges to make things easier. If something was hard for me, that didn't mean I couldn't do it—it meant I had to find a way through it. And in the most intense moments of my life, I realized how invaluable that was.

Some people grow up with everything handed to them. Some people have their paths cleared and their obstacles removed. But those people never feel the deep satisfaction that comes from knowing, unequivocally, that you earned your place. The world wasn't modified to fit me, and I was better for it. Forcing the uncomfortable yields enormous gains. Because once you've done something you thought impossible, you know you can do it again.

For so long, I had felt like an outsider, struggling to fit into a world that didn't make sense to me. But Dad always knew that the world wouldn't change for me—I would have to change for the world. High school was all about appearances, but real life was about substance. Back then, social skills had been currency. Now, in adulthood, currency was resilience, hard work, and the ability to push through adversity. Dad had been right all along: Self-esteem wasn't given. It was earned.

And for the first time, I knew I had earned mine.

Chapter Sixteen

WAR CHANGES YOU

"Nothing is what it seems."

I used to think about that line from *The Recruit*, the movie where Al Pacino plays a CIA recruiter.[1] In the Middle East, that wasn't just a clever saying; it was a survival lesson. It took me a while to understand the arcs of power, to see beyond the immediate chaos and recognize the patterns. Governments, militants, even so-called democracy movements—everyone had an agenda. And the most important skill wasn't just reporting the facts; it was figuring out what those facts really meant. I had to learn this quickly because if you took things at face value, you wouldn't last long.

I spent three more years in the Middle East after the Arab Spring, and if covering revolutions had been about watching history unfold, the years that followed were about understanding what came next. What happened when the rebels took power? When the strongmen fell? When ideology collided with reality? That was when the true nature of the region revealed itself. You couldn't believe anything. Not from the governments. Not from the militants. Back home, people generally assumed they were being told the truth—at least a version of it. In the Middle East, truth was malleable, shaped to fit whatever story someone needed you to believe.

Born Lucky

London had been an escape, one I hadn't realized I needed. After two months of running with rebels, dodging bombs, and watching regimes collapse, I stepped back into a world that was clean, structured, and familiar. I made it. But the thing about making it—especially as a journalist—is that you don't stop. Success isn't a finish line; it's a revolving door. One moment you're sitting in the US ambassador's residence in London, and the next you're back in Jerusalem, standing across from a man who spent years plotting how to kill people like you. The break was over. The world had moved on, and so had I. I was back in the Middle East, and this time, I wasn't covering revolutions. I was staring into the minds of the people who planned them.

I was in Ramallah once, meeting with a Palestinian press liaison, a woman named Hanan Ashrawi, who had been a fixture in the foreign press scene for decades. She was young and striking during the days of Peter Jennings, rumored to be one of his girlfriends in the region. Over tea and dates, she asked me, "What brought you to the Middle East?"

Without thinking, I said, "I wanted to have the Peter Jennings experience."

She smirked and replied, "We can arrange that."

I quickly learned that everything and everyone had layers. My fixer in the Palestinian parts of the West Bank, Shadi, was a prime example. A *fixer* is someone who operates behind the scenes to make things happen— part translator, part local insider, part problem-solver. They know the right people, the right favors, and the right stories to tell to keep you moving safely. Shadi looked like he had stepped out of central casting: He spoke six languages, knew everyone, and could get anything done. He had worked for Fox for a while, and when my parents came to Bethlehem for Christmas, I was reporting at the top of Manger Square on Christmas Eve. Palestinian Security Services had closed the area off, so Shadi went down and smuggled Dad through closed Palestinian security checkpoints by wrapping him in a keffiyeh. My Jewish father from St. Louis strolled into Manger Square like he belonged there, all with Shadi's help.

WAR CHANGES YOU

And then one day, Shadi disappeared. Maybe Israeli intelligence picked him up. Maybe he skipped town to avoid that fate. We never really knew. That was the Middle East. Nothing was what it seemed.

Even the concept of democracy wasn't what we imagined. When the US pushed for democratic elections in Egypt, the people voted in the Muslim Brotherhood. In Libya, removing Gaddafi didn't bring freedom—it brought chaos. It turned out that strongmen weren't just holding power for themselves; they were the only thing preventing their countries from imploding.

The attack on Benghazi was proof of that chaos. On September 11, 2012, militants stormed the US consulate there, setting fire to buildings and killing four Americans, including Ambassador Christopher Stevens.[2] Hours later, they turned their sights on the CIA annex, where a small team of former SEALs and intelligence officers made their stand. One of them was my friend Glen Doherty. Glen was in Tripoli when the attack started. He and his team could have stayed there, safe. Instead, they volunteered to fly into an active firefight. He made it to Benghazi, fought through the night, and was killed on the rooftop of the annex on the morning of September 12. When I landed in Cairo, mass riots filled the streets. Our local team threw me into the back of a van, covered me with prayer rugs, and smuggled me downtown. On that drive, I learned Glen was dead.

I sent Fox the pictures I had taken of Glen at Shorewood when he visited just weeks before, so they could use them on-air. Then, I went straight to work, reporting from the riots outside the US embassy in Cairo. Days later, Glen's family stood at Dover Air Force Base, watching his casket carried off the plane in a dignified transfer ceremony. I watched from my hotel room in Cairo, with tear gas filtering into the room from the riot below.

And then, not long after, I sat face-to-face with the man who helped inspire it—the brother of Ayman al-Zawahiri, who at the time was the leader of al-Qaeda.

That interview was one of the last of its kind. Before ISIS made journalist kidnappings and beheadings their primary form of propaganda, terrorist leaders still saw value in talking to Western reporters. They wanted to be understood—wanted to justify themselves, to sell their version of history. Muhammad al-Zawahiri was no different. They all fancied themselves as freedom fighters. It's cliché but true in the Middle East: "One man's terrorist is another man's freedom fighter." They're true believers, and they want to show you that.

I got al-Zawahiri to agree to an interview at a hotel in neutral territory. But I had a purpose, and it wasn't to give him a platform. It was to prove, once and for all, that the attacks in Benghazi and Cairo weren't about some offensive YouTube video about the Prophet Muhammad as the Obama administration claimed.

I had learned by then how to shut off my emotions, a skill honed in childhood when I had to endure the daily gauntlet of being bullied. I learned to read the smallest shifts in body language, the pauses between words, the tension in a room—because survival depended on it. Emotional detachment wasn't just useful in the Middle East. If I let fear or anger cloud my thinking, I wouldn't be able to see what was happening. It was remarkably easy to detach, to separate myself from the horrors around me because I had been doing it my entire life.

Dad had prepared me for this. He had drilled into me the importance of reading people, of understanding their motivations, of never taking things at face value. He had taught me how to focus intensely, to listen more than I spoke, to see what others missed. The tapping-the-watch lesson came to mind, his quiet way of teaching me timing, restraint, and awareness. Learning to read a room wasn't only about understanding people; it was about knowing when to speak and when to stay silent. The learned skill of observing people—understanding what they truly wanted rather than what they said—became second nature. He believed social awareness wasn't solely a result of instinct; it could be developed, refined, and mastered. That discipline became essential, especially when dealing with someone who wanted to manipulate or mislead. In moments like this, it was invaluable.

That detachment allowed me to sit across from al-Zawahiri and focus entirely on what I needed to get from him. It allowed me to ignore the anger of Glen's murder, to suppress the knowledge that I was staring into the face of someone whose ideology had directly led to the murder of my friend and others. I wasn't there for vengeance or outrage. I was there for the truth. And I got it. On camera, al-Zawahiri admitted he had never even seen the video that supposedly sparked the Benghazi attack. That single admission unraveled the entire public narrative surrounding Benghazi. But it didn't bring the people back. It didn't change the fact that nothing—not truth, not reality—would stop these men from believing in their righteousness.

The only thing that mattered to them was the cause. And that was the terrifying realization: Evil doesn't see itself as evil. It justifies, rationalizes, and moves forward with conviction. I had seen it in Benghazi, and I would see it again in Gaza, sitting across from someone who had once been willing to sacrifice everything for what she believed was righteous.

Seeing the World as It Is

As a kid, Dad taught me to see the best in the world. Every night before bed, I'd spin the globe in my room, close my eyes, and let my finger land on a random country. Wherever it stopped, Dad would tell me about that place—its people, its history, what made it unique. If he didn't know much, we'd pull out an encyclopedia and learn together. It was our ritual, a way of exploring a world that seemed endless.

Back then, the world felt like an adventure waiting to happen. Dad was and remains an idealist. He believed in the best of people, the potential for good, the power of democracy. And he taught me to believe in it too. But the Middle East stripped that away. I saw the world and came back. I left as an idealist and came home as a realist. I had seen too much to think otherwise.

Maya Angelou once said, "When someone shows you who they are, believe them the first time."[3] The Islamic terror groups had shown the world who they were over and over again, yet the West kept believing that if only they were given peace, they would take it. I had watched people in Tahrir Square believe that democracy would change everything, only to see the Muslim Brotherhood rise to power in Egypt. I had seen the fall of Gaddafi in Libya, only for the country to collapse into war. The hard truth was that some places were held together by force because that was the only way they could function. The world is a dangerous place, and there is absolute evil in it. That was the world I was living in. A place where survival depended on knowing that no one's words could be taken at face value. Which is why I was so intrigued when I got the opportunity to interview a failed suicide bomber.

She was a young girl when she accidentally poured a pot of boiling water over herself in Gaza. The Israelis medevaced her out and spent fifteen years giving her the best medical treatment available, free of charge. She became one of the few Palestinians who had permission to move freely between Gaza and Israel for treatment. And then, one day, Fatah militants recruited her to be a suicide bomber. They gave her three target choices: a bus, a café, or the hospital that had saved her life. She chose the hospital. She got to the checkpoint from Gaza to Israel. The Israelis discovered the bomb. She tried to detonate it but it didn't go off. The Israelis arrested and imprisoned her. While in jail, she continued to receive medical care. She got her degree. Years later, she was released in the Gilad Shalit prisoner swap. I thought this could be a redemption story, a chance to show that people could change.

I traveled to Gaza, went to her home, and showed the Israeli surveillance video of her at the checkpoint, trying to detonate the bomb. She had never seen it before.

I asked, "How do you feel watching this now?"

Her eyes widened as she watched. She took a deep breath, looked at me and said, "I thought I was going to get to Paradise."

I pressed her. "Hard to watch?"

She didn't hesitate. "I would do it again tomorrow if I could."

That was it. That was the moment I understood. There was no hope of changing people like her. No amount of reasoning or compassion could undo what had been embedded in her since childhood. This wasn't about oppression or desperation. This was about belief. I left Gaza that day without an ounce of doubt left in my mind. The world was not as we wanted it to be. Evil wasn't theoretical. It wasn't something you debated in classrooms. It was real. And I had just looked it in the eyes.

One Last Assignment

By late 2013, I knew my chapter as a foreign correspondent needed to end. The job wasn't teaching me anything new. I had seen the fall of regimes, the rise of new ones, and the cycles of violence that followed. I had watched the promise of democracy dissolve into chaos in Egypt, Libya, and Syria. At some point, I realized I wasn't learning anymore. I was chasing danger for the sake of it, feeding off adrenaline. In war zones a cruel gallows humor set in. I often joked about eating war for breakfast, refugees for lunch, and drinking my dinner. The joke betrayed the calluses I needed to protect myself emotionally while witnessing the worst of humanity. And drinking my dinner often involved enough Johnnie Walker Black to numb the pain of seeing the unthinkable all day. The juice wasn't worth the squeeze. I missed America.

The closest thing you'll ever have to eternal job security is being a Middle East network correspondent. There would always be another war, another uprising, another attack. But I knew it wasn't going to advance my career any further. If I wanted to move up, I had to get out.

I also knew I was teetering on a dangerous edge. I didn't want to be one of those journalists who lived off the high—going to the front, coming back, filing the report, drinking until I couldn't feel the emotional pain of war, then going back out to the front the next day. I had seen it happen to others, and I could feel it happening to me. At one point, Mom called and said, "I think you are drinking too much." She was right, so I replaced drinking scotch with running. The adrenaline was addictive, and I worried I was starting to need it just to feel normal.

Being overseas meant I got a few "home leave" trips in addition to normal vacation time. Home leave included a stop at Fox headquarters in New York.

Dianne Brandi, Fox News's head of business affairs general counsel, had other plans. "We want to re-sign you," she told me in her office.

"I'm not re-signing while I'm in the Middle East," I said.

She slid an offer across the table: more money, more vacation, more trips home. That wasn't what I was looking for. I needed to be in New York where the next step in my career could happen. Staying in the Middle East meant being stuck. In New York I could fill in at the anchor desk, get sent to the White House, be in the rooms where bigger opportunities happened. If I wasn't there, I wasn't in the conversation. "If you're not home in a year," Dianne told me, "you can leave the network."

"I don't think you understand," I said. "I'm not signing in the Middle East, so either bring me home or I'm not re-signing. I'm not going to learn any more in the Middle East. It's been fun. It's been wonderful. It's time for me to come home."

I could see she didn't believe me. "Well, you have to counter us," she said. "I have to take something back to Roger." She meant Fox News founder and chairman Roger Ailes.

"You have a piece of paper?" I asked.

She handed me one, and I wrote: "$1 million, $2 million, $3 million"—for years one, two, and three of my contract.

She looked at it and laughed. "This is a nonstarter."

"So is me staying in the Middle East for three more years."

WAR CHANGES YOU

As negotiations dragged on that fall, I decided to ask Bill Shine for a meeting. Shine, who was the executive vice president of Fox News, was the first senior executive I'd met in 2010 when I was gunning for that network correspondent job in the Middle East. After meeting twenty executives over the course of my interviews, Dad asked me, "What do you think of all these people? Do you like them? Do you trust them?"

I told him, "Well, there's one guy named Bill Shine. I don't know, but I think you and he would be friends." Of all the people I met, something about him said this man was of exceptional character. And I knew that's all that mattered to Dad.

I had very little interaction with Shine during my time in the Middle East, and getting a meeting with him was never easy. He was the number two at Fox News, reporting directly to chairman and CEO Roger Ailes. Shine's time was dominated by running Fox's biggest programs: *The Sean Hannity Show*, *The O'Reilly Factor*, and *Fox & Friends*. He and the head of news, Michael Clemente, were considered equal deputies to Ailes, but Shine was the first among equals. I technically worked for Clemente, but I had always liked Shine more. So in November 2013, desperate to come home, I pushed hard for a meeting—and finally got one during the next home leave visit in the fall.

"Have you ever anchored before?" Shine asked.

"Yeah, in Denver," I told him.

"Send me a tape," he said.

I did, and to my surprise, a month or so later I got word they would give me a chance. Over Christmas 2013, he brought me back to New York to fill in as an anchor for five days over Christmas.

I was terrified. This was the biggest opportunity of my career, and I knew the stakes. My parents and Liberty came to town to spend the holiday with me. I was literally anchoring on Christmas Day. The night before, I was so nervous I threw up.

Dad didn't understand. "You've done this before," he said. "Why are you so nervous?" To him, it was just another newscast. But to me, it was my one shot to prove I belonged at the anchor desk. In this business, if you flopped, you didn't get a second chance. If I screwed this up, I was done.

As expected, I was raw. The last time I had anchored was in Colorado, for God's sake, at a local station—prominent, yet tiny compared to Fox News. Now, I was anchoring on a national stage. This was the big leagues. I stumbled over the teleprompter, lost my place during interviews, and struggled to match the pace of seasoned anchors. Often off-rhythm, I just kept talking. I can still remember the bloopers. But Shine believed in me. Even while on his Christmas vacation, he took the time to send me encouraging notes: "Just keep being you" or "You're doing great." Those small messages steadied me when I felt like I was floundering.

After New Year's, I was out skiing when Shine called: "You did good, kid. You're coming home."

And then nothing happened for months. They kept promising to bring me home, but nothing changed.

So I made a move. I went out and got another offer from a station in St. Louis. I called Dianne in late April and said, "I have another offer."

"Do you want that job more than you want to be at Fox News?" Dianne asked.

"No," I said. "But I want it more than being at Fox News in Jerusalem. And if you're not bringing me home now, you never will." That was the right answer.

Shine called me a few hours later and said, "You'll have a contract to come home in forty-eight hours." I got it the next day.

Before I left, I had one more assignment in Ukraine. It was early 2014, and Russian President Vladimir Putin was making his move on Crimea. Russian special forces—"Little green men"—were on the ground in Donetsk and eastern Ukraine.[4] I had covered wars before, but this was different. The press was beginning to go from a protected class to a target. Russian Special Forces operating in eastern Ukraine in 2014 understood Western journalists were to be handled carefully, but they also wanted to send a message. Other than Libya, Ukraine was the most terrifying situation I faced overseas. We had gone back and forth to the front lines multiple times, navigating unpredictable checkpoints manned by armed, often drunk, Russian-backed separatists with new AK-47s and Russian-issued gear. Each trip was a gamble, and we knew the rules could change in an instant.

One morning, I was supposed to go to the front lines with a group of other reporters—Sky News, CBS, and others. We had been threatened before, but it was usually manageable. The key was to go out in the morning because the villagers-turned-Russian-militia-men would be drunk by noon.

That morning, something felt off. I woke up and told my team, "I don't feel like going out today. I have a bad feeling." The other journalists went. They got grabbed. Beaten up. Held for hours before being released.

Ukraine also proved emotional in a different way. As you know, my dad's family came from Ukraine as Jewish refugees at the turn of the century. Driving through the towns with Soviet-era apartment blocks and abject desperation, I couldn't help but see my relatives. It made me so grateful for their sacrifice and so proud to be an American. John McCain said, "I fell in love with my country when I was a prisoner in someone else's."[5] I understood what he meant.

That was my last war zone.

Packing up my things, I came across the flag I had taken from the checkpoint in Libya, the one that nearly cost me my life.

As I folded it, another memento caught my eye.

I can't remember which Gaza war it was, but our producer, Yonat Friling, was with us. The Israelis rarely wore their flak jackets and helmets. One night, I was live on-air with Megyn Kelly, and you could see Hamas rockets and Iron Dome interceptors lighting up the sky behind me. I had my heavy flak jacket on, with the helmet clipped to a loop on my shoulder, ready to be put on. (Let's be honest—nobody looks good on TV with a helmet.) We had been on for about thirty minutes when Megyn suddenly said, "Leland, your mother called, and she would like you to put your helmet on." So, on-air, I clipped my helmet on and kept going.

The sirens went off as Hamas fired multiple rockets, trying to break through the Iron Dome. We could hear the incoming rounds and knew they were going to be close. Yonat didn't have her helmet or flak jacket on, so I threw her down behind a huge rock and covered her with my body. A rocket landed on the other side. That was my other memento: a piece of shrapnel from the near miss. That whine, that hot shriek of incoming artillery—there's no sound scarier in the world.

Moments like that had been my life for years. But how much longer could I keep rolling the dice? Eventually the wrong number would come up. I had covered a war, an uprising, and revolutions. I had learned all I could as a foreign correspondent. If I wanted to keep growing, I had to move on.

In May 2014, Mom came to Israel to fly home with me. We spent a few days saying goodbye—goodbye to the place where I had pushed myself to the limits, where I had chased stories through war zones, and where I had been tested in ways I never imagined. Most difficult was saying goodbye to those that I had gone to war with. They were staying in Israel; I was starting a new adventure—but they will always be family.

As I walked through the familiar streets one last time, I reflected on everything I was leaving behind. But I also knew it was time to step away, to take on a new challenge, and to return to life in America.

Before leaving Jerusalem, I went to the Western Wall. Jews go there to leave notes of prayers; it's the holiest spot in the Jewish faith. Standing there, I felt the weight of the years I had spent there, the close calls, the moments of fear, and the straight line that had brought me to this point in my life. I pulled out my wallet, where I kept some cards with my name on them, and wrote a note.

Thank you for keeping me safe.

I tucked the paper into the wall and headed to the airport.

Chapter Seventeen

JUST BE YOU

It was almost midnight on May 31, 2014, when I left Tel Aviv. It had been four years of war zones, front lines, dodging artillery, and reporting on history as it unfolded in ways I never could have imagined when I first set foot in Jerusalem at twenty-eight. And then, just like that, I was on a plane, leaving it all behind.

By the time the wheels touched down in Newark, the Middle East felt like a dream. The overnight flight from Tel Aviv landed around 5:30 a.m., and while most passengers sleepily shuffled toward customs, I was flagged immediately. Too many trips in and out of conflict zones, too many stamps from places that make US Homeland Security nervous.

A customs agent glanced at my passport and sighed.

"We need a supervisor for you," he said. The big red "X" across my customs slip meant one thing: secondary screening.

So there I was, at the crack of dawn, stopped at customs with my entire life crammed into eight duffel bags. Mom, meanwhile, strolled through customs without an issue.

"Go ahead, Mom," I said. She took the luggage cart piled high with my bags and walked to the other side. If I was a national security threat, she was my trusted ally in smuggling whatever horrible stuff was in those bags. She turned and waved while I was led into a holding area for questioning—standing there in a T-shirt and sweatpants next to a group of people who looked like they had just emerged from a decade spent in a cave in Afghanistan.

The supervisor arrived, looking as annoyed as the first agent. I had probably flown through Newark thirty times during my four years as a network correspondent in the Middle East. As I stood there, the supervisor typed on his computer. He scanned the screen, paused, and asked, "Have you been to Turkey lately?"

"All the time," I said.

"Why?" he questioned.

"I'm a foreign correspondent for Fox News Channel," I told him.

He sighed again. "Do you have any checked bags?"

"My mom has them," I said. "She's checking them through to Traverse City."

A long pause. "They let your mom take all your checked bags?!"

I nodded in agreement.

"Oh my God." He shook his head. "This is so screwed up."

It was obvious they had flagged me because of my travel patterns, thinking I was doing something nefarious. At the time, Americans joining ISIS headed to Syria via Turkey. And yet, my mother had walked out with everything they assumed needed searching. Eventually, they photocopied my Fox News press credentials and sent me on my way. That was my welcome home.

Mom and I caught our next flight to Chicago, landing at O'Hare around 10 a.m. "Why don't we go downtown to Joe's Stone Crab?" she suggested. That was the restaurant where, four years earlier, I had met my parents and told them I was taking the foreign correspondent job in the Middle East. The place where I had sat across from them and explained that yes, I understood the risks, and yes, I knew it was dangerous, and no, I wasn't going to change my mind. Now, walking into that same restaurant, I saw Dad at a table, waiting to surprise me.

I had come full circle. Four years before, I had told them I was leaving for the most dangerous job of my life. But I had come back in one piece.

"So," Dad asked, "what's next?"

"Just Be You"

Returning to the States in 2014, the next step was clear: get on-air in the anchor chair. I had done my time in the Middle East and paid my dues in war zones, and now it was time to prove myself stateside. The plan was simple: Start as a fill-in anchor in Washington, DC, make myself indispensable, and work my way up.

At Fox, the only way to get ahead was to say yes. Will you work the overnight shift? Yes. Will you fill in on Christmas Eve? Yes. It became a game of endurance—how many times I could say yes, because every yes led to another opportunity, another chance to prove I belonged. I was the journeyman jack-of-all-trades.

As I've mentioned, the currency of DC is equally as screwed up as in high school; power and influence matter infinitely more than character. The Fox bureau there was no different—a viper pit of ambition, alliances, and rivalries. I wasn't a "DC guy." I wasn't part of the club. That meant I had to work twice as hard just to be noticed. Dad had always believed in good people, but I had to teach him that in TV, people often aren't inherently good—they can be nice, but in the end, most people just do what is best for them. Promises are made and broken as easily as a segment rundown. But every rule has an exception, and Bill Shine was one of them. It seemed as if he was always looking out for me.

When you have a hard time in life, you never forget the people who are kind to you. In 2014, I had one of those moments with Martha MacCallum. It was my first time filling in for Bill Hemmer on *America's Newsroom*, a major step up and a clear sign that Shine was putting me in the line of succession at Fox. The twelfth floor of Fox was where it all happened— the *America's Newsroom* set, the green room, the makeup chairs where guests prepped, and the small private area where anchors could catch their breath. That morning, I walked in knowing this was my moment, but also knowing I was completely in over my head. I had as much business anchoring with Martha as I did teeing off at Augusta in the Masters. Hours of breaking news were in front of me, and I was sitting next to a seasoned pro.

From the color on my face and the perspiration on my brow, it was clear I had no idea what I was doing.

Martha could have let me flounder, but instead, she leaned over, patted my arm, and said, "It's going to be okay. I got you." She carried the broadcast that day and talked 80 percent of the time, but now and then, she teed up a perfect question for me—just enough to let me take a swing and feel like I belonged. That moment stuck with me. True confidence isn't about proving how good you are—it's about being secure enough to help others shine, a quality in TV as rare as flawless diamonds.

For years at Fox, I hardly spoke to Bill Shine. I went to New York maybe ten times over the years, and every time I'd email and say, "Can I have an appointment with you?" We spent maybe four hours together in the seven years we overlapped. To use a sports analogy, he was the head coach on a back-to-back Super Bowl–winning team, and I was a quarterback on the practice squad who occasionally got to dress for the game. But even from a distance, I knew he had my back. And in a business like television—where almost no one sticks their neck out for you—that meant everything. TV news isn't known for gentlemanly behavior. It's a world where alliances shift fast, and the same people shaking your hand in the hallway might be maneuvering against you behind closed doors. I had my share of that at Fox.

Between the infighting in the DC bureau, Clemente trying to box me out, and the general cutthroat nature of the business, it felt like I was constantly fighting uphill. But Shine was different. It was clear to me that he was always moving the chess pieces to protect me. When you've spent most of your life feeling like you're on your own, the moment you realize someone is in your corner, that's your guy.

Eventually, I went to him for advice. By 2015, I had fought my way into a weekend anchor slot, co-anchoring *America's News HQ*. But I wanted more.

I sat down across from Shine in New York and said, "Coach, give me some swing tips. How do I get better?"

He looked at me and said, "You're doing great!"

"Yeah," I said, "but how do I get better?"

"You're doing great," he repeated. "Just be you."

I pushed again, hoping for some secret formula, some road map to success. This was the guy who had created *Hannity*, *O'Reilly*, *Fox & Friends*, and *On the Record with Greta Van Susteren*. He was an architect of Fox News. And here I was, a thirty-three-year-old weekend anchor, just trying so hard to prove I belonged in a world where no one my age was on the anchor desk at that time.

Instead, he said: "Look, I can sit here from now until tomorrow morning watching tape with you and helping and critiquing your tape . . ." I sat there thinking he was about to give me the insightful coaching he would give a prime-time star. "But until you learn how to be you, I can't help you. Once you're you, then I can help shape you. Just be you."

At the time, I didn't fully get it. I walked out of that meeting still searching for the magic formula, still hoping for a clearer road map.

But something about what he said lingered.

A Call I Couldn't Ignore

By the spring of 2015, frustration was building. I had returned from the Middle East expecting a clear trajectory: anchor more, report less from the field. Instead, I found myself stuck in a tug-of-war at Fox, caught in the middle of a power struggle between Shine and Clemente. Shine was pushing me toward the anchor chair, Clemente had his own ideas that did not involve me, and I was left somewhere in between.

My time on the desk in DC became sporadic. On one minute, off the next, depending on who had the upper hand. It felt like I was in limbo, waiting for the next move to be made by someone other than me.

I had gone up to New York to try to meet with Shine, but he was tied up. Frustrated with the back-and-forth of my role and the infighting at the DC studio, I was doing my best to ignore work altogether. But that night my phone started ringing. The bureau chief in DC kept calling. Again. And again. And again. I ignored it. Finally, after what felt like the tenth call, I picked up.

"I need to talk to you," he said.

"You guys can go fly a kite," I shot back. "You brought me home to anchor, and I'm not anchoring. I'm going out with my friends."

"I get it. We're going to work out what's going on here," he said. "But I need you to get to Baltimore."

I paused. "What do you mean you need me to get to Baltimore?" I looked down at my seersucker suit ready to head out for a spring night. "I am going out in New York."

"You're the only person who can handle themselves in a hostile environment," he said. "Go to the train station, buy a ticket, and get to Baltimore."

I begrudgingly agreed, hung up, and bought a pair of khakis and a denim shirt on my way to Penn Station. By the time I was on the train, I was already mapping out where I needed to go: North and Penn, the center of unrest in Baltimore following the death of Freddie Gray. I called Mom on the train; she was in Michigan, and I was bored.

"Where in Baltimore?" she asked.

"North and Penn," I told her.

Mom had gone to college in Baltimore, so she knew the area. "I staffed a Red Cross aid station at a Black church at North and Penn during the riots in '68 when Martin Luther King Jr. was assassinated," she said. Two days into the riots, I would end up in that same church.

The scene when I arrived that first night was something out of the Middle East. This was the first truly lawless moment in recent American history. The police had retreated, and I found myself standing between them and the rioters, asking protesters how looting liquor stores and setting cars on fire was going to fix anything.[1] They were angry about Gray's death—understandably so.

That night, our photographers had their SUV tires slashed. Gunshots rang out, tear gas canisters filled the streets, and we took cover behind vehicles. At one point, Fox sent in contracted security. They had hired an off-duty officer from some tiny police department on Maryland's Eastern Shore. He showed up—overweight, middle-aged, wearing a bulletproof vest under a polo shirt and khakis.

"You Leland?" he asked.

"Yeah." I nodded.

"I'm your security," he said. "Don't worry. I'm carrying."

I looked around at the rioters. "Guess what?" I said. "So are about a hundred other people here, and they've got way more rounds than you do. Stay behind me. I don't want you anywhere around me. You're gonna get us all shot."

Around midnight, as we were on TV, a car came barreling toward us, its tires screeching as it swerved down the street. It was impossible to tell if the driver had lost control or if we were about to become targets. I yelled for the crew to get up on the stoop of a Baltimore row house. Just as we scrambled to safety on the front steps, the car slammed into something right in front of us.

It was a night of mayhem. I had been in war zones before, but this was the first time I felt under threat in America. I told Megyn Kelly on-air that night, "I've seen this in the Middle East. I never thought I'd see it here."

The next forty-eight hours were a blur of live hits, reporting on the ground, and very little sleep. Baltimore felt lawless. I saw police stand back and watch looters destroy businesses. I was wandering the streets live on television, sticking out my hand to people and saying, "I'm

Leland." A friendly greeting kept us alive and uncovered a few good stories.

What I saw backed up what my police sources had told me: The mayor had given a stand-down order, telling police, "Let them loot. It's only property." I watched officers retreat, restricted, their hands tied. Business owners were furious as their livelihoods got looted, destroyed, and burned to the ground while police looked on from a distance.

We heard the mayor was making an appearance, so we drove over and waited in the hall for her to come down. When she finally emerged, surrounded by Reverend Al Sharpton and others, I calmly asked if I could ask some questions. She was the only one uninterested in engaging. I asked her directly about the stand-down order, but she ignored me. "The Rev" tried to step in and promised a press conference but started to get handsy with me and put his hand in my face. Then the mayor's security grabbed me and shoved me to the ground. "Hey! Why can't we ask questions?" I asked. The mayor spoke at the event, then ducked out. No answers, and certainly not Sharpton's promised press conference. It was all on tape; the picture of "Sharpton's shove" ended up on the top of the Drudge Report and became the talk of cable news.

After three days of nonstop reporting, I finally crashed in the wee hours to get some rest. At 8 a.m., I got a call from a producer. "Come downstairs," he said.

"What do you mean?" I said. "I just got to sleep."

"No," he said, "come downstairs."

I stumbled down to the lobby, half asleep, to find a producer standing there with a big bag of clothes. "I was told to deliver these to you," he said. Shine's wife, Darla, had told her husband, "Get that kid some new clothes." I was still wearing the same denim shirt I had left New York in three days earlier. It reminded me that even in the chaos of Fox, Bill (and Darla) had my back.

That wouldn't last forever. Two years later, Shine was forced out, fired after *The New York Times* painted him as the man who kept Ailes's empire running while the scandals piled up. He was never accused of anything himself but according to the *Times* was guilty by association. It appeared that Fox wanted a clean break from the Ailes era, and Shine was the easiest sacrifice. No defending him. No pushing back on the narrative. Shine wasn't just fired; he was made an example of.

He had made it clear to me that the next anchor job in New York was mine, an opportunity to finally move up and out of DC. And then suddenly, he was gone. Without him, I was an anchor without a protector. The rocket-ship trajectory I had been on was suddenly in free fall. I went from being the first among equals, anchoring weekends and filling in for everyone, to slowly disappearing into weekend TV irrelevance. In the years that followed, I watched others get the opportunities I had been promised, but in television, nothing is guaranteed. As I've said, it's a game of alliances, and my biggest ally had just been forced out.

It reminded me of something Dad always said: There are very few people in life who truly share your values. Shine and I had that. If Fox News was that winning football team, he was the head coach who identified talent, developed it, and called the plays. And just like a backup or practice squad quarterback trusts his coach, I trusted him. When he left, I didn't just lose an ally—I lost the person who had always seen something in me, the one who gave me a shot. With him gone, I started realizing my future at Fox had already been decided without me.

Play It as It Lies

In the winter of 2017, shortly after Trump's inauguration, as the Fox executive shake-up was underway, I was working weekends in DC, and Dad was at Pritikin, a health retreat Mom sent him to in order to lose weight. He was miserable and depressed. He wouldn't leave his room, wouldn't engage with anyone. He just sat there watching his two TVs—one for CNBC and another for Fox News. Mom called me and said, "You need to go down there."

Born Lucky

I was co-anchoring *America's News HQ*, which meant I had most weekdays off. So I flew down to Florida and tried to cheer him up.

"Let's go for a walk on the beach," I said. *No.* "Let's go do something." *No.* Finally, I spotted a golf course and threw out an idea. "Let's play golf."

He scoffed. "I'm not playing unless you play too."

Dad golfed nearly every day as I grew up. He had picked up the sport in his late thirties and turned into a very good player.

"I don't know how to golf," I said.

"Fine," he said.

Finally, to get him out of the room, I relented. That was the deal. If I wanted him to go outside, I had to pick up a club. Okay, fine. I agreed. We got a caddie, grabbed some clubs, and started walking the golf course. I had no interest in playing. We were just going to try to walk nine holes, but by the third hole, Dad turned to me and said, "Why don't you just try it?" He handed me a nine-iron and said, "Just take a swing."

I hesitated. Golf had never been my thing. But in that moment, with Dad watching, I swung. Somehow, the ball flew toward the green and landed on it. I looked at Dad, and he was beaming. "Let me try that again," I said on the next hole. And then again on the one after that. By the last few holes, I had strung together enough solid shots that the caddie turned to Dad and said, "I'm seeing someone fall in love with golf."

That round changed everything. For Dad, it was like winning a lottery he didn't even realize he had bought a ticket for. We had never really done anything together. Other fathers and sons talked about football or baseball, but we never had that. Our relationship had always been intense, filled with difficult moments and serious conversations. And then, suddenly, we had something light. Something simple. Something that didn't carry weight.

From that day forward, golf became our thing. We'd call each other, talk about swings, courses, and shots we wished we could take back. He even wrote a column about it, reflecting on how we had finally found this wonderful common ground.

And then at the age of 35 he fell for golf—and that was something I could do—and still can, but not very well... But we could do it together. Together. It has been wonderful—he has and is planning golf trips—we compare clubs, talk about the rules and etiquette, and who we want to play with. This Sunday, I was in a car and he called to give me a shot-by-shot, putt-by-putt account of the last holes in the exciting Houston Open—unbelievably he was excited—and for a far, far separate reason, so was I.[2]

For the first time, we had something that was purely ours, something that didn't need to mean anything—yet somehow meant everything.

One day, during a round of golf together, I got a call from work. Something minor—an assignment change or a scheduling shift—but it completely threw me off my game. My swing fell apart, and my focus shattered. I was frustrated and rattled. Dad watched me struggle for a while before I finally turned to him and asked, "Was this what it was like when I would call you on the golf course?"

He doubled over laughing. "You have no idea!" he said. "I can't tell you how many of the best rounds of my life I had on the twelfth or thirteenth hole, and then I'd get the call."

Back when I was in school, there was no cell reception on the golf course. So if I was having a bad day, I would go to the pay phone outside the commons, the spot where kids hung out after lunch at Burroughs, and call the clubhouse. "I need you to go find my dad," I'd say. The staff would track him down, pulling him off whatever hole he was on, and he'd drive his cart back to the clubhouse. He'd listen as I unloaded whatever had gone wrong—what someone had said, how mean people had been—and when we were done talking, he'd get back in the cart, return to his round, and finish the hole. Years later, standing there on the fairway, struggling after my phone call had thrown me off—for something stupid, no less—I finally understood. All those times I thought he was just golfing, he was also carrying the weight of my worries with him, never once letting me know what it had cost *him*.

It was the first time I truly understood. The first time I could equate my frustration over a ruined round of golf with the emotional weight he had carried for me. He had never once complained. He had always just been there. As kids, we think our parents are invincible, that their sacrifices come easily. But standing on that golf course, completely thrown off by one simple, stupid phone call, I got it. I finally saw the silent sacrifices he had made.

Golf became our connection, but it was also a metaphor for everything Dad taught me. No improving your position, no preferred lies, no taking the easy way out. You deal with the reality in front of you, no matter how unfair it might seem. It was a game of patience, discipline, and, above all, integrity. Dad made sure of that. You didn't move the ball. You didn't give yourself a better lie. Every penalty counted. Every stroke was tallied. You did the right thing when nobody was watching. He drilled into me the idea that golf wasn't about beating anyone else; it was about playing against yourself, against your own discipline and honor. You paid your bets immediately. And from the very beginning, it was about setting goals.

I was a terrible golfer at first. So we started with small victories: how many bogeys I could make in a round versus how many pars he got. We would play for an ice cream cone after the round. It never mattered how old I was. Even when I was thirty-eight, Dad was still betting me ice cream. That's how he was.

The biggest lesson, though: You play the ball as it lies, and you never give up on a hole. No matter how deep into the woods your tee shot goes, you keep grinding. "You never know what the other guy is going to do," Dad would remind me. We probably hold the record for most penalties called on ourselves in a round, and that was a point of pride. Honor mattered more than winning.

It was never just about golf. It was about life. Play the ball as it lies. And never, ever quit.

Chapter Eighteen

SPEAKING THE TRUTH

Saturday, March 16, 2019, started like any other weekend at Fox News. The newsroom buzzed with routine—producers clicking away at keyboards, teleprompters scrolling, screens flashing the latest headlines.

I had spent nearly five years at the DC bureau and had settled into my role as co-anchor of *America's News HQ*. In addition to my weekend anchoring duties, I often filled in as a substitute host on other Fox News programs, including *Fox & Friends*, *America's Newsroom*, and *Happening Now*. I knew the rhythm of weekends in cable news: a mix of politics, policy discussions, and the occasional breaking story. But this Saturday felt particularly ordinary.

At the time, the biggest political story was President Donald Trump's recent veto of Congress's attempt to overturn his national emergency declaration. He was determined to shift federal funds to build the US-Mexico border wall, despite bipartisan opposition to doing it through declaring a national emergency. That morning, we lined up an interview with Wisconsin Republican Congressman Sean Duffy to discuss the issue. As we went live, I posed what I thought was a straightforward constitutional question: "Article One clearly says the power of the purse is with Congress. If all of a sudden you're using executive action and emergency powers to move that funding around, how is that not changing the law?"

Duffy, as expected, defended the president's decision, arguing that national security necessitated bold action. I pushed again: "Is this precedent worth it, to get a border wall or get funding for part of a border wall, for Congress to continue to give away more and more authority?" The segment wrapped, and I moved on with my day. There was no controversy, no on-air fireworks—just a normal weekend political interview about executive action and constitutional scholarship.

Then, the next morning, my phone buzzed with a notification. It was a tweet from President Trump, buried in a Sunday morning tweet storm that also included opinions on General Motors and the previous night's *Saturday Night Live*.

> Were @FoxNews weekend anchors, @ArthelNeville and @LelandVittert, trained by CNN prior to their ratings collapse? In any event, that's where they should be working, along with their lowest-rated anchor, Shepard Smith![1]

I had been here before. On March 5, 2016, two days after the Republican primary debate in Detroit, Trump took direct aim at me in real time during a breakdown of the debate on *America's News HQ*. As my co-anchor, Elizabeth Prann, and I dissected the performances of Trump, Ted Cruz, Marco Rubio, and John Kasich, a tweet came through from "Trump Force One" while he was flying between campaign stops:

> I am watching two clown announcers on @FoxNews as they try to build up failed presidential candidate #LittleMarco. Fox News is in the bag![2]

It wasn't unusual for Trump to watch Fox News and tweet his reactions. There are pictures of him tuning in on weekends, me anchoring on Fox News while he watched on TV from his airplane and Trump National Golf Club in DC. Back in 2016, getting tweeted at by Trump was seen almost as a badge of honor. If the front-runner for the presidency was irritated by my reporting, it meant I was doing real journalism. But by 2019, the meaning of a Trump tweet had changed.

Later that day, I got a phone call from a mid-level Fox executive. "Stay strong to your beliefs," they said. "You've got to cover everybody fairly." It was subtle, but I could hear the shift in tone. The landscape was changing.

Of course, there were stories I covered that Trump *loved*—like when I reported from the first coal mine to open in Pennsylvania after his election. He tweeted about it, and it became the banner headline on the Drudge Report and one of the top stories on FoxNews.com. That was the whole point of journalism as I knew it: call balls and strikes.

Part of being on the spectrum is seeing things very literally. Between 2017 and 2020, the rise of terms like "your truth" and "alternative facts" never made sense to me. That was completely contrary to what Dad taught me—and what his father demanded. There wasn't "your truth" or "my truth"—there was only *the* truth.

And it was my job to report it.

"Respect the Audience"

By mid-2020, tensions across the country were at a boiling point. The pandemic, social unrest, and a deeply divisive political landscape had created an environment where news coverage could be as volatile as the events themselves. As a journalist, I was caught in a no-man's-land between public opinion of Fox News, which had long been a target for progressives, and President Trump, whose growing frustration with the network, not to mention his previous ire of me, was making headlines of its own leading up to his reelection bid.

On May 30, I was assigned to cover the protests outside the White House, which were part of a broader wave of demonstrations triggered by the killing of George Floyd. By then, protests had spread to over one hundred cities across the country, many escalating into clashes between demonstrators and law enforcement. Lafayette Park, a symbolic area adjacent to the White House that witnessed civil rights protests in the 1960s, became a focal point for the protests in DC.

Protests were nothing new for me, but the Floyd protests were beginning to get out of hand. Earlier that day, the White House had been put on lockdown and reporters moved inside. By 1 a.m., my crew, including cameraman Christian Galdabini and two security staffers, were reporting live from Lafayette Park. We had nondescript microphones and equipment, but that didn't stop a group of masked protesters from recognizing me as a Fox News journalist. It started with shouted obscenities, then quickly escalated. Within moments, we were surrounded.

Then chants: "Fuck Fox News!" Over and over.

A mob chased us through the park, hurling water bottles and other projectiles. My cameraman's equipment was smashed, and one of our security guards was punched and knocked to the ground. We linked arms and hiked out to finally find the protection of a DC police riot squad on standby a few blocks away. The scene was eerily reminiscent of my experience covering the Arab Spring in Egypt when a mob chased us through Tahrir Square.

That night became a flashpoint. Fox News had become a symbol, reviled by the left for its perceived alignment with Trump, yet increasingly criticized by Trump himself for not being loyal enough. I was caught somewhere in the middle, reporting from a place where neither side trusted me. The attacks weren't just about Fox News; they were about what the network represented in an increasingly fractured America.

The Right Thing

Leading up to the 2020 election, my role at Fox News continued to shrink. Once, I had been a rising star with a clear trajectory, filling in on major network shows and frequently anchoring breaking news coverage. But when Shine, my biggest advocate at Fox, was pushed out in 2017, the tide started turning against me. Without his advocacy, I went from being in line for a coveted anchor spot in New York to floundering in the DC bureau, where it became increasingly clear that I was no longer a priority. My assignments grew less significant and my airtime more limited. It was a slow but deliberate sidelining.

Up until this point, none of the decisions had been ethical ones—I wasn't being asked to say things that were untrue or to frame stories dishonestly. But the network had spent over twenty years and billions of dollars cultivating the Trump audience, and as the 2020 election approached, they became terrified of losing them. I started to sense the shift—not in outright fabrications, but in quiet, calculated decisions about what to emphasize, what to ignore, and who to sideline.

That unease reminded me of a story Dad used to tell. In 1971, at just twenty-two years old, he was invited to meet with President Richard Nixon. The Twenty-Sixth Amendment had just passed, lowering the voting age to eighteen, and Dad had recently sold his company that marketed directly to America's college students. The Nixon administration wanted him to help do the same—to sell the president to the country's youth. But the morning of the meeting, Dad changed his mind. He'd already met several members of Nixon's team and found them lacking in character. Dad, barely out of college, made a decision most people twice his age wouldn't have—he canceled. He always said it was the most important decision of his life, second only to asking Mom to marry him. "If I had taken that meeting," he told me, "I would have been completely entwined in Watergate." To him, character was everything. And now, standing at my own crossroads, I started to understand what he meant.

Born Lucky

When election night arrived on November 3, I was stationed at the Hay-Adams Hotel in DC, a luxurious but distant perch from the real action. It was a clear sign that Fox executives wanted me away from the spotlight. I was placed at a location that all but guaranteed I wouldn't be on-air unless something catastrophic happened, like mass riots or the White House going up in flames. I wasn't going to be a key player in the network's coverage.

On election night, Fox made the fateful call, declaring Arizona for Joe Biden days earlier than any other network. The backlash was instant. Trump's base erupted in fury, branding Fox as disloyal and untrustworthy. In the days that followed, results remained unconfirmed, and tensions grew as both campaigns braced for what would come next. Then, when Fox called the election on that Saturday, it set off a political firestorm. I wasn't involved in the call, but as one of the network's weekend anchors, I was on-air the day Biden won the presidency and quickly found myself caught in the crossfire.

As the anger boiled over, so did the protests. "Stop the Steal" rallies swept through the country, and because I anchored weekends, I was inevitably the one covering them for Fox.

On November 14, 2020, one week after Fox made its call, I found myself in an intense, combative interview with Erin Perrine, a Trump campaign spokesperson. She rattled off claims of election fraud, but when I pressed her for evidence, she had none. The exchange turned heated as we went back and forth. Perrine dodged, deflected, and repeated unfounded allegations of voter fraud in places like Detroit and Philadelphia.

There was no data to support Trump's claims. No truth versus alternative facts. Nothing had been proven. And in that moment, I knew exactly where I stood. Dad had taught me to tell the truth, no matter how inconvenient or uncomfortable. That meant telling the truth on TV—not playing cutesy with conspiracy theories.

"I'm trying to ask you, very simply, where are you going to find the votes?" I asked Perrine. "You say you want to count every vote, conceivably because you think you're going to pull ahead. Where are the votes in a path to 270? Where?"

"We are taking every legal avenue that exists in these states to make sure that legal votes are counted and illegal votes are [not] counted," she told me. "For every Democrat and every talking head on the news, how much fraud is okay? How many dead people can vote and you're okay with that?"

"Who are you lumping everyone together with?" I asked. "*You guys?* The media in general? Now it's just you attack everybody if they don't agree with you. Okay, not much else to say." I ended the interview.[3]

The reaction was immediate. The interview went viral. Millions of views. News outlets picked it up. Suddenly, I wasn't just another Fox News anchor. I was the Fox News anchor publicly challenging Trump's campaign. And then came the call from an executive. "You need to respect the audience," they said. I asked what that meant. The response was vague but unmistakable: Fox's audience loved Trump, and I wasn't being respectful. It was a warning.

That same weekend, a few articles online noted I was tough on a Democrat. I had just gone toe to toe with Adam Smith, the congressman from Washington state, on something. It was equally combative—but nobody cared about that interview. Going tough on a Democrat wasn't cause for a phone call from an executive. I wasn't trying to be some crazed contrarian. I wasn't trying to be a rebel at Fox News. I was just being a journalist. I would later find out in the Dominion voting systems lawsuit against Fox News just how much was happening behind the scenes.

By early December, the ax fell. The number two person in the DC bureau called me. "After the first of the year, you're not anchoring again," she said, her voice hesitant, almost apologetic as she passed along the news.

It wasn't a conversation. It was a decision.

"Was anybody else going to tell me?" I asked.

"No," she admitted. "But they've asked me to assign you as a reporter on weekend mornings."

That was it—my punishment. Going from the anchor desk to a weekend morning reporter was like being demoted from the practice squad to shagging balls during practice, knowing you'd never see the field again. The message was clear: I was being humiliated, sidelined, made an example for anyone else who might step out of line. It was a complete F-you.

"Well, that's interesting," I said. "But I have about a hundred comp days saved up. So I'm letting you know now—I'm taking every other Saturday and Sunday off for the next two years. You're going to have to find someone else to cover those shifts. This isn't personal to you, but I'm not gonna get screwed like this."

"I understand," she said. "Don't worry. I'll take care of it."

A few days later, she called back. "This doesn't start until after the first of the year," she said. "And you won't have to work weekends. We'll figure it out."

I knew what was happening. Fox wasn't going to fire me outright. It was like private school—they weren't expelling me, but I was being very clearly invited not to return. The decision had been made: I would never anchor at Fox News again.

On January 1, 2021, I stood in the bathroom, staring at my reflection in the mirror as I prepared for what I knew would be my last time anchoring at Fox News. COVID protocols meant there were no makeup artists, so I applied my own. As I walked out, it hit me: *This is the last show you'll ever anchor here.* I finished the broadcast, packed up my briefcase, and took one last look around the studio. I gathered what little remained in my office, the things that mattered, and walked out the door. Hours later, I was on a plane, heading to spend a few days with my parents before I started my new reporting schedule at Fox News.

Liberty needed help moving to DC so I drove with her and her dog back to Washington on January 6, checking into a hotel near the Capitol with nothing but a backpack and a couple of suits. A few weeks before, my longtime relationship had ended, and I was waiting to move into a new apartment. That morning, as I left for the studio, I was cornered in the hotel bathroom by a group of January 6 protesters. They didn't recognize me at first, but once they did, the questioning began.

"Are you a patriot?" one asked, stepping closer. "What are you doing here?"

"I'm a journalist," I answered.

"We don't like you very much," one of them said.

I glanced over, saw an opening, and slipped out. I walked through the Capitol grounds, through the swelling riot, heading to the Fox News studio to work. I covered the day's chaos from the studio and returned the next day for more reporting.

Then, on January 8, I woke up feeling off. At first, I dismissed it as exhaustion, but as the hours passed, I felt a deep fatigue setting in. By midday, the fever started. Then the chills. On top of everything else, I had COVID. I stayed in my hotel room, hoping rest would help, but each day, I got worse. I felt like I'd been hit by a truck. Just a week earlier, I'd been running five miles in forty minutes. Now, walking to the bathroom felt like a marathon. I tried everything—steroids, vitamins—to keep myself from getting worse. But nothing stopped the downward spiral. I was alone, growing weaker, waiting for my body to turn a corner.

By January 15, I was barely able to stand. I crawled from the bathroom to the bedroom in my hotel room—fifteen feet, but it felt like miles. I knew I couldn't keep going like this.

I called Liberty. "You need to take me to the hospital," I said.

By the time I arrived at Sibley Memorial, my oxygen levels were dangerously low. Doctors moved quickly, stabilizing me, and prescribing Remdesivir. Doctors gave me my first dose on January 16, and slowly, I started recovering. I was released from the hospital after four days, the day before the inauguration. I had lost twenty pounds in ten days and could barely move. I went to my new apartment in DC, but it didn't feel like home. My sister had gone over earlier to oversee the installation of the TV, but aside from that, the place was empty—just a couch, a bed, and the TV mounted on the wall. I sank into the couch, exhausted, staring at the blank ceiling, uncertain of what came next. My body was weak, my career was in limbo, and I had no idea what to do.

About six days later, Fox called. They knew I was sick, and to their credit, they were supportive. Fox had always been good about taking care of its employees, and I believed they meant it. But the following week, the bureau chief and someone from HR called. "You can take six months of paid leave because of COVID," they said. "We'll send you the paperwork. Take as much time as you want."

Officially, it was company policy, but it felt like something else. At the time, Fox News had already cut ties with Bill Sammon and Chris Stirewalt—two others who had found themselves on the wrong side of the Arizona call. I had been through months of vitriol, from both Fox News's audience and my colleagues. Fox wasn't firing me outright, but it was clear: They didn't want me back on the air.

And truthfully, I needed the time away. I was still weak, unable to walk a tenth of a mile without feeling winded. I thought I would convalesce on the beach, rebuild my strength, and figure out what came next. At that point, all I knew was that I needed the time to recover—physically, mentally, and emotionally. I took the leave, packed my few belongings into a backpack, and flew to Florida to recover at my parents' house. I had no job. No relationship. Just a backpack, a few clothes, and the weight of everything that had happened pressing down on me.

The silence was deafening. The phone stopped ringing. The career I had built over the years had vanished in a matter of months. I had gone from anchoring national news to watching. I wasn't just an outsider; I was toxic. People I had once considered colleagues were now keeping their distance. I didn't blame them. There was an unspoken fear hanging over everyone at Fox News, an understanding that stepping out of line could mean losing everything. I had lived it firsthand.

But I had done my job. I had pressed for the truth. And even though I had lost everything, I had my integrity intact.

SPEAKING THE TRUTH

In the quiet of my parents' guest bedroom, I thought about Dad. About his lessons. He had always told me, "You only have one shot to be known as a person of honor." That meant something now more than ever. When I was eight and he made me write "I will always tell the truth" hundreds of times, I thought it was a punishment. Now, I realized it was the foundation of everything.

Fox News had made their choice. I had made mine. I did what was right, and that came with consequences. But Dad was right: Good things happen when you do the right thing. Maybe not immediately, maybe not in ways you expect.

But they do happen.

Chapter Nineteen

LEARNING TO BE ME

"Good evening, I'm Leland Vittert."

The crane camera glided in from above, sweeping over the studio as I sat beneath the bright lights, reading from the teleprompter. That was it—the debut of *On Balance with Leland Vittert*. My name on the screen. My show. My voice leading the conversation.

In TV, every night is just another night. You push the boulder up the hill all day—booking guests, chasing stories, preparing questions—only to deliver the show and watch the boulder roll right back down as you drive home. The next morning, the boulder waits at the bottom of the hill and you do it all over again. Success and failure are impostors, as Kipling said; you treat them both the same. Success can be fleeting, and I knew that better than most.

People on the spectrum often bring an intense focus—some would call it obsessive. As a kid, I was the one who couldn't let things go, who didn't understand when to stop asking questions, who got stuck on the smallest details. But in TV, where every day is a clean slate, that kind of focus isn't just useful—it's required.

After the first show, I took the team out for drinks and tried to enjoy the moment. But as they toasted, I found myself thinking back to how I got there: the uncertainty, the waiting, the months without a job. The road to that moment had been anything but smooth. A few months earlier, my time at Fox News had ended, and not on my terms. Four months off the air, waiting to announce my next step. Then, on a Friday at 4 p.m., a press release I never saw coming: "Fox News Parts Ways With Anchor Leland Vittert." No warning. No chance for me to announce the next move the way I wanted to.

I could have fought back. Given interviews. Set the record straight. But I thought about another lesson from Dad: Let your work do the talking. Revenge is a messy business. The Jewish proverb says, *If you seek revenge, you dig two graves.*

I could have gone to *The New York Times* and aired it all out, but it didn't feel right. Reporters were calling, messaging, wanting the inside story on Fox News. I could have given them exactly what they wanted—although, at that point, we didn't yet have the text messages to prove what I already knew. I could have been a hero for one news cycle, then forgotten the next. That wasn't how Dad taught me to respond.

I wasn't going to waste energy pounding my chest about morality or fairness. I already had another job lined up. NewsNation was launching something new, and I was ready to work again. Truthfully, I was relieved to be done at Fox News. I had been working for people I no longer respected and could no longer trust.

The place where I had started, the one that once prided itself on fair and balanced reporting, had become something else entirely. When Shine left Fox, the network's North Star shifted, catering more and more to an audience they were afraid to upset. Journalism became a secondary concern.

During the worst times in high school, Dad always promised me that the bullies—and even some teachers—would eventually get what they deserved. It felt like a weak promise. I wanted to believe him, but it was hard to imagine these people, who loomed so large on campus, could ever fail or be exposed. He would say, "The world is a round place," meaning that what goes around comes around. And he was right. The currency of high school—popularity, power, and perception—rarely holds its value in the real world. Those who chase profit and fame at the expense of integrity almost always get exposed. Fox News's $787.5 million payout to settle the Dominion lawsuit spoke far louder than anything I could have said about them.[1]

Dad always asked me about Shine after he left Fox News in 2017. After all, I had told him that Shine was the one executive he would have respected—because, for Dad, values and character were all that mattered. A few months after Shine's departure, I tracked down his number and gave him a call.

"Hey, it's Leland. Whatever you do next, I'm a Bill Shine guy," I said. "I want to come with you."

He brushed it off. "I'm done," he said. "I'm not doing anything new."

I didn't buy it. "You're not done," I told him. "Whatever you do next, I want to come with you."

From the time Shine left Fox News in 2017 until the 2020 election, we had spoken half a dozen times about my options. He had moved on to the White House—which, of course, I didn't. Then, one day shortly after the November 2020 election, my phone rang. Shine had taken a consulting job at NewsNation, an unknown cable news start-up. "What are you doing tomorrow?" Shine asked. I didn't have anything.

"Your phone's gonna ring at two," he told me. "The guy who runs NewsNation wants to talk to you."

That call came on November 16—less than two weeks after the election and two days after my viral moment questioning Trump's claims, which earned me a reprimand. At Fox during the last contract negotiation, the message had been clear: no raise, no promotion. I was on thin ice. NewsNation, on the other hand, was offering me something Fox never would—my own evening show.

After our conversation, I sent NewsNation executive Sean Compton an email: *Your idea to "talk about the news" in a way that holds both sides equally accountable is appealing to me, as it is what I aim to do every time I take a seat in the anchor chair.*

Compton is a legend—the architect behind much of modern conservative talk radio and a genius TV programmer. Like me, he's from Midwest roots—Indiana—and he understood something rare among network executives: New York and DC aren't real life. Years earlier, he envisioned a cable channel for the millions of people in the middle who see the world in terms of right and wrong, not left and right. Now, he was offering me a chance to bring Midwest common sense to prime time. It was the opportunity of a lifetime.

To put it in sports terms: I had just been cut from the Kansas City Chiefs' practice squad. And now I was being offered the starting quarterback job at an expansion franchise. Compton had a lot of choices for his new network. The "beach," as TV insiders call it, is crowded with big names fired from one network, waiting for their next job—familiar faces who make you wonder: *Whatever happened to them?* I wasn't one of those big names. I was a weekend anchor with no prime-time experience and no track record. Compton could have made a safer choice, but he had a vision for what NewsNation could be.

Compton and I didn't have many conversations, but the ones we did have never centered around politics. We talked about values. Compton instinctively knows what matters to people outside the media bubbles of Washington and New York—a rare, dare I say nonexistent, quality among most network executives. For me, it was an opportunity to learn from someone who truly understood the audience.

Not long after, I was packing up my life again. But this time, I wasn't just starting over—I was heading to Chicago to build something new: my own show at NewsNation.

Expect the Unexpected

I landed in Chicago on May 16, 2021, the day before my first day at NewsNation. Sitting on the small regional jet from St. Louis, taxiing around O'Hare, my phone buzzed. It was a text from an old college friend who still lived in the area.

"I hear you moved to Chicago," she wrote.

"Yeah," I replied. "I just landed."

"Welcome!" she said. "I hear you're single."

I told her I was.

"Great," she responded. "I'm going to find you your wife."

I shook my head and texted back, "I don't want a wife. I don't want a girlfriend. I just got a condo downtown. I'm going to have the greatest summer of my life."

She ignored me. The next day, she texted a picture of a girl named Rachel and wrote, "I found your wife."

I moved to Chicago determined to focus on work. I wasn't looking for anything other than launching the show and proving myself. That lasted about twenty-four hours. Something about Rachel intrigued me. "Hi Rachel. Leland here," I texted. "So I guess some people think we should meet."

We made plans for Saturday, but twenty minutes later, she texted back. "Can't do Saturday. It's my birthday." She had forgotten her birthday? There were plenty of ways to back out of a date, but this was a new one. Then she followed up with, "How about next Tuesday?" And that was it.

We were having drinks ahead of our dinner reservation, and when she got up to walk to the table, I thought to myself, *I'm going to marry this girl*. I couldn't explain it, but I knew. Three dates later, we had dinner plans for a Wednesday night when Dad called.

"Hey," he said. "I'm in town for a meeting."

"Great," I told him. "I have a date tonight."

"I'll come along!" he replied. To Dad, this seemed like perfectly normal behavior. I was, and always will be, his little boy. More importantly, why *wouldn't* I want him to come along?

I texted Rachel. "Really sorry, but my dad's in town, and he wants to come to dinner. Do you mind meeting him?" She later told me she immediately texted her friends in a panic. What kind of guy invites his dad to dinner on the fourth date? Eventually, her council of elders decided she should go—if only to witness whatever strange situation she had gotten herself into.

At the end of dinner, after she went home, Dad turned to me and said, "You're going to marry that girl."

He was right.

For the moment, work quickly took over. In the first two months at NewsNation, I filled in on the anchor desk, traveled to Switzerland to cover the summit between President Joe Biden and Russian President Vladimir Putin, and began building a team for my show's launch. I wanted something different—something that didn't cater to one audience but held everyone accountable.

But like in any newsroom, bullies existed at NewsNation, and I was an easy target. I've grown a lot since high school, but some things never change. A few weeks into my time at NewsNation, the company held an all-hands meeting to announce some changes, including the official launch date for my show and the expansion of our small but growing network. It should have been a moment of celebration. Instead, it turned into a disaster.

The network president, Michael Corn, announced, "Leland's primetime show will launch on July 19." A few people clapped. Then came the Q&A.

One of the founding anchors stood up and said, "When we started here at NewsNation, we were promised the chance to do unbiased news. I think I speak for a lot of people when I say that if we're bringing in a little Tucker Carlson, that isn't what we were promised." That was my big moment—my announcement, my vindication. And there it was again: another high school bully.

I stood in the back of the newsroom, listening and almost shaking with anger. To his credit, Corn pushed back and defended me. But the anchor wouldn't let it go, continuing to make a scene in front of everyone. Uncomfortable doesn't even begin to describe the situation.

This anchor had all the credentials and a résumé with one of the big alphabet networks (NBC, ABC, CBS), and yet he ran the newsroom like a high school bully ran recess.

I left the meeting, picked up the phone, and called Dad. "I made a horrible mistake," I told him.

But then something happened that had never happened before. Compton, who had been listening to the meeting on Zoom, called me that night. Not only to apologize—but to commiserate and promise that things would work out. *Wow.* This was new. And Compton's word proved good. The bully left the company a few weeks later. For a lot of reasons, Compton's clearheaded decision took guts. It was the right call—but a tough one.

Finally, I had someone fighting for me.

On July 19, launch night arrived—the culmination of years of preparation. The cameras rolled, the lights came on, and I delivered my first monologue.

Among the people who made that night special was my friend Mike Allen. A founder of *Axios* and *Politico*, and one of the sharpest minds in journalism, Mike had always been someone I deeply respected. We first connected years earlier when he texted me about a comment I made on-air at Fox News. That exchange led to drinks, then to a friendship built on shared values. Mike flew in just to be there for my first show. He took a picture of the set, put it in *Axios AM*, and wrote, "Congratulations, Leland." It was an incredible gesture and a guarantee everybody in DC would see where I was now.

The only other thing I remember from that night was signing off:

> As Tom Brokaw said, I'm simply the most conspicuous part of this large team, and we are grateful for your time and your trust. We pledge to earn it every show, and to that end, we will approach every night without fear or favor to those we interview or the stories we cover. And while you might not always agree with our guests or our point of view, we do hope you'll be smarter for the discussion.

That mindset came from Dad. Achievement, he always told me, is something that's quietly acknowledged. It's not about the applause or the headlines. It's not about *you*! You do something because you can do it—not because the world has to notice. He drilled that into me about flying when I was a kid. That was a strange concept for someone who would spend his career in front of a camera, but it stuck.

For all the focus on launch day, the next morning I woke up in my Chicago condo and started pushing the boulder up the hill again—preparing for the second show. And then the next. And the next.

I wasn't focused on "making it." Success wasn't about one moment or one show; it was about showing up and doing the work, day after day. I wasn't caught up in the idea of the first show being a milestone. I was thinking about the thirtieth show. Then the hundredth.

Every night, I analyzed what worked, what didn't, and how we could improve. Some nights, I'd leave the studio feeling like we'd nailed it. Others, I'd walk out frustrated, convinced we'd missed the mark. Either way, the next morning, we started fresh.

The ratings come out every day at 4 p.m. A few months into the show, around mid-fall, the overnight ratings were up big. I called Shine, ecstatic.

"God, have you seen the numbers?" I asked.

"Oh yeah," he said. "They're great."

I kept going on and on.

Finally, he cut me off. "Are you done?"

"What do you mean?" I asked.

"Are you done?" he repeated.

"I guess," I said.

"Okay." And just like that, he moved on to that night's show.

I sat there, phone pressed to my ear. *Wasn't he excited?* I wondered. A couple of weeks later, we had a show that tanked. The ratings were terrible. I called Shine again, totally beside myself. "This is a disaster."

He listened for five minutes while I vented.

Then, calmly: "Are you done?"

I hesitated. "Yeah."

"Remember two weeks ago when you were so excited and I asked if you were done?" he asked. I nodded, even if he couldn't see me. "You've got five minutes. Doesn't matter if the ratings are great or if they're bad. Look at them for five minutes, and then move on. You've got a show to do."

That stuck with me. *Five minutes.* Whether it was a win or a loss, you took the lesson, processed it, and then you got back to work. That's how Dad always taught me to see the world. There are days of great triumph, and there are days of great disappointment. But you get five minutes—then you move on.

A year into *On Balance*, Shine finally started critiquing me.

I want you to show more personality. Smile more. Have more emotion when you read this. Let the audience see who you are. Talk about loving golf. Talk about Rachel.

It reminded me of the time at Fox News when he told me: "Until you learn to be you, I can't make you better." The day Shine finally started critiquing my tape at NewsNation was one of the great professional moments of my life. Not the first show, not the high ratings, but when Shine thought I was worth coaching. It meant I had learned how to be me.

As a young weekend anchor at Fox News, the weekday news anchors saw me as a threat, someone to push aside rather than mentor. But that all changed at NewsNation. As a prime-time anchor, I finally had the chance to learn from the greats.

Bill O'Reilly, a larger-than-life figure during my time at Fox News, has become a frequent guest, mentor, and friend. He's sold more books than any nonfiction author in history and hosted the number one cable news show of all time for almost two decades. Now, we've even done a few hour-long specials together—though "together" might be generous. They were his specials; I just asked a few questions. But learning how to engage an audience from the King of Cable News is the kind of opportunity you only dream about.

Then there's George Will. When I was bored in Jerusalem, I would watch George's speeches and lectures on YouTube, trying to mimic his speaking style and learn his timing. Today, he's not only a guest on my show but a dear friend. I'll never hope to write like he does, but I'm starting to understand how he thinks—and that's a gift.

NewsNation is everything I always dreamed journalism—and cable TV—could be.

If you had told someone that a kid like me—the one who couldn't look people in the eye, who failed basic spelling tests, and who couldn't read a room—would end up talking on national television every night, they would have rightfully questioned your sanity. That's the thing about autism: It doesn't always look the way people expect. In the end, I didn't have to prove the world wrong—I just had to prove to myself that I belonged, not just in front of the camera, but in the life I built.

As usual, Dad's words proved prophetic: Do the right thing, even if it's painful, and good things happen. Everything had led to learning how to be me.

Chapter Twenty

THE ROAD AHEAD

Six months into our relationship, Rachel knocked on my apartment door. I had told her to come by before our Thursday night dinner date. When she stepped inside, though, she froze. Sitting on my couch, a beautiful chocolate lab named Sage lifted her head.

"Is she yours?" Rachel asked, smiling with the excitement of a little girl seeing a horse and carriage. Before I could answer, Sage was off the couch and in Rachel's arms, her tail wagging. Rachel, all dressed up for dinner, dropped to the floor, laughing as Sage licked her face.

"No," I told her. "We're just dog sitting for the weekend."

One of our executives was heading out of town, and when I heard she had a dog, I insisted Sage stay with me instead of going to a kennel. I knew Rachel loved dogs. You might recall that I grew up with Newfoundlands—after Sally came Bessie, Daisy, and Donut. Rachel grew up with boxers. On one of our first dates, she told me about Brando, the boxer who climbed into bed with her during nightmares, a gesture he continued until he passed away. We bonded over our love of big dogs.

Sage, with her sweet and gentle disposition, won us over. She preferred tummy rubs to fetch, unusual for a lab. When the weekend ended and Sage's owner texted that she was downstairs, I called Sage to the door.

As Rachel said goodbye, I saw a tear in her eye. The moment I saw that tear, I knew a dog was in our future.

I called Sage's breeder the next day.

When I told a friend about my plan, he laughed. "Dogs are gateway drugs—for marriage and kids." In any previous relationship, those words would have ended my desire for a dog. But with Rachel, they didn't scare me at all.

The breeder didn't have puppies at the time, but she had kept back one dog from a litter to show and breed. At two years old, though, Dutch would lie down for tummy rubs instead of prancing in the ring. Not exactly competition material, but he was perfect for us—a failed show dog because he was too lazy and thus not desirable to breed.

On a frigid January night, I brought him to Chicago. Rachel picked us up at the airport. He was terrified—and honestly, I was too. This was the start of responsibility. I told friends I got Dutch as an insurance policy so Rachel would never leave. Rachel shot back, "All insurance policies have deductibles and coverage limits." (To be fair, she disputes ever saying this.)

A few weeks later, on February 24, 2022, Putin's tanks rolled across the Ukrainian border.[1] Rachel and I were spending three or four nights a week together by then, but that night, she was at her apartment a few blocks away. When our bosses decided that Marni Hughes and I would anchor all night, I called Rachel and asked if she could come over to take care of Dutch.

Rachel never left.

For the next four months, Marni and I pulled double duty—anchoring our own shows and then a late-hour broadcast. For me, saying yes to another assignment felt natural. It reminded me of my days in Little Rock and Orlando, living close to the station so I could jump on breaking news. Saying yes gets you a long way in life.

Rachel got her first real taste of what a TV relationship meant. She would leave for work early in the morning, and I wouldn't get home until after she'd gone to bed. Once or twice a week, we'd meet at a Costco near work for a dinner date—me in a suit and TV makeup, her in work clothes, eating pizza at the food court.

It was perfect.

Real Success

For so long, I had thought career success would give me the ultimate validation. If I could just get the right job and build the right show, then I'd know I'd made it. But the further I got into my career, the more I realized that wasn't it at all—Dad was right again. The moments that matter aren't the launch of a show or the headline-grabbing interviews. They are the golf games with Dad; the bottles of wine with Mom sitting on the kitchen floor late into the night; the phone calls with Liberty as she travels (the only time she will pick up my calls); and the quiet dinners alone with Rachel.

It's funny how life works. If I had stayed at Fox News, if things had gone the way I thought they were supposed to, none of this would have happened. I wouldn't have my own show, I wouldn't have had the opportunity to build something at NewsNation, and I wouldn't have met Rachel. In the end, that door closing was the best thing that could have happened.

Just after New Year's in 2025, Compton decided to take another chance on me and move my show into the 9 p.m. prime-time slot. Naturally, bosses, friends, and colleagues all hyped up launch week: "Oh my God. Who's your first guest?" Maybe it's my ability to have this intense focus, but the crazier everybody else gets, the calmer I get.

At work, I had finally found what I wanted: a network and bosses who believed in me, giving me the freedom to just do the news. I poured myself into every show like it was the first. But even as I pushed myself harder, something unexpected had changed. For the first time, something mattered more than work.

For years, I had assumed the kind of love Mom and Dad have was something other people found. At nearly forty, I was still single, and nothing in my dating life had ever quite measured up to the bar my parents had set. Then I met Rachel.

She saw me in a way few people ever had. While Dad had always been the one tapping his watch, gently guiding me when I got lost in my own world, Rachel had her own way of keeping me grounded. She understood my intensity, knew how my mind raced ahead of me, and never tried to change it—just slowed me down when I needed it. With her, I didn't have to explain myself. I could just be.

It didn't hurt that Rachel's parents had the same kind of fierce love and partnership mine do. We had both waited for the kind of relationship our parents modeled.

And somehow, against all odds, we found it.

More Than a Label

There are singular moments that could have defined me. Mom and Dad sitting in the preschool room as the teacher told them I should be tested. Dad visiting school in fourth grade, only to find me placed with the girls in PE because I was being bullied. The teacher telling my parents that kids thought I was weird, and that she did too. The art teacher comparing me unfavorably to his dog's ass. The IQ test that put me on two opposite ends of the spectrum, definitive proof that something was wrong.

Any one of those moments could have been a stopping point. A reason to define me, to box me in. My parents could have taken the easy way out. They could have accepted the diagnosis as an answer instead of a challenge. They could have let me be the weird kid, accepted the label, adjusted the world around me, and let me live within the safety of lowered expectations. They could have listened to the teachers, the experts, the

THE ROAD AHEAD

system that said, "This is who he is. There's only so much you can do." But they didn't. Because they believed I could be more.

Instead, Dad waited at the end of the driveway every day to put me back together again. He didn't tell me life was unfair; he showed me how to live in it anyway. He didn't let me define myself by what was hard; he taught me how to push through it and demanded that I did. When I sat at dinner, disrupting the conversation, he tapped his watch to teach me timing. When I didn't understand how to interact, he taught me to analyze the rhythm of conversation and learn how to talk to people. He didn't change the world for me. He changed me for the world.

Because that was the lesson: The world isn't going to change. And if you expect it to, you're going to spend your life waiting.

It would have been simpler if they had just accepted I was different and softened the road ahead. They could have homeschooled me through high school. They could have demanded accommodations that would have reshaped the world for me. Instead, Dad gave up his life and put me back together again, day after day, school after school, setback after setback. It wasn't easy. But I learned. I learned that autism—or whatever label you want to give it—wasn't a limitation unless I let it be. No label is.

I remember my rowing coach telling us we could stop running stairs as a team when the second guy puked. That was the standard. And if you live life that way—if you keep running when others quit—you're going to be successful, because most people won't do it. That ability to obsess over something, to work harder, became my greatest strength.

I still catch myself talking too much, misreading moments, trying too hard to land a joke that falls flat. For me, the human equation is a learned skill and a discipline. Even now, I embarrassingly miss social cues. You might not notice it on TV or over a cocktail—Dad taught me how to compensate. But if we played golf or had dinner, you'd see glimpses. They're still there.

I will always be who I am. I still have moments where I think, *God, Lucky, why did you do that? Why did you say that? Why couldn't you stop talking? Dad was right, you* are not *funny!* There are times when I keep arguing, keep repeating myself, and let anger get the best of me.

But I'm profoundly grateful for the people who understand me—Mom, Dad, Liberty, and now Rachel. Beyond them, I don't have many friends. The few who stick around possess a rare kind of patience and insight. They see past the awkward moments, the occasional temper, the emotional blind spots. They don't ask me to be someone I'm not. They just accept me. I'll never be part of the cool kids club, but I've come to realize I'd rather have a handful of people who really get me than a roomful who never did.

There isn't a cure for autism. But Dad taught me how to think about others—how to listen, the beginnings of the incredible empathy he possesses, and how to bring out the best in people by championing and empowering them. It's a learned skill. And as that psychologist said so many years ago: *You have to want it.* I would add, *every day.* But that's no different from anything else in life.

Dad once told me that the only thing he ever wanted was for his own father to be proud of him. He lived his life fighting for that, holding himself to the standard of the letter he received when he was sixteen. I never worried about whether Dad was proud of me. I always knew. He tells me, but he doesn't have to. I knew it in the way he showed up. In the sacrifices he made. In the way he never let me quit.

I think back to that summer at Shorewood, when Dad put me up on the ledge of the tree and told me to jump. I hesitated—just for a second. But then I dove toward his outstretched arms.

And he caught me.

His message was simple: *You can always trust me to catch you.*

Physically catching me became a metaphor for so much more.

He always did catch me. And even now, things are different—our lives busier, our roles changed—but some things stay the same. He is still my best friend, we still talk a few times a day, and I still call him every night to say good night.

THE ROAD AHEAD

I was—and remain—profoundly lucky. Lucky to be alive. Lucky to have the parents I do. Lucky that, through hard work and my mother's sainthood, their marriage withstood the strain of my challenges despite studies showing an 80 percent divorce rate among parents with kids who have disabilities.[2] Lucky to have met Rachel. Lucky for the people who stood up for me when it mattered most.

Dad's only real rule for me, his ultimate lesson, was this: You don't have to be defined by a diagnosis. You get to decide who you are.

That message is powerful because it applies to everyone. It doesn't matter if you're on the spectrum, have a physical disability, struggle with anxiety, a speech impediment, or a cleft palate—whatever challenge you face, it doesn't have to define you. What matters is defining yourself on your terms, no matter what the world wants to call you. It sounds hokey, but it's true. The flip side is also true: If you let it define you . . . it will, forever.

My story isn't a prescription or an answer. It's just proof. Proof of what dedication, love, and an unwillingness to accept limits can do. Because in the end, you don't have to be what people say you are. You don't have to be what they assume.

All I ever wanted in life was to belong. But what I realized was belonging doesn't come from being just like everyone else. It comes from knowing exactly who you are and embracing that.

When my first girlfriend said, "You're more like your dad than he is," I didn't really understand what she meant. It was an incredibly perceptive thought; maybe that's how she saw through my awkward seventeen-year-old self. But now I know she was right in so many ways. I am more like my dad—sometimes more intense than he ever was. But there's more to it than that. He couldn't have understood me so well if he hadn't struggled in some of the same ways. In today's language, I was farther on the spectrum than he was. That's why he got me. That's why he knew what I needed.

Until I met Rachel, I never seriously considered having kids. In fact, I told every woman I dated—including her—that I didn't want them.

The truth? I couldn't imagine taking on that kind of responsibility. That sounds a lot like Dad. I know how much effort, heartache, sacrifice, and emotion Dad poured into raising me—or at least I think I know. The truth is, I probably don't know half of it. Second only to giving others hope, the most important part of writing this book is to say thank you to the man who believed in me, taught me, and, in many ways, created me.

At a very young age, he realized I was alone. All I had was him and Mom. So he resolved *never* to show disappointment. "I knew it would crush you," he once told me. I've never doubted that he was proud of me—but first in my mind remains living up to the sacrifice and dedication he showed me.

I built a successful career, threw it all away on principle, and fought my way back to the top—realizing along the way that success wasn't what I first believed it to be. I found a selfless, kind woman to build a life with.

But there's still one more challenge.

I never thought I could be the kind of father my dad was—*is*. I'm still not sure I can.

But because of his example I'm inspired to try.

AFTERWORD FROM DAD

As you have already read, Lucky, decades ago, placed me on a pedestal.

This occurred simply as a result of his fundamental needs, that there was no one else, no other man, to help him and hold him. Consequently, it might appear in this book that I offered him support as a secure and knowledgeable father. That was not true.

I was scared for years. I still am to a degree, uncertain quite often and holding on for my family till sleep comes, bringing a few hours of peace.

For all of us who are in the most difficult and complex battle to help our special children survive, there is no finish line.

I am positive that every father and mother engaged in the monumental effort to help and protect and love our challenged children are dealing with the same issues.

Believe me, despite Lucky's admiration, I did only what any father would want to do.

All of us in this battle, this fight against what feels like the world has left our side, are in the same place.

We all feel enormous love and responsibility to those little ones who are absolutely lost and, without us, alone. Mothers and fathers need to know that there is definitely hope.

I am not that smart nor capable to have known what to do for him, except to love him and listen always to his cries for help, and to enlist

AFTERWORD

a couple of personal rules that seemed to make sense in a frightening circumstance.

Let me say that his mother, Carol, was the unsung angel here. She not only had to hold Lucky, but also me.

I really did not know what was ahead, who could help, or if the verdict was just "give up." Well, the purpose of this book is to offer hope, real hope. Here are the principles that I wrote down for myself when Lucky was diagnosed:

1. Have no expectations about the future.
2. Under no circumstances let your child feel that they have ever disappointed you. *EVER*, under no circumstance.
3. You are the depository of their hurt, their frustration, and their humiliations. You must listen and listen—morning before school and late into the night.
4. Tell them that they have the right stuff for life. That the currency of high school, etc., is not the currency of life. There are many more years after the six years of junior high and high school.

There were times where I reflexively responded to a seemingly endless difficult day with temper. Those were the most regrettable of times.

I fully understand that so many had and will have far more significant challenges and difficulties than we had.

You will need to remember that your child will continue, no matter the advancement, to simply be themselves. This is not a broken arm that heals; it is the way they were made.

Together, whatever the circumstance or how dire the situation, there is hope, good hope, but it will require endless understanding and the firm belief that your child can be better.

With the advent of so much bullying and other negative effects from today's social media culture, it will be hard to escape. We did not have to address that issue.

AFTERWORD

We did not discuss Lucky's issues or label with anyone, nor did we seek outside assistance. Perhaps that would have been better. I do not know.

Whatever your child's issue, I believe their best chance to progress is you and your love and patience and, in particular, your unwavering belief in them.

It was felt that writing this book could possibly help. There are so many of us who were and are lost in the nightmare of this despair.

If you are in this fight, it will be a challenge that is the most worthwhile of your life. It will probably take years and years, but it will be worth it.

If someone would have told me about what the future held for our little boy, I would have likely yielded right then. I would have been terribly wrong to do so.

If I can do it, you can. You can make an enormous difference for the ones you love dearly.

With all my heart, I wish for you and your child a future that you will make better together.

—Mark Vittert

ACKNOWLEDGMENTS

By now you have noticed I did not use the names of people who were mean to me in the book. This endeavor isn't about settling scores. As I began writing, I thought I would be far more emotional about people who were mean. Those would be the hardest memories to process. In fact, I became the most emotional remembering the good times and the people who believed in me. Many are noted in the pages you have read, and I am so grateful.

Specifically, there are a few people who deserve special thanks:

Don Yaeger, for his friendship and unbelievable storytelling ability.

Don's son Will, for the inspiration.

Barbara Fedida Brill, for understanding me and how this story could help others, and doggedly pushing me to write it.

Our agent, Ian Kleinert, for believing in the project based on eight hundred words and a New York diner breakfast.

Matt Baugher, our editor at HarperCollins, for understanding what the story was really about.

Reliving so much of my childhood to tell this story took an emotional toll on Mom, Dad, and Liberty. We all agreed that the pain is worth the hope that, through our story, other families will find hope. That said, I am grateful beyond words to the three of them.

Rachel, for never complaining about me coming home late from work

ACKNOWLEDGMENTS

and then diving into yet another project. Often she had to deal with the emotional fallout of my reopening the wounds of early life that I have tried to forget.

Michael Farr, for his constant encouragement, long conversations about why this project mattered, and friendship.

NOTES

Foreword by George F. Will
1. "When a Child Turns 18..." Children's University, accessed June 12, 2025, https://www.childrensuniversity.co.uk/media/1151/percentage-of-time-outside-the-classroom.pdf.

Chapter 3: The Measure of a Man
1. "Millionaires: Campus Conquistador," *Time* magazine, March 8, 1971, https://time.com/archive/6838640/millionaires-campus-conquistador/.

Chapter 6: Do It Right the First Time, Every Time
1. "Charles Lindbergh Completes the First Solo, Nonstop Transatlantic Flight," History.com, updated March 2, 2025, https://www.history.com/this-day-in-history/May-21/lindbergh-lands-in-paris.

Chapter 7: Walking Through Hell
1. Tom Brokaw, Emory University Commencement Address, Atlanta, May 16, 2005, https://www.americanrhetoric.com/speeches/tombrokawemorycommencement.htm.

Chapter 10: Practice Your Craft
1. Attributed to Winston Churchill in *Oxford Essential Quotations*, 5th ed., ed. Susan Ratcliffe (Oxford University Press, 2017), https://www.oxfordreference.com/display/10.1093/acref/9780191826719.001.0001/q-oro-ed4-00008442.

NOTES

CHAPTER 14: I'LL TELL MY KIDS ABOUT IT

1. "Egypt Unrest: 846 Killed in Protests—Official Toll," BBC News, April 19, 2011, https://www.bbc.com/news/world-middle-east-13134956.

CHAPTER 15: MOM, NO MATTER WHAT YOU SEE ON TV, I'M OKAY

1. "Libyan War Planes Strike Rebel Positions," Fox News Insider, YouTube, posted March 9, 2011, https://www.youtube.com/watch?v=CXvI8t TEbb4https://www.youtube.com/watch?v=mXJzehUPz-k.

CHAPTER 16: WAR CHANGES YOU

1. *The Recruit*, dir. Roger Donaldson, Touchstone Pictures, 2003.
2. "2012 Benghazi Attacks," *Encyclopedia Britannica*, updated May 17, 2025, https://www.britannica.com/event/2012-Benghazi-attacks.
3. Maya Angelou (@MayaAngelou), "When someone shows you who they are, believe them the first time," Facebook, January 6, 2022, https://www.facebook.com/share/p/1BCVKaGTon/.
4. "The Crisis in Crimea and Eastern Ukraine," *Encyclopedia Britannica*, updated June 11, 2025, https://www.britannica.com/place/Ukraine/The-crisis-in-Crimea-and-eastern-Ukraine.
5. "McCain Remembrances," Brookings, accessed June 11, 2025, https://www.brookings.edu/mccain-remembrances/.

CHAPTER 17: JUST BE YOU

1. Andrew Kirell, "The Worst Moment of Fox's Baltimore Riot Coverage," Mediaite, April 28, 2015, https://www.mediaite.com/tv/the-worst-moment-of-foxs-baltimore-riot-coverage/.
2. Mark Vittart, "Mark Vittart's Reflections: For a Far Separate Reason," *St. Louis Business Journal*, April 5, 2018, https://www.bizjournals.com/stlouis/news/2018/04/05/mark-vitterts-reflections-for-a-far-separate.html.

CHAPTER 18: SPEAKING THE TRUTH

1. Donald J. Trump (@realDonaldTrump), "Were @FoxNews weekend anchors, @ArthelNeville and @LelandVittert, trained by CNN prior to their ratings collapse? In any event, that's where they should be working,

NOTES

along with their lowest rated anchor, Shepard Smith!" Twitter/X, March 17, 2019, https://x.com/realdonaldtrump/status/1107345541724291072.
2. Donald J. Trump (@realDonaldTrump), "I am watching two clown announcers on @FoxNews as they try to build up failed presidential candidate #LittleMarco. Fox News is in the bag!" Twitter/X, March 5, 2016, https://x.com/realDonaldTrump/status/706179933480099840.
3. Peter Wade, "Fox Host's Simple Question Derails Interview with Trump Aide," *Rolling Stone*, November 14, 2020, https://www.rollingstone.com/politics/politics-news/fox-news-interview-with-trump-aide-derails-quickly-1090623/.

CHAPTER 19: LEARNING TO BE ME

1. David Bauder, Randall Chase, and Geoff Mulvihill, "Fox, Dominion Reach $787M Settlement Over Election Claims," AP, April 18, 2023, https://apnews.com/article/fox-news-dominion-lawsuit-trial-trump-2020-0ac71f75acfacc52ea80b3e747fb0afe.

CHAPTER 20: THE ROAD AHEAD

1. Elliott Davis Jr. and Madeline Fitzgerald, "Russia Invades Ukraine: A Timeline of the Crisis," *U.S. News & World Report*, March 18, 2025, https://www.usnews.com/news/best-countries/slideshows/a-timeline-of-the-russia-ukraine-conflict.
2. Ann Gold Buscho, "Divorce and Special Needs Children," *Psychology Today*, February 28, 2023, https://www.psychologytoday.com/us/blog/a-better-divorce/202302/divorce-and-special-needs-children.

ABOUT THE AUTHOR

Leland Vittert is the host of *On Balance with Leland Vittert* and serves as NewsNation's chief Washington anchor. A veteran journalist, Vittert joined NewsNation in May 2021, where he has been pivotal in covering national affairs and delivering special reports across the network's primetime weeknight newscasts. Before joining NewsNation, Vittert worked for Fox News from 2010 to 2021, serving as a foreign correspondent based in Jerusalem and later an anchor and correspondent in Washington.

Don Yaeger is a twelve-time *New York Times* bestselling author, longtime associate editor for *Sports Illustrated*, and one of the most in-demand public speakers on the corporate circuit. Throughout his writing career, he has developed a reputation as a world-class storyteller and has been invited as a guest on numerous major talk and news shows—from *The Oprah Winfrey Show* to *Nightline* and *Good Morning America*. In addition to writing and speaking, Yaeger is the host of the highly rated *Corporate Competitor Podcast*.